A Kaleidoscope of Digital American Literature

by Martha L. Brogan

with assistance from

Daphnée Rentfrow

Council on Library and Information Resources

Digital Library Federation

Washington, D.C.

September 2005

The author's text was submitted for publication in May 2005.
All URLs included in this report were valid as of July 2005.

Published by:

Council on Library and Information Resources
Digital Library Federation
1755 Massachusetts Avenue, NW, Suite 500
Washington, DC 20036
Web sites at http://www.clir.org
and http://www.diglib.org

ISBN 1-932326-17-0
ISBN 978-1-932326-17-8
CLIR Publication No. 132

Additional copies are available for $30 per copy. Orders must be placed through CLIR's or DLF's Web site. This publication is also available online at no charge at http://www.clir.org/pubs/abstract/pub132abst.html and at http://purl.oclc.org/DLF/brogan0505

 The paper in this publication meets the minimum requirements of the American National Standard for Information Sciences—Permanence of Paper for Printed Library Materials ANSI Z39.48-1984.

Library of Congress Cataloging-in-Publication Data

Brogan, Martha L.
  A kaleidoscope of digital American literature / Martha L. Brogan ; with assistance from Daphnée Rentfrow.
    p. cm.
  Includes bibliographical references and indexes.
  ISBN-13: 978-1-932326-17-8 (alk. paper)
  ISBN-10: 1-932326-17-0 (alk. paper)
  1. American literature--Research--Computer network resources. 2. American literature--History and criticism--Computer network resources. 3. American literature--Bibliography--Computer network resources. 4. American literature--History and criticism--Data processing. 5. American literature--Bibliography--Data processing. 6. American literature--Research--Data processing. 7. American literature--Computer network resources. 8. American literature--Data processing. I. Rentfrow, Daphnée. II. Title.
  PS51.B76 2005
  025.06'81--dc22
                    2005022693

Contents

Appendixes

Acknowledgments

A multitude of people made this report possible, and I would like to thank them, starting with Donald J. Waters of The Andrew W. Mellon Foundation, who entrusted me with the preliminary report that served as the foundation for this expanded version. J. Paul Hunter (University of Virginia) offered expert advice as a consultant to the Mellon Foundation on the original report. Second, I am indebted to the many outstanding digital scholars and practitioners who participated in telephone interviews, generously sharing their knowledge and opinions; their names are listed in Appendix 1. Third, I appreciate the guidance and patience of the Council on Library and Information Resources and the Digital Library Federation, particularly David Seaman, whose commitment to this report never flagged. Daphnée Rentfrow, a former CLIR Postdoctoral Fellow and independent scholar, agreed to assist me with the report in its final stage. She is the lead author for section 3.5, Collections by Design. In addition, she provided valuable feedback and editorial advice about the entire report.

I also owe thanks to a number of specialists who answered my e-mail inquiries and provided additional information, including Willard McCarty (King's College London) for prepublication access to the manuscript of *Humanities Computing* (forthcoming Palgrave 2005); Kenneth M. Roemer (University of Texas, Arlington) for valuable advice; Mary Mark Ockerbloom for clarifications about the Web resource Celebration of Women Writers; Mary Beth Barilla of Blackwell Publishing for a review copy of *A Companion to Digital Humanities* (Schreibman et al. 2004); Marge Gammon (NetLibrary) for a copy of her American Library Association (ALA) Midwinter 2005 PowerPoint presentation; Lou Burnard, of the TEI Consortium, for pointing me to *Electronic Textual Editing* (2004) and answering my questions; Edward M. Griffin (University of Minnesota) and Edward J. Gallagher (Lehigh University) for information about their presentations at the Society of Early Americanists' 2005 conference; David Nicholls (MLA Book Publications) for arranging permission to reprint excerpts from "Guiding Questions for Vetters of Scholarly Editions" in Appendix 2; Deborah Thomas (Library of Congress) for providing a copy of her ALA Midwinter 2005 PowerPoint presentation about the National Digital Newspaper Program; Tom Franklin for answering questions about the Digital Book Index; Dayna Holz for answering questions about the California Digital Library's eScholarship program; Daniel J. Cohen (George Mason University) for responding to inquiries about SyllabusFinder; Jill Fluvog (DiMeMa Inc.) for information about CONTENTdm® Digital Collection Management Software; and John L. Bryant (Hofstra University) for updates regarding the Melville Society's Web site.

Nor would the report have been possible without a variety of publishers providing me with trial access to their products, including ProQuest (EEBO, LION); the Modern Language Association (ADE [Association of Departments of English] Web site); Choice/Association of College & Research Libraries (ChoiceReviews.Online); Readex (Evans and Shaw-Shoemaker Digital Editions, Early American Newspapers); Thomson Gale (ECCO, LitFinder); Columbia University Press (Gutenberg-e); University of Virginia Press (Rotunda collection); OCLC (First Search/WorldCat); and Alexander Street Press (Black Short Fiction, Women and Social Movements, North American Theatre Online).

A number of specialists read drafts of different sections of this report. Their comments improved it substantially. These reviewers include Edward L. Ayers (University of Virginia); Angela Courtney (Indiana University Libraries); Shawn Martin, Mark Sandler, and Perry Willett (University of Michigan Libraries); and John Unsworth (University of Illinois, Champaign-Urbana).

Martha L. Brogan
New Haven, August 2005

About the Authors

Martha L. Brogan is an independent library consultant with two decades of experience in academic libraries, most recently as associate dean and director of collection development at Indiana University Libraries-Bloomington. During her five-year tenure at Indiana University, Ms. Brogan helped launch the Wright American Fiction project within the Committee on Institutional Cooperation. Previously, she served as a social sciences librarian at Yale University and as a Western European library specialist and assistant to the provost and vice president of academic affairs at the University of Minnesota. In 2003, the Digital Library Federation commissioned Ms. Brogan to write *A Survey of Digital Library Aggregation Services*. She was a fellow in the Frye Leadership Institute sponsored by the Council on Library and Information Resources, Educause, and Emory University in 2001.

Daphnée Rentfrow has spent the past five years investigating the use of digital projects in course development. She holds a Ph.D. in comparative literature from Brown University, where from 2001–2004 she was on the research faculty with an appointment in the Department of Modern Culture and Media. She was a senior editor and project manager for the Modernist Journals Project at Brown, where she developed materials for students and scholars using this digital collection. She recently held a CLIR Postdoctoral Fellowship in Scholarly and Information Resources for Humanists at Yale University, where she concentrated on teaching and learning support in the use of digital text and images.

Foreword

The study of American literature is not limited to schools and colleges in the United States; "Am Lit" is a popular course of study all over the world, as a glimpse at the Web-usage statistics of any of the sites in this report would make abundantly clear. Given this need, and mindful of the rich holdings of manuscript, typescript, and printed materials that fill our libraries and archives, it is not surprising that from the earliest digitizing experiments, librarians turned their attention to American cultural heritage materials, and that both scholarly and amateur sites devoted to American authors have flourished from the early days of the Web.

Compared with students in many other humanistic disciplines, students specializing in American literature are well served with online primary works and related manuscripts or other contextual material—from the earliest novels to licensed, copyrighted works from twentieth-century poets and dramatists. This richness, however, is scattered and fragmentary: Some material is publicly accessible, and some is subscription based; some is full of insights from scholars, and some is the work of hobbyists; some is accurately digitized, and some distractingly not so. And nowhere is all this material gathered and categorized, revealed, and reviewed.

Around this mass of material and its somewhat uncoordinated activity swirl all the fears and debates about the value of digital scholarship; the role and nature of peer review in this arena; the stifling effect of current copyright (especially in regard to so-called orphaned works, whose owners are impossible to find); the need for easier and more-powerful tools to capture, enrich, and analyze this material; and the excitement of new research and teaching possibilities.

These factors, coupled with the growing availability of American literature resources online, make this report, commissioned as an internal document by The Andrew W. Mellon Foundation and expanded for publication through a partnership between the Council on Library and Information Resources and the Digital Library Federation, a timely and much needed work. Martha Brogan has done a splendid job of analyzing a complex digital landscape and of synthesizing the feedback of nearly 40 scholars and librarians.

The results, part annotated survey of resources divided by type (e.g., subject gateways, author studies) and part analysis of prevailing trends and opinions, should help us discover what exists already, identify major resource gaps, and, on this basis, pull together the multiple shards of opinion and observation into a coherent narrative.

This report will be useful to anyone interested in the current state of online American literature resources. It will also be of use to individuals with a general interest in the shifts in scholarly communication and pedagogy that our universities and colleges are experiencing, and in humanities scholars' responses to the opportunities and pitfalls afforded by digital library collections and services.

David Seaman, Executive Director
Digital Library Federation

x

... this rainbow looked like Hope—
Quite a celestial Kaleidoscope.
—Lord Byron, *Don Juan*, II, XCIII

1. INTRODUCTION

The word *kaleidoscope* comes from a Greek phrase meaning "to view a beautiful form," and this report makes the leap of faith that "all scholarship is beautiful" (Ayers 2005b). The point here is not to pit one medium against another but to explore what digital resources offer to the study of American literature. This report recognizes myriad digital projects, attempting to reveal and lay out the various brightly colored shards into a provisional pattern of coherence. Its purpose is twofold: to offer a sampling of the types of digital resources currently available or under development in support of American literature; and to identify the prevailing concerns of specialists in the field as expressed during interviews conducted between July 2004 and May 2005. Part two of the report consolidates the results of these interviews with an exploration of resources currently available to illustrate, on the one hand, a kaleidoscope of differing attitudes and assessments, and, on the other, an underlying design that gives shape to the parts. Part three examines six categories of digital work in progress: (1) quality-controlled subject gateways, (2) author studies, (3) public domain e-book collections and alternative publishing models, (4) proprietary reference resources and full-text primary source collections, (5) collections by design, and (6) teaching applications. This survey is informed by a selective review of the recent literature, focusing especially on contributions by scholars appearing in discipline-based journals.

1.1 Scope

1.1.1 What Is American Literature?

The study of American literature is inseparable from an examination of its cultural context. From the era of exploration and discovery through the Revolutionary period, American literature is found in diverse forms: in poetry, captivity narratives, essays, letters, speeches, travel accounts, religious tracts, sermons, political and commercial documents, and diaries. The study of early American literature, in particular, is inherently interdisciplinary, drawing from history, religion, economics, geography, and political philosophy, and difficult to separate from the social sciences. Moreover, American literature before the nineteenth century cannot easily be divorced from English literature, since until the early nineteenth century, publishers and most readers were located in England. Adding to this confusion, the study of American literature of the past two centuries has traditionally been organized by author and genre—notably, fiction, poetry, drama, and prose nonfiction.

Kenneth Roemer (University of Texas, Arlington) at his Web site Covers, Titles, and Tables: The Formations of American Literary Canons provides insight to the changing conception of the subject by gathering in one place the tables of contents of important histories and anthologies of American literature published from 1829 up to the present. As these listings make clear, a few simple questions recur, but have different answers, as the decades go by:

- When did American literature start? Roemer notes the following:

  1607 (Tyler) and 1620 (Parrington) suggest different British, English language origins (John Smith and Bradford). The opening essays in Spiller and Bercovitch focus on early European explorers and chroniclers; Elliott's history goes back thousands of years to American Indian rock art and oral literature; for Pattee "American" commences in 1770. The shifting dates provoke basic questions about whether the "American" in our literature is primarily English and monolingual, European multicultural, trans-Atlantic multicultural, or defined primarily by legal and political concepts.

- What defines it?

  The tables of contents of histories also imply differing views of how American literature should be "told": as an authoritative historical chronicle (Tyler); as expressions of important ideals, themes, and unities (Parrington, Pattee, and Spiller); or as a reflection of both the unities and multiplicities of American cultures (Elliott and Bercovitch).

- Which writers belong?

  The radical shifts in the number of authors included in anthologies also reflect critical and institutional changes in the history of the field. In 1919, one year before the formation of the MLA's [Modern Language Association] American Literature Section, the substantial number of authors (more than 100) represented in Fred Lewis Pattee's anthology reflects an understandable desire to announce that there was enough American literature to justify courses and extensive study. The radical shrinking of that number in William Gibson and George Arm's *Twelve American Writers* (1962) . . . reflects . . . the obvious attempt to prove that American has produced "masterpieces." . . . The significant increase in numbers of authors and types of written and oral literatures represented in recent anthologies (e.g., the Jehlen-Warner table of contents of English literatures "of America" before 1800 lists 201 selections) makes the "expanding canon" dramatically clear to students (Roemer 1999).

1.1.2 Parameters

These changing definitions influence the curriculum, the organization of scholarly societies, and the scope of scholarly resources. They are also manifest in the different priorities, needs, and expectations of stakeholders who use and create digital resources to support the field. This survey reflects the enormous breadth of academic inquiry in American literature, extending from the Early Americas Digital Archive, a growing collection of electronic editions of early texts originally written in or about the Americas (circa 1492–1820) and culminating with the Electronic Literature Directory, created by the Electronic Literature Organization to provide easy access to "cutting-edge literature" and new forms of writing.[1]

Despite its breadth, the survey is by no means exhaustive. It highlights representative projects to illustrate the types of resources available and how they might be put to use. It also attempts to summarize the current trends and prevailing issues in the application of digital technologies to teaching and research in American literature. Given the formidable expertise of the respondents, the growing body of literature, and the proliferation of digital materials, a report such as this can best be understood as a starting point for deeper inquiry and as an invitation for more-extensive conversations among its many stakeholders.

The preponderance of resources under review predate 1923, reflecting the constraints of making copyrighted materials available online. Twentieth-century literature and new forms of the literary avant-garde are, regrettably, largely ignored with the notable exception of the work of the Electronic Literature Organization. The report draws examples from major genres, including fiction, poetry, drama, and prose nonfiction, but various subgenres are excluded, for example, literary history, children's literature, history of the book, film studies, and literary criticism and theory.[2] While there are examples drawn from women's, ethnic, and regional literature, these fields are not covered systematically. Applications of new technology to composition and creative writing are excluded. In terms of formats, books and electronic full-text resources take precedence over periodicals and newspapers.[3] The discussion of commercial databases

---

[1] For discussions about contemporary new media, refer to the *Electronic Book Review* available at http://www.electronicbookreview.com/.

[2] Refer to the regular columns about Internet resources in *College & Research Libraries* for guides to these and other topics. See, for example, Mach 2004 on twentieth-century authors; Roberson, Richey, and Kratzert 2002 on literary theory; Shirkey 2003 on e-poetry; and Werre and Story-Huffman 2000 on children's literature. See also Sparr 2003 about poetry journals on the Web.

[3] For an elaboration about the influence of American eighteenth-century periodical and newspaper content, refer to Kamrath 2002.

is restricted primarily to reference resources and full-text primary source collections. A discussion of commercial e-book providers such as NetLibrary and eBrary was beyond the scope of this report. Finally, the report excludes Web resources that point users primarily to printed works, such as PAL: Perspectives in American Literature—A Research and Reference Guide (edited by Paul P. Reuben, California State University-Stanislaus) and the Outline of American Literature, sponsored by the U.S. Department of State, International Information Programs (edited by Kathryn VanSpanckeren, University of Tampa).

1.1.3 Typologies

Resources are grouped into broad categories in order to identify common characteristics, trends, and challenges. In the absence of any agreed-upon vocabulary, typology, or taxonomy for digital genres in this field, the author identified a few broad categories as a convenient way to focus the discussion in areas of high activity. The placement of any particular resource is open to debate, and many resources could have been discussed under a variety of rubrics. As one frustrated scholar suggested, there must be some labels other than the ones he has been using— "magnet sites, sponge sites, mall sites, tentacled sites, etc." The report does rely to the extent practicable on two digital manifestations, or genres, that enjoy some degree of definition: quality-controlled subject gateway (Koch 2000), and thematic research collections (Unsworth 2000b; Palmer 2004). The concept of electronic scholarly editions is also well documented thanks to the publication of *Electronic Textual Editing* (Burnard et al. 2004) and the Modern Language Association of America's revised "Guidelines for Editors of Scholarly Editions" (MLA 2005).

The various genres need more-precise definition so as to indicate what is unique about them. More than terminology is at stake, as Brown University's Julia Flanders, editor of Women Writers Online, suggests in her provocative essay "Trusting the Electronic Edition." Scholars need to make a distinction, she writes, between "editions which are primarily pedagogical in their aims, those which aim above all at scholarly authority, and those which attempt to provide textual information as high-quality data which can be analyzed and processed" (Flanders 1998, 301). In practice, many scholars use the term *electronic archives* (e.g., The Walt Whitman Archive, Dickinson Electronic Archives) in preference to either *thematic research collections* or *electronic scholarly editions*. As the editors of The William Blake Archive explain:

> Though "archive" is the term we have fallen back on, in fact we envision a unique resource unlike any other currently available for the study of Blake—a hybrid all-in-one edition, catalogue, database, and set of scholarly tools capable of taking full advantage of the opportunities offered by new information technology. (See explanation of the word *archive* at http://www.blakearchive.org/.)

1.2 Interviews

Between July 2004 and May 2005, the author conducted telephone and e-mail interviews with nearly 40 scholars, librarians, and practitioners (Appendix 1). This cohort represents practicing digital specialists as well as representative organizational leaders. Although the interviewees figure among the best-known experts in their respective fields, each made a point of referring the author to several other colleagues who are also doing important digital work. The interviews were open-ended and unstructured, often using the person's particular digital project as a starting point, but endeavoring to learn how well scholars of American literature in general are served by existing digital resources and what is most needed to advance digital scholarship. What are the immediate priorities: ramping up the speed of full-text digitization, creating a more cohesive and integrated portal, developing tools for text mining and manipulation, or promoting innovative training models? How much attention should be devoted to standards, promotion-and-tenure practices, and preservation of data? Has the technology begun transforming instruction and research? If not, what are the barriers? Part two of this report is an attempt to summarize the major issues and concerns revealed by these interviews.

1.3 Resource Descriptions

The resource annotations in this report are not intended as original, evaluative critiques. Most are taken from the descriptions at the provider's Web site with little or no editing. Readers should refer to James L. Harner's *Literary Research Guide: An Annotated Listing of Reference Sources in English Literary Studies* (2002) for qualitative annotations of reference sources and consult his ongoing list of updated entries that is freely available online. *The Charleston Advisor: Critical Reviews of Web Products for Information Professionals*, a modestly priced subscription journal, provides free online access to some resource reviews (e.g., Google Scholar, December 2004) and columns (e.g., the interview with Ted Koppel of The Library Corporation on Standards, April 2005). It is an excellent source for critical evaluations of tools and Web trends across all disciplines. In addition, the regular columns in *C&RL News* on Internet resources on specific topics, including many related to American literature, provide good overviews of Web sites (1998–present). Previously published reviews are freely accessible to all through the American Library Association, Association of College & Research Libraries (ACRL) Web site. It is unfortunate that current updates are restricted to ACRL members, since many people would benefit from being able to obtain the most current listings.[4]

---

4 See the References section for some relevant examples or refer to http://www.ala.org/ala/acrl/acrlpubs/crlnews/internetresourcestopic.htm.

1.4 Delving Deeper into the Literature

This report examines developments only over the past dozen years, that is, since the ascendance of the Web. The history of humanities computing and its application to literary studies extends back decades. Readers seeking a deeper historical context should refer to Susan Hockey's *Electronic Texts in the Humanities* (2000) and her chapter "The History of Humanities Computing" in *A Companion to Digital Humanities* (Schreibman et al. 2004). Thomas Rommel's chapter in Schreibman's volume also places literary studies into a historical context. Librarians new to the field will find useful discussions in Betty H. Day and William A. Wortman's *Literature in English: A Guide for Librarians in the Digital Age* (2000), which includes implications for collection management, library instruction, and reference among other topics.[5] Finally, among the recent outstanding works exploring issues only touched upon in this report, readers should refer to the essays in *Electronic Textual Editing* (Burnard et al. 2004); *A Companion to Digital Humanities* (Schreibman et al. 2004); *Humanities Computing* (McCarty 2005); and the readings cited at A Networked Interface for Nineteenth-Century Electronic Scholarship (NINES.org) Web site. In closing, readers can look forward to the recommendations of the American Council of Learned Societies (ACLS) Commission on Cyberinfrastructure for the Humanities and Social Sciences later in 2005. These recommendations will, no doubt, provide a blueprint for the future that complements many of the findings in this report.

1.5 A Word about the Audience

This report gives an overview of areas of concentrated activity in digital American literature. It is intended primarily for the non-specialist—librarian, instructor, publisher, university administrator—who seeks an introduction to the field and wants to know more about the prevailing issues and the types of digital resources available. Experts in any given aspect of digital work—scholarly editing, text conversion, metadata, the preservation and archiving of data, American literature Web sites, textual theory—may discover little new here in their area of specialization and find reason to object to the casual treatment of complicated topics. Whatever its shortcomings, the report aims to stimulate a productive dialogue in the wider community and lead to a better understanding of what is at stake in the world of digital scholarship.

---

[5] See Stebelman 2000 for an earlier article discussing Internet resources in English and American literature.

2. SUMMARY OF FINDINGS

2.1 "A Revolution Led from Above"

Lest anyone forget the extent to which the academy now relies on digital media, Edward L. Ayers, dean of the College and Graduate School of Arts and Sciences at the University of Virginia—in a series of hopeful talks delivered around the country on scholarship in the digital age—emphatically reminds everyone of the transformation that has taken place in the past decade.[6] Citing technological advances in networking, mass storage, digital conversion, and speed, Ayers notes that millions of objects—scanned, transcribed, and cataloged, including (as borne out in this report) books, articles, diaries, letters, newspapers, films, artifacts, oral histories, and images—are now available to millions of people. He recalls those days, not very long ago, when scholars denounced the disappearing library card catalog and its conversion to an online environment. Creating digital copies of journal articles (enter JSTOR) likewise met with initial disapprobation. Now, a few short years later, scholars realize the power of linking directly from the library's online catalog and a host of specialized databases to digital objects of all types. As Ayers remarks, scholars are now "demanding" around-the-clock online access not only from their offices but also from their lakeside cabins and, librarians would add, from their sabbatical and fellowship posts around the globe.

While the texts of their trade are rapidly becoming available anywhere, anytime, humanities scholars, who might have much to gain from digital media's potential to spread their scholarship, remain firmly committed to traditional forms. Why is it, Ayers wonders, that humanities scholarship is dedicated to constant change and innovation, "yet the institutions in which it is embedded, maybe especially the monograph and the scholarly article, have been remarkably, even stubbornly, stable?" He argues that scholarship should be able to take any form as long as it adheres to the fundamental principles of "documented research and rigorous, anonymous peer review." But humanities scholars, in large part, have resisted change, viewing digital media as "a dissolution, distraction, a diversion" from their "real work." Recent Ph.D.s interviewed for this report bear witness to even harsher judgments by established faculty in English departments about the value of digital media: It is irrelevant to scholarship, a matter of indifference to them, or not even in their consciousness.

It is, then, no wonder that Ayers credits visionary librarians, professional societies, and their supporters in the philanthropic world with spearheading the transformation. It is "a revolution led from above," he asserts, by powerful and prestigious agencies such as the American Historical Association (AHA), the American Council on Learned Societies (ACLS), the Council on Library and Information Resources (CLIR), the Digital Library Federation (DLF), and The

---

6 Unless noted otherwise, this summary and quotes are from Ayers 2005b and from notes Ayers provided the author from his talk "Revolution in the Archives" (2005a).

Andrew W. Mellon Foundation. These national organizations have "sponsored ambitious efforts to create electronic monograph series and to foster new kinds of scholarship," as also made evident by the review of resources in this report. Deploying multifaceted approaches, they have sponsored initiatives to encourage a new cadre of specialists who can, in the words of Ayers, both "walk the walk of a discipline and talk the talk of the digital world." These national leaders, however, mindful of trends in society at large and concerned that the humanities keep pace, "are not waiting for scholars to build new things" before taking further action. Rather than risk being left behind, they hope to establish the requisite infrastructure by creating a digital "vacuum" that scholarship will rush to fill. While most of the scholars and practitioners interviewed for this report applaud these efforts—in fact, many of them are directly involved—they are renegades. Shifting the campus culture in the humanities, and perhaps especially in English departments, is a slow proposition. To paraphrase one senior campus administrator, you have to let people come to accept digital media on their own; you can't force it on them. His institution encourages experimentation and adoption by offering training and professional development support, but is moving "incrementally" while waiting for the next generation of faculty to accelerate the process.

2.2 Creating a Culture of Innovation

The University of Virginia repeatedly emerges as *the* place where digital innovation happens in the humanities. Ayers's trajectory of scholarship is a case study of how this paradigm shift occurred, giving his observations considerable weight. A decade ago, his Valley of the Shadow: Two Communities in the American Civil War, along with The Complete Writings and Pictures of Dante Gabriel Rossetti: A Hypermedia Research Archive, developed by his English department colleague Jerome McGann, formed the cornerstones of the newly created Institute for Advanced Technology in the Humanities (IATH) at the University of Virginia (UVa). Today, both innovators are award-winning, nationally recognized digital scholars. When they embarked on these projects in 1993, however, they were charting new territory. The Web had just presented itself as a new medium for the production and dissemination of scholarship, and because there were few standards, best practices, or computing tools to facilitate their work, Ayers and McGann had to invent them.

John Unsworth, the prescient former director of IATH and now dean and professor of the Graduate School of Library and Information Science at the University of Illinois at Urbana-Champaign, attributes IATH's success to two innovations. First, senior computing administrators insisted that all its projects focus on research, envisioning IATH as a fulcrum to leverage change in the institutional culture. By targeting research, rather than teaching with technology—which has a shorter developmental life cycle—they set the stage for serious long-term investigations. Moreover, Unsworth understood that teaching would be strengthened as a natural outcome of research because "the curriculum rests on scholarship" (Chodorow 1997). Second, in direct support of the first principle, IATH fellows were given generous two-year appointments "in residence" with a half-year teaching release time. "Forbidden from grant-writing during the first year," they were forced to delve into their work before going out in search of external funds.[7]

In his award-winning book *Radiant Textuality: Literature after the World Wide Web*, McGann explains how IATH's commitment to the Web caused a fundamental shift in the character of his project:

> On the technical side, a major challenge for the institute and its fellows was to pursue long-term, large-scale humanities computing research projects with an almost ascetic rejection of the surface effects and short-term gains offered by proprietary software and proprietary data standards. In an apparently paradoxical way, IATH's W3 commitment drove its projects to make rigorous logical design a fundamental goal. This pursuit reflected a dedication to portability and the abstraction that enables it—even if it also entailed doing without good tools for creating or disseminating the scholarly work in the short run. As it happened, that commitment was to induce a profound shift in the principal focus and goals of The Rossetti Archive—moving it, in fact, from an editorial project per se to a machine for exploring the nature of textuality in more general and theoretical ways. (McGann 2001, 10–11)

By bringing fellows together in a central, shared, intentional space, IATH fosters a sense of community and enables networking among scholars long after their residencies end. Time and again in this report, the premier examples of digital innovation emanate from IATH, although their influence now extends beyond the University of Virginia: The William Blake Archive, The Complete Writings and Pictures of Dante Gabriel Rossetti: A Hypermedia Research Archive, The Dickinson Electronic Archives, The Walt Whitman Archive, Uncle Tom's Cabin & American Culture: A Multi-Media Archive, and The Salem Witch Trials Documentary Archive and Transcripton Project, among others.[8] Unsworth calls these "thematic research collections," and while their specific research agendas vary, he has identified the following characteristics that they have in common:
1. necessarily electronic (because of the cost of 2, 3, 8)
2. constituted of heterogeneous data types (multimedia)
3. extensive but thematically coherent
4. structured but open-ended
5. designed to support research
6. authored (and usually multiauthored)

---

[7] Unless cited otherwise, Unsworth's quotes are from a telephone interview conducted on March 10, 2005.

[8] For a critical evaluation of this genre and scholarly electronic editions, refer to Karlsson and Malm 2004.

7. interdisciplinary
8. collections of *digital primary resources* (and they themselves are *second-generation digital resources*) (Unsworth 2000b)

Unsworth's colleague Carole L. Palmer has reworked this list of attributes in an effort to separate content and function as reproduced in figure 1.

Fig. 1. Features of thematic research collections

Content	Function

Basic elements
    Digital
    Thematic
	Research support

Variable characteristics
    Coherent
    Heterogeneous
    Structured
    Open-ended
	Scholarly contribution
	Contextual mass
	Interdisciplinary platform
	Activity support

Source: Palmer 2004, 350

While thematic research collections emerged as IATH's signature contribution to scholarship, IATH also helped spawn parallel innovations in teaching and library services—often working in tandem with the UVa Library's Electronic Text Center. The net result is an impressive array of digital multimedia archives; easy-to-use teaching tools and interpretative Web sites; experimentation with hybrid public-commercial publishing; prodigious digital-conversion projects; advanced humanities computing tools; and an emerging infrastructure in the form of a digital-object repository (e.g., Fedora) with a commitment to long-term data preservation, migration, and access.

2.3 Building Cyberinfrastructure for the Humanities and Social Sciences

Apart from experts such as those interviewed for this report, it is safe to assume that most scholars of American literature could not begin to articulate, let alone imagine, what constitutes a cyberinfrastructure or why they would ever need it. Unsworth, who chairs the ACLS Commission on Cyberinfrastructure for the Humanities and Social Sciences, has quipped that the name itself has been the biggest obstacle to explaining the goals of the commission. Coined by the National Science Foundation (NSF) "to describe the new research environments in which capabilities of the highest level of computing tools are available to researchers in an interoperable network," the word *cyberinfrastructure,* according to Unsworth, refers to any shared resource that "has utility beyond a particular project or institution," e.g., people, tools, standards, or collections.[9]

---

[9] ACLS Commission on Cyberinfrastructure for the Humanities and Social Sciences Web site. Available at http://www.acls.org/cyberinfrastructure/cyber_what_is.htm.

The investigations of the ACLS commission, which was formed in 2004, go much deeper into critical issues that are only touched upon in this report.[10] Readers are encouraged to review the papers of prominent constituents delivered in a series of public hearings held by the commission. The observations of noted classicist and digital innovator James O'Donnell (2004), provost of Georgetown University, and of Martin Mueller (2004), professor of classics and English at Northwestern University, echo the concerns of forward-looking campus administrators and literary scholars interviewed for this report. After a period of public commentary, says Unsworth, the commission's final report will be released later in 2005 with recommendations, outcomes, and next steps. Because the humanities and social sciences do not have any agency that is equivalent to the NSF to coordinate their research agendas, the commission will look to a coalition of private and public agencies, including the ACLS and other scholarly societies, private foundations, and government agencies, to fill the void.

2.4 Shaping the Future

When seeking innovative models relevant to American literature, the author repeatedly came upon ways in which the history profession has been actively engaged in an open, highly visible dialogue about the application of digital resources toward a transformation of their discipline. In contrast to their counterparts in literature, the AHA and the Organization of American Historians (OAH) have played leading roles in fostering innovation through large-scale partnerships such as the following:

- The History Cooperative, "a pioneering nonprofit humanities resource offering top-level online history scholarship," including full-text access to a growing number of premier journals in the discipline;
- Gutenberg-e, an experimental program of the AHA and Columbia University Press to publish, upon "rigorous academic review," electronic monographs by recent Ph.D.s whose work represents "the most distinguished and innovative scholarship delivered with creative and thoughtful use of digital technology";
- The ACLS History E-Book Project, a collaboration with eight learned societies (including AHA and OAH) and 60 contributing publishers "to assist scholars in the electronic publishing of high-quality works in history, to explore the intellectual possibilities of new technologies, and to help assure the continued viability of history writing in today's changing publishing environment";
- History Matters, a nationally recognized, sophisticated gateway to original essays and peer-reviewed Web sites designed for high school and college teachers of U.S. history courses, sponsored by the Center for History and New Media at George Mason University and the American Social History Project/Center for Media and Learning, City University of New York Graduate Center;

---

10 For background information, see Goldenberg-Hart 2004.

- Recent Scholarship Online, a searchable, cumulative database of history-related citations available to members of the OAH that offers personalized e-mail updates and the ability to save, edit, and e-mail bibliographies;
- A freely accessible Web site that serves as a companion to the Textbooks and Teaching section published each year by the *Journal of American History* (*JAH*) with syllabi and other supplemental material from the authors as well as the full text of the print articles; and
- Echo: Exploring & Collecting History Online, developed by the Center for History and New Media at George Mason University with funding from the Alfred P. Sloan Foundation. This Web site has four components: it catalogs, annotates, and reviews more than 5,000 sites on the history of science, technology, and industry; maintains a directory of Web sites that emphasize the online collection of historical materials; provides a Tools Center of any and all tools applicable to the practice of digital history; and, through a Resource Center, offers a practical guide to the best practices for doing digital history.

A sampling of recent issues of core journals in American literature turned up very few articles testing the concept of digital scholarship (comparable to the article by Thomas and Ayers 2003); frankly assessing experimental programs (cf. Manning 2004); reviewing Web resources (as has the *JAH* since 2001); debating digital media's "transformative" impact on teaching (cf. Brown 2004a and 2004b, and others in *Rethinking History*; cf. Kornblith and Lasser 2003, in a collection of essays in the *JAH*; cf. Sklar 2002); or probing open-access issues (cf. Rosenzweig 2005).

Martha Nell Smith's "Computing: What's American Literary Study Got to Do with IT?" in the December 2002 issue of *American Literature*, stands out as a rare contribution from a practicing digital scholar. The article attempts to explain the advantages of digital media and is based on her considerable experience as editor of the Dickinson Electronic Archives and director of the Maryland Institute for Technology in the Humanities (MITH). Also singular is Joanna Brooks's "New Media's Prospect: A Review of Web Resources in Early American Studies," appearing in *Early American Literature* in 2004. It is in keeping with this slow acceptance of digital technology by scholars in the field that Jerome McGann's 2001 book *Radiant Textuality: Literature after the World Wide Web*, which garnered the Modern Language Association's James Russell Lowell Prize in 2002, was reviewed in *American Literature* only in 2004 (Ramirez 2004). More important, these are isolated achievements, unrelated to programmatic initiatives by the profession as a whole such as those now routinely emerging in American history.

Modern Language Association of America. It is only natural to turn to the powerful MLA, which represents the interests of scholars in American literature within ACLS, to inquire about its leadership role in advancing digital scholarship. According to Executive Director Rosemary Feal, the MLA has three primary functions: (1) to promote and protect the scholarship of its members; (2) to continually adapt and evolve as a publisher to make publications that are useful for the research community; and (3) in collaboration with librarians, publishers, the ACLS, and other groups, to grapple with the changing environment and to chart a direction for the future. In support of these goals, Feal cites the following activities:

- The MLA's Task Force on Evaluating Scholarship for Tenure and Promotion—working in 2004 and 2005—will examine the criteria and procedures used to assess the scholarly work of faculty members being reviewed for tenure or promotion, will consider the effects of the widely discussed crisis in scholarly publishing on the review process, and will recommend evaluation guidelines for discussion and possible adoption by the field. It is conducting a representative survey of 500 departments to inventory their promotion-and-tenure practices and ascertain whether standards are shifting. It hopes to discover how departments evaluate contributions other than print media for promotion and tenure. The results of the survey are anticipated in fall 2005. (The MLA Executive Council approved a "Statement on Publication in Electronic Journals" at its October 2003 meeting.)

- Since Stephen Greenblatt, writing on behalf of the MLA's Executive Council, issued a "Call for Action on Problems in Scholarly Book Publishing" to members in May 2002, and since the Ad Hoc Committee subsequently issued its report on the Future of Scholarly Publishing (available at MLA's Web site), the MLA has continued to seek ways to support the mission of university presses. The 2004 issue of *Profession*, MLA's annual journal of opinion, featured a forum on the publishing and tenure crises.

- Through its revised "Guidelines for Editors of Scholarly Editions" (August 3, 2005), including the series of "Guiding Questions for Vetters of Scholarly Editions" pertaining specifically to electronic editions (see Appendix 2), the MLA's Committee on Scholarly Editions (CSE) helps set standards for evaluation of electronic scholarly publications so that they receive the same treatment as their print counterparts. With the TEI (Text-Encoding Initiative) Consortium, CSE cosponsored publication of *Electronic Textual Editing* (Burnard et al. 2004), a collection of essays that incorporates these guidelines. The CSE is poised to give its approval to electronic scholarly editions.

- The *MLA International Bibliography* indexes peer-reviewed electronic publications including e-books, e-journals (95 titles), and online bibliographies; where possible, as with JSTOR, they link directly to full-text content.

- The *MLA Newsletter* is available online for members. *PMLA*, the journal of MLA, and *Profession*, an annual publication of MLA, are available by electronic subscription through *Ingenta* (a comprehensive collection of academic and professional publications). Back files of *PMLA* are accessible from JSTOR.

- The MLA's American Literature section sponsors *American Literature: A Journal of Literary History, Criticism, and Bibliography*.

- The next edition of James Harner's *Literary Research Guide: An Annotated Listing of Reference Sources in English Literary Studies*, published by the MLA, will have an electronic version or electronic updates and may be developed as a portal to research in the field. More generally, the MLA is thinking about how technology can facilitate rapid updating so that publications are not frozen in time, making it possible, for example, to turn bibliographies into e-resources for easy updating.
- Within five years, some version of the *MLA Handbook for Writers of Research Papers*, edited by Joseph Gibaldi, will become available in an electronic format. The MLA is consulting with librarians and reviewing which sections of the handbook are best suited to this change.
- The Committee on Information Technology, which issues the MLA's "Minimal Guidelines for Authors of Web Pages," is involved with instructional technology, and sponsors poster sessions about teaching with technology at MLA conventions.

Finally, Feal notes that the MLA tries to be responsive when approached by its members about what it might to do to influence peer-review processes, especially for those who develop e-resources of high quality.

This summary of the MLA's involvement is praiseworthy, and to this list should be added the prizes awarded by the organization to McGann's *Radiant Textuality* and to Morris Eaves (University of Rochester), Robert N. Essick (University of California, Riverside), and Joseph Viscomi (University of North Carolina, Chapel Hill) for The William Blake Archive in 2001–02—the first electronic edition to win the Distinguished Scholarly Edition award. Nevertheless, if the consensus of scholars interviewed in this report reflects the sentiments of the MLA's wider membership, its digital accomplishments are minor compared with what remains to be done—pointing at the very least to a public relations issue. One literature specialist, while noting numerous obstacles to more-widespread adoption of digital scholarship, referred to the lack of engagement by scholarly societies in general as the most serious problem of all. In reference to the MLA's leadership role in testing new forms of scholarly publication, another scholar asserted that it is "not even on the radar screen." Yet another called the MLA Executive Council's stance on the crisis in scholarly publishing and tenure "hardly worth reading . . . completely misguided," concluding that they "do *not* understand." Two others spoke of "frustration" when trying to accomplish their work through MLA committees, having achieved their ultimate goal "despite" the parent organization. Finally, one disaffected member explains that the MLA has in recent decades become a "political organization, not a scholarly one" in which "literature is just a tool, not the true subject." The most charitable observer noted that the MLA is trying harder, though its enormous size is a considerable hindrance. There is "more and more activity," he acknowledges, but the organization is slow and lumbering, like "a big elephant."

American Studies Association. While many interviewees believe that the MLA is curiously missing in action, they note substantial participation from another ACLS member, the American Studies Association (ASA). ASA is a major sponsor of The Visible Knowledge Project, a large-scale, five-year collaboration (discussed more fully in the Teaching Applications, section 3.6) that "aims to improve the quality of college and university teaching by focusing on both student learning and faculty development in technology-enhanced environments." ASA's Web site features communities based around the curriculum, technology and learning, and reference and research. Its flagship journal *American Quarterly* (*AQ*) has recently launched a new Web site, providing online access to its contents. Under a heading labeled "New Forms of Writing," the *AQ* solicits "proposals for and submissions of visual essays and essays that include hyperlink and online supplements, such as video and audio clips, additional images, [and] links to online sources for key archival information. . . . As we continue to build our Web site," it advises, "we are interested in proposals for essays and reviews that can be published online." In addition to regular reviews of exhibitions, "the *American Quarterly* is open to proposals for reviews of other cultural forms that are of interest to American studies scholars, including reviews of films, television shows, web sites, and CDs." Recently, the *AQ* has called for papers to be published in a special issue (September 2006) entitled "Rewiring the Nation: The Place of Technology in American Studies."

American Literature Association. The American Literature Association (ALA), according to its founder and Executive Board member, James Nagel (University of Georgia), is a "no-budget operation" that charges no dues and wants none. It serves its 10,000 members as an umbrella organization for almost 150 author societies and coordinates the meeting space for the annual conferences of these societies, which are held simultaneously. ALA does not publish its own scholarly journal; hence, it does not meet one of the key criteria for membership in the ACLS. Many or most of the author societies, while low-budget operations, do publish journals and maintain Web sites that are a rich source of information about American writers. ALA's Web site features a directory of affiliated societies (in need of updating) and of members.

Nagel figures among the most vociferous of those interviewed in denouncing the quality of many online books, calling some efforts a "terrible waste of resources because the books placed online are from corrupt editions rather than from first editions," rendering them unsuitable for scholarship. Attributing the problem to the "ignorance of the technical people," he is not alone in decrying the absence of textual integrity or accurate bibliographical information about editions placed online.[11] As one example, Nagel notes that Hemingway's

---

[11] For an elaboration of the importance of textual scholarship in the digital environment, refer to McGann's October 3, 2002, lecture "Textonics: Literary and Cultural Studies in a Quantum World," delivered in conjunction with the Richard W. Lyman Award, which is presented by the National Humanities Center (Research Triangle Park, N.C.). McGann calls "restoring intimate relations between literarians and librarians" a "pressing current need" in service to electronic scholarship.

novel *The Sun Also Rises*, first published in 1926, was changed in 1934 to expunge anti-Semitic remarks. He also recognizes the huge problem of keeping up with single-author publications, estimating that some 3,500 journals produce some 60,000 articles, and an unknown number of books, about American authors annually. Keeping up with Hemingway alone is a full-time job, with some 600 articles and scores of books published about him annually. Nagel acknowledges that even the projects that he criticizes are exploring the right concepts by making materials more widely accessible. His primary concern is the lack of quality control and the need to coordinate "technical people and scholars." He has suggested that ALA could help do this in areas such as text selection by identifying a member of each constituent author society to serve as a digital project liaison. Singling out Networked Interface for Nineteenth-Century Electronic Scholarship, or NINES (see 2.5 and 3.3.5.3), as a worthwhile effort, ALA has recently joined this initiative as an affiliated group.[12]

Other Professional Organizations. Many other disciplinary and specialized professional associations, with their own journals and conferences, serve the needs of the primary cohort discussed in this report. They include scholarly societies organized by period, movement, or constituent group, such as the Society of Early Americanists, the North American Society for the Study of Romanticism, and the Society for the Study of American Women Writers. This group also embraces various organizations at the intersection of humanities computing and literary studies, including the Society for Textual Scholarship, the Association for Literary and Linguistic Computing, the Association for Computers and the Humanities, the TEI Consortium, the Association for Documentary Editing, and the Electronic Literature Organization.

2.5 Communities of Practice

The most frequent refrain heard from interviewees was the call for the development of a common agenda—a coming together of scholars, practitioners, publishers, and funding agencies to agree on priorities, standards, best practices, and next steps. One scholar cried out for a "larger sense of community," along with the "critical space" to see what developments are taking place across a variety of fronts—by different people in different fields: a "clearinghouse" of projects under development would be a start. Another asserted the need for "a more integrated approach by developers and grant agencies." "Developers," he continued, "must have the goal to integrate [their technical work] into a national site." There is a need for "strategic planning" and developing "paths of evolution" among practitioners, scholars, and major granting agencies, he concluded. This theme was echoed by a librarian, frustrated with overlapping and redundant projects, who regrets the lack of coordination. We need

---

[12] Based on telephone interview with Nagel conducted on August 11, 2004, and on e-mail correspondence of May 12, 2005.

to find ways to make the field less fragmentary, he recommended, adding that "throwing money" at the problem is no way to fix it. New models are called for, but what would be most useful: "Why not bring people together to ask?" he wondered. There are communities of practice developing in related fields, for example, the Digital Medievalist Project, established in 2003 "to help scholars meet the increasingly sophisticated demands faced by designers of contemporary digital projects."[13]

In direct support of scholars in nineteenth-century British and American literature, Jerome McGann created NINES, a multifaceted project "to found a publishing environment for integrated, peer-reviewed online scholarship." NINES is rapidly garnering support from a growing group of affiliates (including the ASA, ALA, and other specialized scholarly societies noted above). In addition to formulating processes for peer-reviewed digital scholarship and creating a publishing environment, NINES is developing analytical tools to support the work of its constituents. The effort as a whole might be construed as an attempt to build a cyberinfrastructure for scholars in nineteenth-century British and American literature. American literary scholars working outside the nineteenth century believe that there is a need for other communities of practice like NINES.

2.6 Tools to the Rescue?

An alarming number of digital projects aimed at the discovery of American literature are maintained by professionals as a labor of love. In particular, those devotees creating gateways and access to online books—Voice of the Shuttle (VoS), Literary Resources on the Net, Alex: Catalogue of Electronic Texts, the Online Books Page, A Celebration of Women Writers—continue their work as a service to the profession, assuredly not because it will lead to fame, fortune, promotion, or tenure. Rather than "expert enthusiast," one practitioner preferred to characterize himself as "a lucky person because my vocation is also my avocation." While that may be the case, without secure funding and full integration to a campus, let alone national, framework, these efforts will last only until the goodwill of their progenitors runs out. Their task was already Sisyphean before Google Print announced its partnership with five prominent research institutions to digitize more than 30 million volumes. Now, it seems truly impossible.[14]

Alan Liu's experience as the founder of the award-winning (now desperately behind) VoS is typical. Created when directory-type access to the Web was the norm, VoS initially offered features unavailable even through commercial services, namely, browsable access to annotated scholarly Internet resources situated in a disciplinary and

---

[13] Information about the Digital Medievalist Project can be found at http://www.digitalmedievalist.org/.

[14] For a general introduction to visualization tools and their application to libraries, refer to Luther, Kelly, and Beagle 2005.

historical framework. However, without a full-fledged technical support staff, VoS suffered a hack attack. The site had to be shut down, and it took three months "to recode the dynamic pages in the background." If the project is to continue, Liu suggests that it is time to redesign it on a national scale, taking advantage of open-source architecture and having it properly set up with a team of developers across the country. At the same time, he acknowledges that it might be more productive to concentrate instead on developing the "tools" to search and find scholarly information.

In the preliminary version of this report, based on interviews with 16 specialists, the term *tools* rarely came up (aside from Liu), except to acknowledge the need for "better search engines" to find out "how to get to these things." Not surprisingly, therefore, when an expert group of faculty, convened by DLF in June 2004, avowed the "severe need for tools customized for a range of scholarly inquiry needs," the federation discovered that "so unfamiliar is this area that we heard from several individuals that they had a hard time articulating precisely what they required from such tools, or what level of software creation skills or consultancy is available to them, and where." Concluding, "we are still in a stage where it is easier to react to an example of an existing tool than to dream them up," DLF decided instead to discuss and demonstrate a variety of software packages (Digital Library Federation 2004a).

Leading theoreticians such as Unsworth and McGann, who traverse the boundaries of humanities computing and literary scholarship, believe that a real breakthrough in digital scholarship hinges on building open, modular, extensible, and reusable tools.[15] These tools must be readily accessible and relatively easy to use and, above all, enable important work, such as literary analysis and interpretation. In reviewing progress over the past 10 years in humanities computing and articulating what would be required to make the necessary leap forward, Unsworth states:

> Building these tools will answer or moot many of the questions we've been discussing . . . and will shift the burden of proof, in effect, from the new modes of scholarship to traditional ones: if we build tools that do allow us to ask new questions and answer old ones, then it will be clear why we have built our digital libraries, and in the disciplines, we will worry about what hasn't changed in scholarly methodology, and not about what has (Unsworth 2003).

What purposes would these tools serve for literary scholars? Unsworth (2000a) identifies six "basic functions common to scholarly activity across disciplines, over time, and independent of theoretical orientation." He refers to them as "scholarly primitives." They are as follows:
1. discovering
2. annotating

---

15 See also Ramsay 2004.

3. comparing
4. referring
5. sampling
6. illustrating

2.6.1 Tool Projects Under Way

Unfortunately, there is no "tools center" to serve literary scholars as does the Echo site for history. A few of the more notable projects (externally supported national collaboratives), geared toward literature, are offered as a starting point for further exploration.

NINES tools are designed to support six basic scholarly tasks while opening rich digital archives and research collections to the interpretive interests of teachers and students. The six tasks (arranging, comparing, transforming, discussing, commenting on, and collecting texts and images) are addressed in a variety of ways by the tool set and by the markup schemes and interfaces NINES supports. These data models and tools are in various stages of development:[16]

- **Juxta** allows a scholar to locate for comparison equivalent textual passages and to display the equivalent image files as well as the transcriptions. It also allows comparisons between comparable pictorial objects or comparable textual and pictorial objects. All such comparisons can also be annotated. The tool will also collate equivalent textual strings (marked and unmarked) and create a schedule of the differences.

- **Ivanhoe** allows multiple "players," or research students, to undertake a collective investigation of a given text or field of texts by manipulating and transforming the material in order to expose features and meanings that the original text or field of texts ignores, suppresses, or puts at the margin. The play space licenses imaginative acts of reinterpretation. This tool is ideally suited for pedagogical and classroom work as well as for high-order investigations of difficult literary questions.

- **The Patacritcal Demon** is projected to release a beta version sometime in 2005. It will allow the formalization of acts of subjective interpretation (such as those developed through the protocols of New Criticism or "close reading"). It will track and visualize in various ways an individual's engagement with an individual text or document.

- **Collex** will allow users of digital resources to assemble and share virtual "collections" and to present annotated "exhibits" and rearrangements of online materials. These critical rearrangements can bring together materials that are variously diverse—materially, formally, historically. This tool set aims to reveal the interpretive possibilities embedded in any digital archive by making the manipulation and annotation of archived resources open to all users.

---

16 These descriptions are abridged versions of the text appearing at the NINES Web site at http://www.nines.org/tools/tools.html.

The NORA project will produce software for discovering, visualizing, and exploring significant patterns across large collections of full-text humanities resources in existing digital libraries and collections.[17] "In search-and-retrieval," Unsworth says, "we pose specific queries and get back answers to those queries; by contrast, the goal of data-mining is to produce new knowledge by exposing unanticipated patterns. Over the past decade, many millions of dollars have been invested in creating digital library collections: the software tools we'll produce in this project will make those collections significantly more useful for research and teaching."

NORA's initial content domain consists of about 5 gigabytes of eighteenth- and nineteenth-century British and American literary texts (about 10,000), including

- 6,000 texts from IATH's projects on Rossetti, Whitman, Dickinson, Blake, and Twain;
- more than 1,000 texts (mostly nineteenth century) from the Library of Southern Literature, University of North Carolina-Chapel Hill;
- 600 to 1,200 texts from the Early American Fiction collection at the University of Virginia;
- 120 texts of nineteenth-century British women poets from the University of California-Davis;
- 175 volumes of American verse plus literary materials from other collections, such as relevant journals from the Making of America;
- 1,100 literary texts from the Wright American Fiction collection, the Victorian Women Writers Project, and the Swinburne Project at Indiana University;
- 40 nineteenth-century literary texts from Brown University's Women Writers Project; and
- nineteenth-century literary texts, including several works by Charles Dickens from the Perseus project at Tufts University. (Kirschenbaum 2004 and NORA project Web site).

National Institute for Technology and Liberal Education (NITLE) Semantic Engine is designed to address the universal problem of accessing and organizing large amounts of unstructured digital text. Using mathematical algorithms to index the latent semantic content of documents, the prototype engine has been demonstrated to reduce drastically, if not eliminate, the need for expensive and time-consuming metadata tagging and to produce results superior to those produced by keyword searches in limited test domains.[18]

DLF Aquifer (see section 3.5.3.1) is a collaborative effort among a dozen DLF members to develop a test-bed of library tools and services for the scholar. Intended to realize the potential of a distributed open digital library, it will initially focus on American culture and

---

[17] This description and quote are extracted from the press release about NORA that is available at its Web site: http://noraproject.org.

[18] Quoted from the NITLE project Web site at http://www.nitle.org/tools/semantic.htm.

life, drawing on quality content from such projects as the American South, the American West, American Memory, Making of America, and Wright American Fiction. DLF Aquifer will provide tools and services for aggregating and distributing content by interoperating with

- repositories that preserve;
- content management systems that provide structure;
- e-learning systems that support the teaching and learning process; and
- personal content management systems that support the scholar.

DLF Aquifer will siphon content from mass-digitization projects.[19] Participating institutions are expected to adhere to consensually developed standards, information architectures, and development agendas that emphasize interoperability and deep resource sharing.

2.7 What's Not to Like?

Scholars of American literature readily recognize certain benefits that digital resources offer. Few would argue about their democratizing impact, making widely available, high-quality ("vetted, not random") digital surrogates on the Web, giving scholars and their students immediate access to primary sources worldwide. All revel in the way in which online access facilitates searching so that users can identify research patterns with "blinding speed." "Searchability of primary source material has been fun," as one scholar put it. It facilitates reading that is (in a positive way) "broad and shallow"—covering vast amounts of digital text and making intellectual connections that were previously impractical, if not impossible. They acknowledge the advantages of online access to peer-reviewed journals through reliable aggregators such as JSTOR. Scholars also appreciate the ability of Internet-accessible resources "to foreground" scholarly work. The Web is a starting point that helps situate literary texts in their cultural, sociopolitical, and historical contexts.

But here the consensus comes to a halt. Few are willing to use digital texts (outside e-journal articles) as the "text of record for a scholarly article"—even those digital resources (texts and archives) produced by their peers, by university libraries, or by otherwise credible publishers.

The obstacles to more-rapid deployment of digital resources in American literature are peppered throughout this report. Three have been highlighted: the absence of a prominent scholarly organization to lead from above and advocate a shared agenda among stakeholders; the need for more communities of practice; and the present state of (not-quite-ready-for-prime time) analytical and interpretative tools. Five more barriers stand clearly visible:

---

[19] Extracted from Aquifer Director Katherine Kott's presentation at the DLF Forum, April 13, 2005. Available at http://www.diglib.org/forums/spring2005/presentations/kott0504.ppt.

1. insufficient peer-review processes for digital scholarship
2. absence of trusted mechanisms to sustain and preserve digital work
3. thorny issues of copyright and permissions
4. paucity of sustainable business models
5. dearth of specialists

2.7.1 Insufficient Peer-Review Processes

Many have reported on the plight of the research monograph—dying with or without cause—and its traditional centrality to the promotion and tenure process (Chodorow 1997, Greenblatt 2002, Davidson 2003 and 2004, Estabrook and Warner 2003, Unsworth 2005). Meanwhile, in a recent survey of promotion-and-tenure practices in humanities departments, Cronin and LaBarre (2004) report "coming away from the data with the clear sense that granting of tenure in humanities departments still requires the production of a research monograph published by a reputable press. Sole authorship is expected," they continue, "and the documents we examined are virtually silent on the issue of collaboration and co-authorship . . ." (increasingly the norm in many other disciplines and a frequent feature of serious digital work). Cronin and LaBarre further note that

> A few institutions acknowledged the acceptability of online, electronic, and digital forms of scholarly production, but most were content to stress the importance of a candidate's work being subjected to peer review while remaining silent on the matter of medium. Overall, new modes of scholarly production and distribution received hardly any direct attention (Cronin and LaBarre 2004, 97).

It will be interesting to learn whether the MLA's promotion-and-tenure survey reveals more-nuanced or more-refined norms to accommodate new sorts of scholarship.

There is a divergence of opinion among faculty members interviewed for this report about the impact of digital scholarship on the promotion-and-tenure process. Many forms of digital scholarship appear without peer review. One scholar observed that some forms of digital peer review already occur but that there is no public record of scholarly transactions when they assess the digital work of their colleagues going up for promotion and tenure, serve as references for new digital scholars in the job market, or evaluate grant proposals in support of digital projects (e.g., by the National Endowment for the Humanities). In the field of history, there is evidence that digital work counts—Ayers tells the "bittersweet" story of William Thomas's success in gaining tenure at the University of Virginia on the basis of his digital scholarly work, only to be snapped up by the University of Nebraska. Individuals with freshly minted Ph.D. degrees in history whose work is featured in Gutenberg-e have secured tenure-track positions across the country. And in the opinion of at least one senior American literature scholar, the promotion-and-tenure issue is grossly exaggerated—the 25 top-tier research institutions may ignore digital scholarship, he contends, but every place else sees it as a definite advantage.

Although many forms of digital scholarship appear without formal peer review, such mechanisms are starting to emerge. Peer-reviewed articles are appearing in leading journals indexed by the MLA's *International Bibliography* such as *Postmodern Culture*, *Americana: The Journal of American Popular Culture*, and *Early Modern Literary Studies*. MLA's adoption of new guidelines for vetting electronic scholarly editions paves the way for digital editions to receive the imprimatur of "CSE-approved editions." NINES also sets out an ambitious agenda that includes creating peer-review processes. Finally, as more university presses initiate electronic imprints, such as the University of Virginia's Rotunda collections, peer review will become more widespread.

The development of formal peer-review mechanisms for digital scholarship will begin to address the concerns of scholars who remain skeptical about the quality of the digital text or the scholar's contribution to knowledge. Fearing that many forms of digital output are merely a way "to outsource the crisis in scholarly publishing to faculty and call it scholarship," one critic, while understanding "the labor of editorial selection or annotating a text as scholarship," stressed the importance of peer review "if a digital work is to be recognized as the archive of record." As the peer-review system is further developed, it will bring to the forefront debates about the value of digital scholarship and eventually help delineate what does or does not constitute bona fide scholarship in the digital world.

2.7.2 Absence of Trusted Mechanisms to Sustain and Preserve Digital Work

When discussing the absence of citations to digital work in the annual review of *American Literary Scholarship* (*AmLS*), one contributor (after noting that these resources are not subject to peer review) stated that there was no official editorial policy to prevent their inclusion but suggested that with a limited amount of space to cover traditional scholarship (peer-reviewed journal articles) most are hesitant to discuss a "resource that may go away."[20] This concern—the ephemeral nature of digital products—resonates with many scholars, who are reluctant, even as they appreciate the myriad advantages, to invest their life's labor into unstable media.

The CLIR report *New-Model Scholarship: How Will It Survive?* addresses these issues more fully (Smith 2003). Carpenter (2005) and Beagrie (2005) discuss digital-preservation activities supported by DLF's U.K. member, the Joint Information Systems Committee. Within the framework of this report, however, it is worth highlighting several initiatives closely tied to scholars of American literature.

---

[20] It is worth noting that *AmLS* does cover scholarship *about* digital archives. For example, M. Jimmie Killingsworth (2003, 69–70, and 2004, 83), when reviewing scholarship on "Whitman and Dickinson," cites Price 2001, "Dollars and Sense in Collaborative Digital Scholarship: The Example of the Walt Whitman Hypertext Archive," and Smith 2002, "Computing: What's American Literary Study Got to Do with IT?"

Preservation, Archiving and Dissemination (PAD) Project, Electronic Literature Organization (ELO). In *Acid-Free Bits: Recommendations for Long-Lasting Electronic Literature*, the ELO's PAD project is a "plea" to writers of born-digital literature "to work pro-actively in archiving their own creations, and to bear these issues in mind even in the act of composition," in the hope that the "creative component does not separate out from the curatorial" (Monfort and Wardrip-Fruin 2004). ELO's 13 principles for creating long-lasting work deserve widespread distribution.

1. Prefer open systems to closed systems.
2. Prefer community-directed systems to corporate-driven systems.
3. Consolidate code, supply comments.
4. Validate code.
5. Prefer plain-text formats to binary formats.
6. Prefer cross-platform options to single-system options.
7. Keep the whole system in mind.
8. Document early, document often.
9. Retain source files.
10. Use common tools and documented capabilities.
11. Maintain metadata and bibliographic information.
12. Allow and encourage duplication and republication.
13. Keep copies on different, durable media.

In a forthcoming report, *Born-Again Bits: A Framework for Migrating Electronic Literature*, the ELO "continues the argument" made in the initial report "by envisioning a technical framework that can not just keep e-lit alive but allow it to come back to life in new forms adapted to evolving technologies and social needs." More technical in nature, this second report is intended to give stakeholders (broadly defined as "authors, publishers, archivists, academics, programmers, grant officers, and others") "just enough of a glimpse of each other's expertise to see how an overall system for maintaining and reviving the life of electronic literature might be possible" (Liu et al. beta version, v1.13 September 2004).

The University of Virginia Library's Model for Sustaining Digital Scholarship. With several mature projects, including NINES, to consider as models, the University of Virginia Library, in consultation with faculty, is developing an institutional framework to support a full array of digital scholarship services. Its Model for Sustaining Digital Scholarship, currently under discussion, describes the workflow for projects selected by the library once they are camera-ready. As the document explains

> . . . "camera-ready" means that digital projects must meet (or be made to meet) all technical standards set by the Library. Production, peer review, editing, and rights management are assumed to be the responsibility of the scholar. The project(s) must have been vetted by a credible peer review group or organization and edited by a credible source (Internal UVa library document, SDS Library Model 4.1, November 9, 2004).

Although this document is still under development, the components described by the University Library represent the types of policy decisions that all academic libraries will soon confront:

Selection and Collection
Selection of born-digital projects for the Library's collections will more closely resemble selection of content for Special Collections. In general, we will favor projects that are open access and can be delivered for free to the public. Projects that have copyright or rights management issues will be considered on a case-by-case basis.

Technical Assessment
Technical assessment will be conducted to insure that technical standards have been met and to identify any technical impediments to delivery. In addition, the Library will work with scholars to find solutions to problems created by dependencies within projects caused when selection and collection does not include the entire project.

Access and Delivery
The Library will maintain and deliver collected digital projects via its established digital library infrastructure. Server and storage/archival space will be provided as part of an institutional infrastructure for supporting digital projects.

The Library may publicize collected projects but will not provide advertising and marketing services for them.

Preservation
The Library will commit to maintain collected projects for as long as it possibly can. Projects will be migrated to new technologies and infrastructure as long as resources allow it and if it is technologically possible to do the migration. It is important to recognize that evolving technologies and infrastructure may impede the ability to preserve a project in its original state. A minimally acceptable preservation method will be determined for digital scholarly projects and will be stated in the project agreement for the project.

Updates and New Editions
The Library will provide clear methods for scholars to update existing collected projects and will include versioning as part of its model. New editions will be expected to follow the same steps for acceptance as the original project.

Going a step farther, the University of Virginia Library is also fleshing out seven levels of collecting, represented by associated technical standards for metadata, files, content relationships, and original delivery formats. All seven levels must have fully compliant metadata. However, to qualify for the most stringent category, or level 1, collections must also have fully compliant files, "exact" content relationships, and "exact" original delivery formats.

Digital Object Repositories and the DLF Registry of Digital Masters. Only by working through the complex set of issues inherent in sustaining digital scholarship will libraries be able to assure scholars that they have the policies and procedures in place to acquire, organize, make accessible, and sustain their digital output. Digital-object repositories (made possible by Fedora, DSpace, and other software) are an essential component. It is noteworthy that the last question in MLA's revised "Guiding Questions for Vetters of Scholarly Editions" asks

> Has a copy of the edition and its images, software, style sheets, and documentation been deposited with a library or other long-term digital object repository? (MLA 2005, Part 2 V. 27.4)

Although most academic libraries have a long way to go before they can demonstrate to MLA, ELO, and other constituents that they have a trustworthy destination for electronic media of all types, digital repositories like the California Digital Library's eScholarship and the University of Virginia's Fedora infrastructure demonstrate what can be done.

The DLF Registry of Digital Masters, maintained by OCLC, is a first coordinated step that institutions may take to signal their intention of preserving and maintaining the accessibility of registered resources over an extended timeframe. The "Record Creation Guidelines" state that

> This implies that materials are digitized, complying with established standards and best practices, and that they are stored in professionally managed systems. When registered, materials should already be digitized, or be in an active queue for digitization. A use copy (a network-accessible, but not necessarily free, copy) of any material registered must be available on-line to the general public. Where digitally reformatted materials are concerned, reproductions should be of meaningful bibliographic entities (DLF 2004b).

2.7.3 Thorny Issues of Copyright and Permissions

More than one scholar identified copyright as the biggest obstacle to advancing digital scholarship in American literature, outstripping by far any technological constraints. Copyright restrictions are especially troublesome to twentieth-century projects, which are the subject of a great deal of academic interest. MLA's "Guiding Questions for Vetters of Scholarly Editions" pose two copyright-related questions.

- Has the editor obtained all necessary permissions—for example, to republish any materials protected by copyright? (Part 2, IV.17.0)
- Does the edition carry a clear statement of the appropriate reuse of its constituent elements, especially those protected by copyright or used by permission? (Part 2, V.22.2)

Case and Green (2004) provide an excellent overview of the issues as they affect electronic editions, giving editors clues about how to investigate copyright and permissions. Typically, authors bear the burden of obtaining permissions. Special collections librarians report that many libraries refuse to make a single copy for authors without proof—in writing—that the owner, agent, or estate executor of the literary property has granted permission. Obtaining such approvals can prove time-consuming, and the results are sometimes inconclusive or subject to dispute. In such situations, scholars may either omit the problematic content or turn to seasoned publishers to help them work through copyright issues. Martha Nell Smith chose to publish Emily Dickinson's Correspondences with the University of Virginia Press's Rotunda electronic imprint not only because she believes it will help to sustain—and lend financial stability to—this edition but also because she can rely on the authority of the press to assist her in negotiating the requisite rights and permissions with its peer agencies (in this case, Harvard University Press).

Who owns and controls primary source materials is of paramount importance to digital scholarship, as Unsworth noted several years ago (Unsworth 2000b). And the issues are only becoming more acute as the number of different players—scholars, libraries, publishers, indexers—flourish, accelerating the production of bodies of digital source materials. While the DLF Registry records a "use copy," thus sparing other libraries the expense of creating a preservation-quality digital master, it does not signal permission for scholars to access or reuse original digital source files. The Million Book Project (MBP) is a source of expertise in the copyright issues surrounding mass-digitization projects and in devising practical workflow issues to address them. Although MBP incorporates "in-copyright" materials and permits online reading, it limits printing and saving to one page at a time. It is too soon to know what practices will emerge among the "Google 5" partners that do include copyrighted books, but if it follows the practices of Google Print, public users will gain access to only a few pages. It is also too soon to know whether or not individual participating institutions will share their source files that have been digitized by Google for scholarly reuse within cooperative frameworks.

There is no U.S.-based shared repository, similar to the Oxford Text Archive, where it is possible to request digital source files (see section 3.3.3.2). Interviews with some librarians revealed that such a model may be unlikely to succeed in the United States. "Why should we give away our digital source files to other scholars?" a prominent librarian asked, arguing that they do not want other scholars to manipulate or repurpose texts owned by the library and created through its labor. There are no accepted norms—even in the special collections world, which enjoys a long history of dealing with primary source materials—in providing digital copies or master images derived from library collections or in the fees charged.

As discussed later in this report, the metadata associated with the digital resource may embody this rights information (see section

3.5.2). Meanwhile, if The New York Public Library (NYPL) serves as a model, there is a complicated set of questions for authors to consider when using digital images. NYPL "provides free and open access to its Digital Gallery and images may be freely downloaded for personal, research and study purposes only." However, "if images are to be used in any nonprofit or commercial publication, broadcast, web site, exhibition, promotional material, etc.," the library charges a usage fee—as the physical rights holder of this material even though most of the images are in the public domain for copyright purposes. The use of images is governed by a licensing agreement:

> Images are not to be used in any manner without the expressed written permission from NYPL. All images are licensed under the terms and conditions as specified in this Agreement and in the written Permissions statement you will receive. No image licenses are valid until NYPL has received payment in full. Image usage without prior payment and NYPL's expressed written permission is strictly prohibited. (NYPL Photographic Services and Permissions, Terms and Conditions, available at http://www.nypl.org/permissions/terms.html.)

The usage fee, NYPL explains, "is not a copyright fee," but helps "ensure that the Library is able to continue to acquire, preserve, and provide access to the accumulated knowledge of the world." It further advises inquirers that they are free to obtain a copy of the requested images from another source, should they so choose. The NYPL's Photographic Services and Permissions FAQ service answers a host of other questions on such matters as the basis for the fee structure, whether the library will reproduce images still in copyright, whether the library's fee still applies when the author also pays a fee to the third-party copyright holder, whether the fees posted on the Use Fee Schedule apply when the author has already paid for a reproduction or downloaded a low-resolution image directly from the Web site, whether a user may link directly to the NYPL Digital Gallery, and so forth.[21]

Given the current state of flux—and the specter of complicated, expensive, or frozen access—the Text Creation Partnership (TCP), headquartered at the University of Michigan University Library, stands out as the only wide-scale initiative aimed at releasing digital master files from proprietary control to unfettered use by its members—and by extension, quite possibly to the public at large. Scholars of stature, such as Martin Mueller, professor of classics and English at Northwestern University, recognize "how important it is to maintain a conversation about how to create and manage sharable sets of our primary textual materials" and urges his colleagues in English departments to take a lesson from scientists and "make the creation of such data sets a partial but integral part of our scholarly lives"

---

[21] NYPL Photographic Services and Permissions FAQ is available at http://www.nypl.org/permissions/faq.html. The use fee schedule is available at http://www.nypl.org/permissions/UseFeeSchedule8_1.PDF.

(Mueller 2004). The University of Michigan is already granting partner institutions the nonexclusive, nontransferable right to use TCP content, subject to the terms and conditions set forth in a formal TCP Local Management Agreement.

2.7.4 Paucity of Sustainable Business Models

Virtually everyone interviewed in this report raised concerns about the high cost of large-scale digital efforts. Publishers and librarians alike look to models such as the TCP as the only economically viable way to produce high-quality, thoroughly edited and encoded texts. Even this public-private cooperative, which hinges on purchasing the corpora first, is beyond the reach of many academic libraries. What will become of graduate students, their faculty mentors wonder, when they leave well-endowed research institutions to teach at places that do not have access to a full spectrum of electronic resources? Is the digital world—with its laudable democratizing potential—really ushering in a new era of haves and have-nots? What can be done to ensure more-equitable access? This report offers no easy answers; it only calls for further investigation into this question. Constituents look to DLF to advocate for new models and support TCP-like efforts.

Many of the projects under review here initially relied on grant funding, and if fortunate, the host institution will bear the continuing cost or developers must devise alternative means to gain revenue, including licensing their product. The costs of major digital projects are not insignificant. To cite two examples: The Wright American Fiction project, which is not the beneficiary of external funds, will cost participating Committee on Institutional Cooperation (CIC) members an estimated $475,000 for about 3,000 fully encoded books. Meanwhile, the production costs for the 30 books expected to be published as part of the grant-funded Gutenberg-e project are estimated at an astonishing average of "slightly under $60,000 per book" (Manning 2004, footnotes 30 and 31). It is no wonder, then, that there has been growth in the number of hybrid access sites, where the general public is provided access to a subset of materials with full service restricted to constituent communities paying fees.

The shift from ownership of content to rental or licensing by contract, which is now affecting all disciplines, is one of the key strategic issues in digital asset management, according to Donald Waters, scholarly communications program officer at The Andrew W. Mellon Foundation. He states, "The shift to electronic publication in its current form represents a dramatic, jump-off-the-cliff shift in the academy from owning scholarly output to renting it." He continues:

> A growing number of senior officers of our colleges and universities—presidents, provosts, and chief financial officers—are beginning to question the huge risk to the future of their institution's core operations because of the growing dependence on the record of scholarship for which the institution is paying substantial sums but on which it has no real claim (Waters 2005).

Institutional digital repositories are envisioned as one component in regaining control and ownership of faculty output, but they, too, are created at considerable expense. Moreover, the concept is a hard sell to many faculty members whose disciplinary allegiance is national rather than local. From the perspective of one disgruntled scholar—who undoubtedly reflects the opinion of many others—the very notion that "every department would publish itself" is a flawed concept. No one is interested in a particular institution's production "outside the context of a discipline," she asserted. Calling it a "nightmare" and "dumb to spend $300,000 to put everything on the Web," this humanist asked, "Why put preliminary work on the Web? Doesn't a published article reflect well upon the institution?" Such questions show the need in the field of American literature for coordinated strategic planning among professional organizations, scholars, librarians, publishers, and funding agencies.

2.7.5 Dearth of Specialists

Many of the faculty members interviewed for this report affirmed the need for more specialists who have grounding in the discipline along with knowledge of new technologies. The Association for Literary and Linguistic Computing's regularly updated taxonomy of "Institutional Models for Humanities Computing," edited by Willard McCarty (King's College, London) and Matthew Kirschenbaum (University of Maryland), gives readers an idea of the types of teaching, research, and technology support structures available to humanists at institutions in the United States and Western Europe. Scholars such as Alan Liu expressed concern about the concentration of expertise in text-encoding and markup-based humanities computing work (starting with the creation of digital text archives but now encompassing other kinds of projects, such as McGann's NINES initiative) along the northeast corridor (e.g., Institute for Advanced Technology in the Humanities, Maryland Institute for Technology in the Humanities, Rutgers University's Center for Electronic Texts in the Humanities, Brown University's Scholarly Technology Group) with only a smattering of significant participation in the Midwest and on the West Coast.[22] As scholarly resources are increasingly developed for presentation on the Web, Liu and others are concerned that too few institutions, including research libraries, have subject specialists with the requisite knowledge of technical standards and encoding protocols. Increasingly, all humanists will need a basic understanding of how technical decisions inform the presentation and longevity of digital content. Stakeholders must formulate strategic plans now and encourage humanities graduate programs around the nation to integrate the tools of technology into pedagogy and research (Rockwell 2003, Liu 2003). If not, who will replace the "next generation of Jerry McGanns?" Liu asks, noting as yet another problem that most of today's scholars came to the Web "with tenure in hand."

[22] Refer to section 3.6 of this report, Teaching Applications, for a model program among six liberal arts colleges to introduce TEI encoding into the undergraduate curriculum (Ebert-Zawasky and Tomasek, n.d.).

CLIR's Postdoctoral Fellowships in Scholarly Information Resources, launched in 2004 in conjunction with a consortium of academic libraries, are designed to meet the needs just outlined. Intended "to establish a new kind of scholarly information professional," the fellowships "will educate new scholars about the challenges and opportunities created by new forms of scholarly research and the information resources that support them, both traditional and digital."23 While some of the faculty members interviewed for this report were unaware of CLIR's program, others were its direct beneficiaries. Many applauded the pilot program, but some would like to see a variety of models developed, including programs lodged in English departments. A national competition among graduate English programs might stimulate alternative ways to integrate technology within the discipline.

Two other professional development opportunities warrant mentioning. Recognizing the importance of supporting scholars with digital project development, NINES offered its first intensive summer workshop for faculty in the summer of 2005. Also in 2005, for the fourth consecutive year, the University of Victoria's Faculty of Humanities and its Humanities Computing and Media Centre, in collaboration with a host of sponsors including the Association for Computers and the Humanities, convened its Humanities Computing Summer Institute in the Digital Humanities. According to its Web site, the institute "provides an environment ideal to discuss, to learn about, and to advance skills in the new computing technologies that influence the way in which those in the Arts and Humanities carry out their teaching and research today."

In the minds of the current cadre of specialists, there is an immediate need for many more graduate fellowships, postdoctoral training programs, and early-career faculty institutes such as these.

2.8 Conclusion: Toward a "Celestial Kaleidoscope"

Until quite recently, the work of American literary scholars engaged in applying new media to their teaching and research has been viewed by their peers with a combination of skepticism and bemusement, tinged by awe, if only at their colleagues' quixotic daring. Laboring on the outskirts of the profession, these scholars have launched their work in the distant harbor of humanities computing, e-text centers, and digital libraries, in isolation from their peers and their home departments. They have been accorded cult-like status as technically savvy mavericks, taking professional risks of considerable consequence. Because their work largely falls outside the safety net of traditional peer review, it has rarely been discussed in the core journals of the discipline unless one of its proponents is inspired to write about his or her experience.

---

23 Information on the CLIR Postdoctoral Fellowship in Scholarly Information Resources is available at http://www.clir.org/fellowships/postdoc/postdoc.html.

Such was the case in December 2002, when Martha Nell Smith in the pages of *American Literature* asked what information technology had to do with the study of literature. On the basis of her experience with the Dickinson Electronic Archives, MITH, and IATH, Smith argued that "digital resources are more than advantages—they are necessities," driven in large part by the dual crises of diminishing funds for scholarly publishing and declining interest in humanities education in an "increasingly corporatized university" (Smith 2002, 836).

This report bears witness to a rich array of digital resources in support of American literature and to dedicated stakeholders developing them. The ACLS Commission on Cyberinfrastructure for the Humanities and Social Sciences, NINES, and the publication of *Electronic Textual Editing*, along with the new guidelines adopted by MLA's Committee on Scholarly Editions, are bringing more than a decade of hard work and accomplishment in digital humanities to national visibility.

After being "mightily preoccupied with the great stacking of the virtual shelves since the WWW hit, with little thought of what we were putting there," as Willard McCarty said, those engaged in digital practice are taking stock of their achievements, making their concerns more visible, and enlarging the circle of debate.[24] How does computing affect "analysis in the humanities beyond simply fetching, counting and formatting data?" McCarty asks (2005). That is, how does it affect "analysis itself rather than its scope, speed or convenience?" he continues. Conveners of the 2005 Transliteracies Conference asked participants: What is new about reading in the age of the network?[25] What are the new genres and forms of publication appropriate to the digital age that Ayers invokes? Smith and others prompt their peers: What benefits do new editorial praxes and technologies bring to electronic scholarly editing? In their efforts to answer tough questions, these seasoned digital leaders are substantiating the ways in which new media are transforming the study of literature. "To change scholarship, we need scholarship," Ayers advises, urging his colleagues to move forward and to do good work with the tools and resources already available. Calling for more models of success, he concludes: "There is no substitute for the passion of scholars and the excitement and credibility of the work those scholars produce."[26]

Looking toward the horizon, these digital scholars now see a "rainbow that looks like Hope." Will their various efforts coalesce into patterns, creating a celestial kaleidoscope? It is too early to give definitive answers, but as readers of these pages will see, there is cause for optimism.

---

[24] E-mail correspondence with McCarty on January 23, 2005.

[25] Information on the conference, held at the University of California, Santa Barbara, June 17–18, 2005, can be found at http://transliteracies.english.ucsb.edu/category/conference-2005.

[26] E-mail correspondence with Ayers on May 12, 2005.

3. REVIEW OF RESOURCES

The following pages provide an overview of selected Web-based resources in six categories: quality-controlled subject gateways, author studies, e-book collections and alternative publishing models, reference resources and full-text primary-source collections, collections by design, and teaching applications. A brief description and URL for each resource noted in these categories can be found at the end of each subsection and is listed according to the number that follows the resource on first mention.

3.1 Quality-Controlled Subject Gateways

This section discusses quality-controlled subject gateways designed to facilitate access to Internet resources in American literature. By necessity, it draws on models from history, American studies, humanities, and literary studies.

3.1.1 Identifying Internet Resources: A History Lesson

Readers who seek a general introduction to finding information on the Internet should refer to the excellent online tutorial prepared by the Teaching Library at the University of California-Berkeley (1). It evaluates generic search engines (Google, Yahoo, and Teoma) and subject directories (Librarians' Index, Infomine, Academic Info, About.com, Google Directory, and Yahoo!) and gives advice about strategies to locate hidden resources on the "invisible Web."

Among these resources, Infomine: Scholarly Resource Collections offers the most sophisticated search options, and its search results distinguish items selected by specialists from those dynamically retrieved "on the fly" through its robotic Web crawler. Infomine has strong coverage of both fee-based and publicly available Internet resources in American literature, including databases, e-journals, e-texts, and other relevant Web sites (2). To illustrate, a search of "Ralph Waldo Emerson" retrieved 12 expert-selected sites, including works by and about Emerson available from Making of America, and 13 robot-selected hits retrieved from such sources as Bartleby.com, Amazon.com, and the University of Virginia's electronic-text collection. Searches can be limited by field or subject category as well as by record origin (expert- and/or robot-selected), resource access (free or fee-based), and resource type (10 options, including electronic texts and books).

If the discipline under review were U.S. history rather than American literature, there would be little debate about where to begin a guided inquiry. The nonprofit History Cooperative (3), which represents the interests of 18 history journals, including the *American Historical Review* (*AHR*) and the *Journal of American History* (*JAH*), advises readers: "We have found no better collection of resources for historians than those at the Center for History and New Media" (4). Winner of the American Historical Association's 2004 James Harvey Robinson Prize for an Outstanding Teaching Aid, History Matters:

The U.S. Survey Course on the Web (5) is a multidimensional site developed with support from national foundations by the American Social History Project, the Center for Media and Learning at the City University of New York Graduate Center, and the Center for History and New Media at George Mason University.

History Matters is discussed again in section 3.6.5, but its annotated guide to Internet resources, WWW.History, deserves special consideration here. In marked contrast to the practice in American literature, the *JAH* has been publishing substantial reviews of Web resources, authored by scholars (with Ph.D.s or other advanced degrees in their fields of specialization) since 2001. The reviews cover resources of interest to American literary scholars as well, for example, the James Fenimore Cooper Society, the Jewish Women's Archive, the Digital Classroom (National Archives and Records Administration), and Studs Terkel: Conversations with America (Chicago Historical Society). The *JAH* reviews, which now number about 100, are integrated into History Matters' publicly accessible Web guide, where they can be browsed by topic or period or searched along with some 750 shorter evaluative annotations prepared by graduate students. The site supports advanced searching that permits users to limit their query by topic, primary source type (e.g., film, letters and diaries, oral history), format (e.g., text, images, audio, video), and section within the site. After completing a simple registration form, users are added to the History Matters' mailing list.

There is no equivalent resource for scholars in American literature. The University of Virginia's census of electronic resources demonstrates the potential of applying a similar model to American studies (6), but it is not as fully developed and does not carry the scholarly imprimatur accorded to History Matters.[27] Graduate students at UVa maintain the census and write the annotations. Resources are grouped into seven broad classifications and then subdivided—in the case of literature, into 14 categories. The site supports advanced searching. Registering as a user allows one to contribute potential entries, pending review.

3.1.2 Directories of American Literature Internet Resources
In the case of the humanities and literature, users have long relied on either the Voice of the Shuttle (VoS) Web site (7) or Literary Resources on the Net (8) as entry points to the field. Created by scholars, these are the only two Internet resource guides that James Harner deemed worthy of inclusion in the 2002 edition of the Modern Language Association's well-regarded and highly selective *Literary Research Guide: An Annotated Listing of Reference Sources in English Literary Studies* (*LRG*). Launched in 1994, VoS was rebuilt in 2001 as a database to serve content dynamically. Both VoS and Literary Resources on the

---

27 In 2000, the American Studies Crossroads Project, sponsored by Georgetown University, regrettably ceased publication of *SiteScene*, its regular reviews of Web resources. The archives, extending back to April 1998, are available at http://www.georgetown.edu/crossroads/asw/sitescene.html.

Net sites are searchable by keyword and provide browsing access to subcategories within "American literature." They cover many of the same resources, although their arrangements differ and VoS links to more subordinate layers than does Literary Resources. VoS has been unable to implement effectively its proposed system of user collaboration that would permit contributors to edit their links. Its long list of "unvetted submissions" dates to 2002. Literary Resources on the Net, which is particularly strong in eighteenth-century resources, appears to lag almost a year behind in refreshing its links. As a result, both Literary Resources and VoS suffer from broken links and an inability to keep up with the growing body of new digital content. It seems inappropriate to judge these efforts too harshly, since both are maintained largely as a labor of love. VoS creator Alan Liu, of the University of California-Santa Barbara, has suggested that it is time to develop a sustainable, collaborative, interinstitutional solution.

Humbul: Humanities Hub (9), a selective annotated catalog to online humanities resources, warrants closer examination as an alternative model. Integral to the United Kingdom's Resource Discovery Network, Humbul meets the definition of a quality-controlled subject gateway:

> Quality-controlled subject gateways are Internet-services which apply a rich set of quality measures to support system resource discovery. Considerable manual effort is used to secure a selection of resources which meet quality criteria and to display a rich description of these resources with standards-based metadata. Regular checking and updating ensure good collection management. A main goal is to provide a high quality of subject access through indexing resources using controlled vocabularies and by offering a deep classification structure for advanced searching and browsing (Koch 2000).

Unlike any of the resources discussed thus far, Humbul makes public its collection-development policy and cataloging guidelines. Within the subject categories of "American Studies" and "English Studies," users can browse all records or browse by resource type, period, or intended audience. Users can also search across the entire catalog or within a subject. Although geared toward British content, the English Case Study demonstrates the potential to create subject guides drawn from Humbul resources. Registering permits users to create an account so that they can access a set of personalization services, including e-mail alerts (based on user subject queries) and the ability to incorporate Humbul records into their own Web pages (with their own annotations). Harner, who intends to add Humbul to the next edition of *LRG*, concludes, "Humbul has the potential to become the principal gateway to online humanities sources; to realize this potential will require a major redesign of the browse screen, maintaining currency of information (especially for major resources) and weeding out defunct sites, and more attention to evaluating—rather than merely cataloging—sites."

Users seeking information on American literature have recourse to the straightforward subject directory of Washington State University's Donna M. Campbell (10). Although it lacks the technical sophistication of previously discussed resources, this handcrafted and well-maintained site is exemplary in its deliberate attempt to adhere to the MLA's "Minimal Guidelines for Authors of Web Pages." In January 2005, Campbell launched a Weblog with regular news about updated links and new content. American Literature has four sections:

- American Authors covers 100 writers, typically providing a portrait image, biographical notes, a select bibliography, and links to works available online.
- Timeline provides a short chronology of events (pre-1650 through 1929) in American history and literature. It is linked to course pages and bibliographies.
- Literary Movements features short essays covering 25 themes, ranging from captivity narratives, transcendentalism, and naturalism to travel narratives and Southwestern humor.
- American Literature Sites links to Web sites in the following categories: American literature, general literature, books online, nineteenth-century periodicals and primary sources, and miscellanea.

Campbell avoids sites with advertising as well as most subscription-based resources unless they offer a significant portion of free content. A search engine retrieves hits not only from the four major sections of the Web site but also from Campbell's course assignments. Perhaps because the site is used in conjunction with regular teaching assignments, there seem to be relatively few broken links. Nonetheless, as is the case with handcrafted sites of this breadth, it is a Sisyphean task to maintain.

Two other frequently cited American literature Web sites, cross-referenced by the aforementioned services, derive from universities in England and Japan. The American Studies program at Keele University's American Literature (11) site features three virtual libraries: Mimi, devoted to eighteenth- and nineteenth-century e-texts and resources; Sally Anne, on the twentieth century; and Writing Black, focused on literature by and about African Americans. American Authors on the Web, maintained by Nagoya University, links to texts by or about almost 750 writers (12). There is no search function, but records can be browsed by author name or by period. Other efforts, such as Göttingen University Library's Anglistik guide (13) and Nagasaki University's American Literature on the Web (14), appear out-of-date and are not worth consulting except for ideas about special features (e.g., Göttingen's resource-rating system and Nagasaki's matrix of timelines and contexts).

3.1.3 Contact Your Librarian

In the absence of a nationally recognized, quality-controlled subject gateway for American literature, library subject specialists across the country create anthologies of Web links for their constituents. The

Directory of Literature Librarians lists members of the Literatures in English section of ACRL and provides links to its subject-based Web sites, many of which take the form of research guides to proprietary and publicly accessible resources (15).

3.1.4 Resource Links

(1) Finding Information on the Internet: A Tutorial (Teaching Library, University of California-Berkeley). An excellent introduction to research-quality Web searching, from formulation of search strategies and types of tools to Web site evaluation and citation formats. Available at http://www.lib.berkeley.edu/TeachingLib/Guides/Internet/FindInfo.html.

(2) Infomine: Scholarly Resource Collections (University of California-Riverside). Built and maintained by librarians as a national collaborative initiative, Infomine is a virtual library of Internet resources selected for an academic audience. It has strong coverage of sources relevant to the study of American literature. Available at http://infomine.ucr.edu/.

(3) History Cooperative (American Historical Association, Organization of American Historians, University of Illinois Press, and National Academies Press). A nonprofit collaborative initiative, History Cooperative delivers high-quality online information to subscribers, most notably the full text of 18 history journals. New collections are added regularly. Available at http://www.historycooperative.org/.

(4) Center for History and New Media (George Mason University). Developer of the History Departments Around the World database and History Matters. Available at http://chnm.gmu.edu/index.php.

(5) History Matters: The U.S. Survey Course on the Web (American Social History Project of the Center for Media and Learning, City University of New York, and the Center for History and New Media at George Mason University). History Matters is a multidimensional resource in support of the study of U.S. history. Available at http://historymatters.gmu.edu/.

- *WWW.History.* This feature of History Matters serves as a selective annotated guide to Internet resources combining a growing set of peer-reviewed sources, published regularly in the *JAH*, with about 750 other individually selected annotated sources. Available at http://historymatters.gmu.edu/browse/wwwhistory/
- *WWW.History* full-search options. Available at http://historymatters.gmu.edu/search.php

(6) Census of Electronic Resources in American Studies (University of Virginia). An annotated catalog of online resources originally designed as part of a larger (now in hiatus) initiative to develop an information community in American Studies. Available at http://infocomm.lib.virginia.edu/toolkit/SPT/SPT--Home.php.

(7) Voice of the Shuttle (University of California-Santa Barbara). Maintained by Alan Liu, Department of English, working primarily with a team of graduate students. Available at http://vos.ucsb.edu.

- Direct link to American literature pages at http://vos.ucsb.edu/browse.asp?id=2739
- *LRG annotation*: unnumbered, page 73

(8) Literary Resources on the Net (Rutgers University-Newark). Created by Jack Lynch, Department of English. Provides more than 6,000 links to other sites. Available at http://andromeda.rutgers.edu/~jlynch/Lit/.

- Direct link to American literature pages at http://andromeda.rutgers.edu/~jlynch/Lit/american.html
- A separate archive of eighteenth-century resources, including Lynch's transcriptions of electronic texts, is available at http://andromeda.rutgers.edu/~jlynch/18th/
- *LRG annotation*: unnumbered, page 74

(9) Humbul Humanities Hub (Resource Discovery Network, Joint Information Systems Committee and Arts and Humanities Research Board, hosted by the University of Oxford). A selective, annotated online catalog of humanities resources relevant to academic users. Available at http://www.humbul.ac.uk/index.html.

- English Case Study, including Internet for English http://www.rdn.ac.uk/casestudies/humbul/
- Use Humbul to export data to your own institution's Web pages http://www.rdn.ac.uk/casestudies/humbul/english/case6.html
- *LRG annotation*: Internet Metapages annotated as item number 500. Available at http://www-english.tamu.edu/pubs/lrg/addenda.html

(10) American Literature: American Authors, Timeline, Literary Movements, and American Literature Sites (Donna M. Campbell, Washington State University). A selective subject directory of links with annotations and original short topical essays. Available at http://www.wsu.edu/~campbelld/.

- **About this Site** with chart of the MLA's "Minimal Guidelines for Authors of Web Pages": http://www.wsu.edu/~campbelld/about.htm
- **American Authors**: http://www.wsu.edu/~campbelld/amlit/aufram.html
- **Timeline** http://www.wsu.edu/~campbelld/amlit/timefram.html
- **Literary Movements** http://www.wsu.edu/~campbelld/amlit/litfram.html
- **American Literature Sites** http://www.wsu.edu/~campbelld/amlit/sites.htm

(11) American Literature (School of American Studies, Keele University). Available at http://www.keele.ac.uk/depts/as/Literature/amlit.html.

- **Mimi**: eighteenth- and nineteenth-century e-texts and resources
  http://www.keele.ac.uk/depts/as/Literature/amlit-mimi.html
- **Sally Anne**: twentieth-century e-texts and resources
  http://www.keele.ac.uk/depts/as/Literature/amlit-sallyanne.html
- **Writing Black**: literature by and on African Americans
  http://www.keele.ac.uk/depts/as/Literature/amlit-black.html

(12) American Authors on the Web (Nagoya University). Links to texts by or about some 750 writers. Available at http://www.lang.nagoya-u.ac.jp/~matsuoka/AmeLit.html.

(13) Anglistik Guide (Göttingen University Library). Out-of-date and uneven coverage, but features an interesting rating method. Available at http://www.anglistikguide.de/.

(14) American Literature on the Web (Nagasaki University of Foreign Studies). Available at http://www.nagasaki-gaigo.ac.jp/ishikawa/amlit/index.htm. No longer actively maintained, but features an interesting matrix of contexts at http://www.nagasaki-gaigo.ac.jp/ishikawa/amlit/17_8/timeline.htm.

(15) Directory of Literature Librarians (Literatures in English Section, ACRL, American Library Association). Directory of English and American literature library subject specialists with links to local subject Web sites. Available at http://www.ala.org/ala/acrlbucket/les/litlibrarians.htm.

3.2 Author Studies

In American literature, the study of individual authors enjoys a strong tradition in the curriculum and research. It comes, therefore, as no surprise to learn that some of the most serious digital scholarly work focuses on individual authors. This section investigates the digital content available from author societies, the evolving forms of scholarly editions, and other author-based content developed by faculty members, independent scholars, digital libraries, broadcast media, and publishers of textbook anthologies. The resources reviewed serve a wide range of purposes, from current awareness to interpretation, and from teaching to research.

3.2.1 Author Societies

More than 100 author societies are affiliated with the American Literature Association (ALA), an umbrella organization with some 10,000 members (1). Most of them have at least a basic Web site with contact information and links to an affiliated society's newsletter or journal. A growing number provide access to significant digital content, including primary and secondary source material. The ALA's Directory of Affiliates—from the Henry Adams Society to the Constance Fenimore Woolsen Society—is a starting point for author-based resource discovery. The directory would be even more useful if it included annotations about the features of its affiliates' Web sites and were more actively maintained. In the absence of any such overview, some sample sites are discussed in the following paragraphs.

The International Theodore Dreiser Society's Web site (2) is maintained by Keith Newlin of the University of North Carolina-Wilmington, president of the society and coeditor of its journal *Dreiser Studies*. The site includes directory information about its officers as well as indexes (since its inception in 1970) and tables of contents (since 1997) to *Dreiser Studies*, with selected articles online. Dreiser Studies also issues an annual checklist of publications simultaneously in print and online at its Web site that supplements *Theodore Dreiser: A Primary Bibliography and Reference Guide* (Pizer et al. 1991). "Dreiser on the Web," compiled by Roger W. Smith and originally appearing in *Dreiser Studies* in 2003, is available at the society's Web site with active hyperlinks and cross-references (3). This selective bibliography serves as a model in its format and coverage, starting with the criteria for inclusion.[28] Divided into 12 sections, it covers such categories as inventories of Dreiser archives, bibliographies, e-texts, teaching aids, and online encyclopedia entries. The twelfth category, titled "Misrepresentation and Misappropriation of Dreiser on the Web," consists of an essay about Web-propagated misinformation about Dreiser, augmented by a link to the ensuing online discussion about this topic.

The Stephen Crane Society's Web site (4), maintained by Donna M. Campbell, provides the table of contents and an author index to its journal *Stephen Crane Studies* from its inception in 1992. The Bibliography section lists secondary scholarship from 1962 to present. The links to Crane sites cover Research Sites (connecting to the finding aids and collection descriptions of major repositories), Biography Sites, and Contemporary Reviews of Crane's Work. The Teaching section features online resources and materials created by teachers. Works Online connects to electronic texts of Crane's stories transcribed especially for the society and to other primary source texts, including titles available for downloading from the Electronic Text Center at the University of Virginia. The site has a basic search engine. Campbell also maintains the Web sites for the Edith Wharton Society (5) and the William Dean Howells Society (6), which share many strong features with the Stephen Crane Society.

The James Fenimore Cooper Society's Web site (7) is maintained by the society's founder Hugh C. MacDougall and hosted by State University of New York College at Oneonta. The site has several unique features, including The Cooper Bookshelf, consisting of two series of short articles—plot summaries of Cooper's short stories and novels and of films and television programs based on his work. Written by MacDougall, the articles first appeared in *The Freeman's*

---

[28] For another worthwhile model, see A Poe Webliography: Edgar Allan Poe on the Internet, compiled and maintained by Heyward Ehrlich, Department of English, Rutgers University-Newark. Available at http://andromeda.rutgers.edu/~ehrlich/poesites.html and from The Edgar Allan Poe Society of Baltimore's Web site at http://www.eapoe.org/.

Journal, a newspaper of Cooperstown, New York, founded in 1808. MacDougall has also transcribed and annotated nine hard-to-find works by Cooper (see Texts of Cooper's Writings), including two foreign editions. The extensive Links section features electronic texts by Cooper in French, Hungarian, Russian, and German, as well as in English.

While many aficionados and students will delight in the content available at the Cooper Society's Web site, Matt Cohen of the English Department at Duke University calls into question the long-term viability and usefulness of the documents, which are encoded in hypertext markup language (HTML) rather than in extensible markup language (XML), as recommended in standards set by the TEI. Cohen concludes his review of the site with the following proviso:

> In an economy and an academy that offer little reward for the maintenance of digital scholarly archives, users can perhaps only be grateful for resources as vast and detailed as this one. But the cost is suggested here: though the site provides a wealth of material, in its current state it cannot serve as a model for similar endeavors and only weakly participates in a wider theoretical conversation about the digitization of humanistic representation (8).

As an editor of the Walt Whitman Archive, Cohen has a considerable investment in meeting the highest standards of scholarly editing: He directs the digitization of nine volumes of Horace Traubel's *With Walt Whitman in Camden*.

3.2.2 Scholarly Editions

To understand the theoretical and practical underpinnings of scholarly editing in the digital world, readers can turn to the landmark volume of essays *Electronic Textual Editing*, edited by Lou Burnard (Oxford University), Katherine O'Brien O'Keeffe (Notre Dame University), and John Unsworth (University of Illinois) (9). Sponsored by the MLA's Committee on Scholarly Editions (CSE) (10) and the TEI Consortium (11), the volume is scheduled for publication by MLA in late 2005, but preview versions of all the essays, in TEI XML format, are now available at the TEI's Web site. A centerpiece of the volume is the complete revision of the CSE "Guidelines for Editors of Scholarly Editions," also available at MLA's Web site (12). The revision includes a new checklist and glossary aimed at vetters of electronic editions (13) and a detailed annotated bibliography of editorial methods. In Principles, the *Electronic Textual Editing* editors describe the five criteria that form the foundation of trustworthiness upon which any scholarly edition is built: accuracy, adequacy, appropriateness, consistency, and explicitness (14). These attributes are applicable to scholarly editions in any form, print or electronic. The rest of the volume consists of 24 contributed essays, grouped under two headings: sources and orientations, and practices and procedures. Written by luminaries in the field, these essays give the reader an appreciation of the many nuanced applications of electronic text editing. Two essays are particularly relevant to this section of the report: "Critical

Editing in a Digital Horizon" (15) by Dino Buzzetti (Universita di Bologna) and Jerome McGann (University of Virginia) and "Documentary Editing" (16) by Bob Rosenberg (Rutgers University), editor of the Thomas Edison papers.

MLA's CSE is a clearinghouse for information about scholarly editing and editorial projects. One of its main functions is to evaluate scholarly editions intended for publication. Editions that conform to professional standards (as set forth in the CSE guidelines) receive a seal of approval from the committee that appears in the published volume. A list of CSE-approved volumes, published and forthcoming, appears at MLA's Web site (17). As of 2004, no electronic scholarly edition had joined these ranks, but a digital archive is under review. Regrettably, there is no registry of digital editions in progress that aims to meet MLA's CSE guidelines. MLA's listing does not offer links to the publisher's or edition's Web sites.

The Association for Documentary Editing (ADE), an organization that encompasses literary and historical editors, maintains a list of ADE-affiliated projects and editions that have made documents or other information available on the Web (18).[29] It further identifies those projects that are part of the Model Editions Partnership, or MEP (19), a consortium that has developed editorial guidelines for publishing historical documents in electronic form. Participants of the MEP are making experimental "mini-editions" available over the Web. As of June 2005, 14 model editions were available.

ADE projects can be browsed by title, keyword, or subject, making it possible for readers to identify authoritative editions of the books and essays of literary authors as well as annotated collections of correspondence, speeches, and diaries of prominent figures in politics, science, social reform, and the arts. American literature is represented by nine authors: Willa Cather, Frederick Douglass, Jonathan Edwards, Ralph Waldo Emerson, Benjamin Franklin, George Santayana, Henry D. Thoreau, Mark Twain, and Walt Whitman. The ADE directory also includes the Modernist Journals Project (20), an effort to make available editions of important journals of the modernist era, and Romantic Circles (21), a scholarly collaborative that has produced digital texts for a decade. Neil Fraistat (University of Maryland) and Steven Jones (Loyola University-Chicago) discuss their editorial experience with Romantic Circles in "The Poem and the Network: Editing Poetry Electronically" in *Electronic Textual Editing* (22).

While the foundational principles remain the same, regardless of the form in which scholarly editions are produced, the approach to print and digital media varies widely. A close examination of a half-dozen authors illustrates these differences. Beginning at one end of the spectrum, still thoroughly lodged in the print world, the scholarly editions of Ralph Waldo Emerson's work that meet MLA's guidelines appear on the Web only as promoted in the publishers'

---

[29] Publication information for a large number of historical documentary editions appears in National Historical Publications and Records Commission 2000.

catalogs (Mississippi State University and Belknap Press [23]). As discussed in 3.2.3, the Centenary Edition of The Complete Works of Ralph Waldo Emerson is fully available on the Web.

The Mark Twain Papers and Project Web site (24) serves primarily to provide information about the comprehensive collections and documents held by the Bancroft Library that support the publication of Twain's papers and works by the University of California Press. An electronic edition of Twain's letters (1876–1880) is available to institutional subscribers through the commercial distributor ebrary or from Amazon.com. The Web site features two digital exhibits about Twain and offers online access to indexes of his letters. Users can search the extensive collection of Outgoing Letters covering all known letters written by Samuel L. Clemens and members of his immediate family or search Incoming Letters, including all known letters written to Clemens and his immediate family in addition to thousands of letters written to and by his extended family and associates. Research Resources describes various physical collections available for on-site consultation.

The Writings of Henry D. Thoreau site is directed by Elizabeth Witherell at Northern Illinois University (25). The site offers biographical information, a database of quotations, and online access to the transcribed, unedited manuscript versions of three volumes of Thoreau's journals. The Thoreau FAQ section answers common but puzzling questions about the writer. The site also features two updated essays written by Witherell with Elizabeth Dubrulle: "Life and Times of Henry David Thoreau" and "Reflections on *Walden*." There are annotated entries about Related Sites. A bibliography of readings rounds out the site. It is complemented by Thoreau's Life & Writings available from the Thoreau Institute at Walden Woods (26).

The beautifully designed and substantive Willa Cather Archive (27) integrates information from *The Willa Cather Scholarly Edition*, published by University of Nebraska Press, into the much larger context of a multifaceted digital research and teaching environment. Founded in 2002 by members of the University of Nebraska-Lincoln Department of English, the Cather Project, according to Director Guy Reynolds, has four distinct features:

- The Willa Cather Archive, which is regularly updated and searchable, publishes unique scholarship and electronic versions of scholarship and Cather-authored texts that have already appeared in hard copy. Additionally, the archive provides access to primary source material from the Cather collections at the University of Nebraska-Lincoln Libraries and elsewhere. Materials appearing on this site have been peer reviewed and vetted in accordance with traditional scholarly standards.

- The *Willa Cather Scholarly Edition*, which is produced in compliance with MLA's Committee on Scholarly Editions' guidelines. As far as copyright allows, electronic versions, encoded in XML format and fully searchable, are made available online.

- *Cather Studies*, the leading forum for scholarship on her work, has issued five editions, all available in digital form at the site, with three more planned by the end of the decade. So far, there have been five editions of *Cather Studies*, which readers can find in digital form through this site.

- The Willa Cather International Seminar, cosponsored with the Willa Cather Pioneer Memorial and Educational Foundation in Red Cloud, Nebraska, serves as the main forum for Cather scholars, enthusiasts, and graduate students to convene and discuss her work and to pursue new areas of inquiry.

The Walt Whitman Archive (28), directed by Ed Folsom (University of Iowa) and Kenneth M. Price (University of Nebraska), is a digital research-and-teaching environment developing the first scholarly edition of Whitman's vast work. The Whitman Archive makes available online both facsimile and e-text versions of all the editions of *Leaves of Grass* and an extended biography of Whitman written by Folsom and Price. Introductions to each edition of *Leaves*, reprinted from *Walt Whitman: An Encyclopedia*, edited by J. R. LeMaster and Donald D. Kummings, are available through an agreement with Garland Publishing Company. In conjunction with the *Walt Whitman Quarterly Review*, the site offers an up-to-date bibliography of books, essays, notes, and reviews about Whitman that is the only comprehensive current bibliography of work about him. The Manuscripts section has four components and includes facsimiles and e-texts of Whitman's poetry (never before systematically collected and edited); links to Whitman's recently recovered notebooks from the 1850s and 1860s, which are housed at the Library of Congress (LC); finding aids to manuscripts in individual repositories; and a unique Integrated Finding Guide to Whitman's Poetry Manuscripts, which brings together dispersed collections and creates collection-level or item-level access through encoded archival description (EAD) finding aids.[30] The Teaching link connects to another rich resource, The Classroom Electric: Dickinson, Whitman, and American Culture, described as a constellation of Web sites on Emily Dickinson, Walt Whitman, and nineteenth-century American culture (29). The Classroom Electric allows users to explore images of original manuscripts, rare photographs, notebooks, scrapbooks, letters, and maps. Each site can be used independently or searched in combination with other sites.

The Dickinson Electronic Archives, or DEA (30), headquartered at the Maryland Institute for Technology in the Humanities, falls outside the net of both MLA and ADE's directories of scholarly editions. It is produced by the Dickinson Editing Collective under the editorship of Martha Nell Smith, Ellen Louis Hart, Marta Werner, and Lara Vetter in consultation with an advisory board. The Web site is divided into four components devoted to writings by the family, responses to Dickinson's writing, critical resources, and teaching resources. Partly because of "copyright conundrums," the DEA is

---

[30] See Walter and Price 2004, "An Online Guide to Walt Whitman's Dispersed Manuscripts."

adopting a hybrid access model to its two major editorial works.[31] The *Writings by Susan Dickinson* is fully accessible without subscription. It comprises the published (out-of-copyright) and unpublished writings of Emily's sister-in-law and literary confidante Susan Dickinson, including her poems, reviews, essays, stories, and personal correspondence. The XML archive is searchable by keyword. Each transcribed text is accompanied by digital facsimiles and editorial notes. The centerpiece of the DEA, *Emily Dickinson's Correspondences*, will be published in fall 2005 by Rotunda, the University of Virginia Press's new electronic imprint (31), limiting access to licensed users. More than one-third of Dickinson's poems appeared in her letters, and *Emily Dickinson's Correspondences* presents the complete transcriptions of her letters, their digital facsimiles, and editorial and bibliographical notes. The XML-based archive allows users to sort and search by subject, date, or correspondent.

Emily Dickinson's Correspondences is the first publication in Rotunda's Nineteenth-Century Literature and Culture Collection. As of mid-2005, the product had not yet been released and price information was unavailable. However, the pricing and license agreement for Rotunda's debut American Founding Era series—the *Dolley Madison Digital Edition*—is available at the University of Virginia Press's Web site (32). Rotunda has also announced the forthcoming electronic edition by renowned Melville scholar John Bryant of *Herman Melville's "Typee": A Fluid-Text Edition.*

As electronic publishing widens to embrace new genres, such as electronic archives and digital scholarly editions, it is too early to know what models or standard practices will gain acceptance to integrate proprietary and public resources. Many of these complex projects were initiated with grant funds and may have no long-term business plans to sustain them. *Typee* was envisioned originally as integral to the Melville Society's proposed electronic library, where it would become part of a hypertext reading room along with other Melville titles (six are publicly accessible from the University of Virginia Electronic Text Center's e-book collection). Now, The Melville Electronic Library (33) is "on hold" until grant funding can "kick-start" it.[32]

The only scholarly editions currently available of Charles Brockden Brown are his novels. However, an international team of scholars is now collaborating to make all of Brown's uncollected writings available in a fully searchable electronic edition, with a textual and critical apparatus, including historical and biographical notes. *The Charles Brockden Brown Electronic Archive and Scholarly Edition* (34), which aims to comply with MLA's CSE guidelines, has requested funding from the National Endowment for the Humanities (NEH) to prepare six print volumes between 2005 and 2016. Construction of the digital versions would begin after the MLA successfully vets each

---

[31] Information from interview with Martha Nell Smith on February 7, 2005.

[32] Correspondence with John L. Bryant on March 22 and 25, 2005.

volume. Project editors hope to integrate the volumes with a planned digitized version of the Bicentennial Edition of Brown's novels published by Kent State University Press (1977–87). In addition to providing information about the scholarly edition and its publication schedule, the project's Web site has a biography, bibliography of primary and secondary sources, teaching resources, and related links. The archive includes the table of contents of two important out-of-print volumes; portions of these texts eventually will be published electronically at the site.

3.2.3 Other Models and Producers of Digital Content

This section discusses five Web sites to illustrate contributions to author studies by independent scholars, digital libraries, and managers of author estates. The sites offer a range of models of access to content by and about specific authors. Operating under various copyright restrictions, the Emerson site relies on the out-of-copyright centenary edition of Emerson's complete works. Among the three digital library examples, the first two draw primarily on out-of-copyright materials from their respective collections, Jack London and Horatio Alger, Jr. The third and most ambitious, Mark Twain's Mississippi, is under development but holds great promise given the combined expertise and holdings represented by the participating institutions. The fifth example centers on Jack Kerouac, an author whose work is still under copyright restrictions. This site, managed by the private foundation that oversees his estate, serves as bookstore and business agent while also providing biographical information and other information for enthusiasts.

RWE.org—The Works of Ralph Waldo Emerson (35) is created and maintained by Jim Manley, who is chair of the Ralph Waldo Emerson Institute, under the general advisement of independent scholar Richard Geldard. The centerpiece of this site is a digitized version of the 12-volume centenary edition of Emerson's complete works, originally published in 1903–1904 by Houghton Mifflin and Company, with notes and commentary by Emerson's son Edward. Pages from these volumes can be printed or e-mailed. AMS Press republished the centenary edition in 1968; a second edition, published in 1979, included a new introduction by Joel Myerson, distinguished professor emeritus at the University of South Carolina, Columbia. The site refers scholars and those interested in the most accurate and recent editions of *The Collected Works* to the Belknap Press series of Harvard University Press, begun in 1979 and now complete through Volume VI. RWE.org also offers access to the Ralph Waldo Emerson Society's archival collections and "A Concordance to the Collected Essays of Ralph Waldo Emerson," compiled by Eugene F. Irey, both hosted by the Walden Institute. This well-designed site serves as a filter and conduit to high-quality information about Emerson, including audio and video access to two bicentennial forums on Emerson held in Boston's Faneuil Hall in 2003.

The Jack London Collection (36) from Berkeley Digital Library SunSITE, (University of California-Berkeley), was developed by Roy

Tennant, user services architect for the California Digital Library, and Jack London scholar Clarice Stasz, professor of social history at Sonoma State University. The site provides a full array of resources related to the writer, including biographical information, audio clips, documents, images, writings, bibliographies, networking resources, and resources for students and teachers. The Documents section includes letters written by London and by his second wife Charmian as well as miscellanea such as his will. There is an extensive collection of London's writings, including the full text of 19 novels and collections of short stories, essays, and nonfiction works. The documents and writings can be browsed or searched.

The Horatio Alger Jr. Digital Repository (37) is a project of the Northern Illinois University Libraries, which has the world's most comprehensive collection of materials by this best-selling boys'-series writer. Housed in the libraries' Special Collections and Rare Books Department, the 4,000-volume collection contains most first, hardcover, soft-cover, and variant editions; serialized titles; manuscripts; letters; and the archives of the Horatio Alger Society. The digital repository contains selected digitized texts from the collection, including Alger's letters, poems, and short stories. The site has no search engine. It does include a biography and bibliography. It also links to other Alger full-text collections and related Web sites.

Mark Twain's Mississippi (38) is a collaborative effort involving the Northern Illinois University Libraries, the Newberry Library, the St. Louis Mercantile Library, Tulane University Libraries, and the Deep South Regional Humanities Center at Tulane University. It aims to provide a fully searchable and indexed digital library of Samuel Clemens's Mississippi novels and reminiscences (*The Adventures of Tom Sawyer*, *The Adventures of Huckleberry Finn*, and *Life on the Mississippi*). It intends to offer original interpretative essays contributed by scholars along with contextual materials from participating libraries, including text, images, and sound.

Jack Kerouac: The Official Web Site (39) is presented by CSM Worldwide, Inc., for the estate of Jack Kerouac. This site provides biographic information (an unsigned essay), quotes, photos, fast facts, and a chronology of his writings. For the community, it links to Tribute Sites submitted by enthusiasts and to Related Sites. This latter category connects to the Jack Kerouac Writers in Residence Project of Orlando, Inc.; an interview with Kerouac's friend David Amram, the composer and author of *Offbeat*; and *Jack Magazine*, a nonprofit e-zine publishing nonmainstream articles in honor of the beat generation and other experimentalists. The site serves as a store for Kerouac's books, videos, and CDs for purchase from Amazon.com and as a place for fans to download free desktop wallpapers and screen savers. Finally, the site manages business inquiries for the use of Kerouac's assets, including photographs, artwork, and sound and video files available through Legends Archive.

3.2.4 Interpretative and Teaching Collections

Stephen Railton, professor of English at the University of Virginia, is widely recognized for his groundbreaking Web sites that provide contextual material in support of the study of authors and their work. Railton's three premier sites are produced in collaboration with the library's Electronic Text Center.

The important role of broadcast media in developing Web resources for educational use in conjunction with television, video, or radio programs is becoming increasingly apparent. These innovative projects exemplify public and private partnerships involving a range of academic institutions, publishers, and professional associations. The sites take advantage of streaming audio and video, bringing the voices and personae of authors into the classroom.

Finally, author-based information is readily available in companion Web sites to major anthologies of American literature.

Mark Twain in His Times (40) created by Railton, features the extensive Twain holdings of the Barrett Library of American Literature. The site is built around six of Twain's full-length works, in standard generalized markup language (SGML)-encoded text and, in the case of *Pudd'nhead Wilson*, accompanied by a graphic facsimile of the first edition. Each of the six titles contains rich contextual information about the work, including its sources and pretexts, advertising, sales prospects, contemporary reviews, and essays about prevailing attitudes and customs of the times. Three other major sections of the Web site explore Clemens's professional life and the evolution of the image of Mark Twain, the ways in which his work was marketed (for example, through subscription sales), and Clemens's career as a lecturer performing Mark Twain. In his Web review of this site, Carl Smith (Northwestern University) concludes that "it is its old-fashioned intellectual rigor and attention to detail, quality of content, and ease of navigation that make this site so engaging and rewarding."

Uncle Tom's Cabin and American Culture: A Multi-Media Archive (41) is also directed by Stephen Railton, with support from the library's Electronic Text Center, the Institute for Advanced Technology in the Humanities, and the Alderman Library Special Collections as well as from the Harriet Beecher Stowe Center in Hartford, Connecticut. The site can be approached in three modes: browse, search, or interpret. At the site's core, *Uncle Tom's Cabin* can be viewed and compared as an evolving text. Also available is the complete text of Stowe's book *The Key to Uncle Tom's Cabin*, defending and documenting how she developed the story. Surrounding *Uncle Tom's Cabin* are Pretexts (1830–52) and Responses (1852–1930)—evidence of the milieu preceding and following the publication of *Uncle Tom's Cabin*. The Interpret mode includes Railton's suggestions for teachers with explanations of how he has incorporated the site's illustrations, movies, music, posters, and Tomitudes (popular commercial products) into his teaching. This Web resource is annotated by History Matters and was the subject of a review in the *JAH* by Ellen Noonan.

According to its editor Stephen Railton, *Absalom, Absalom!* Electronic, Interactive! Chronology (42) is an experimental site "designed to help first-time readers orient themselves inside the stories William Faulkner is telling in *Absalom, Absalom!* while preserving some aspect of the experience of reading it." The site is also intended to give more-experienced readers new ways of understanding the novel's design, achieved through an interactive chronology mapping the structure of the work. The site is augmented by digital audio files of talks that Faulkner gave at UVa in 1957 and 1958, and page images from Faulkner's notes on the chronology, which are housed in the Alderman Library's Special Collections.

Wired for Books (43), from WOUB Online Radio at Ohio University, provides access to author interviews, spoken poetry and stories, and children's literature in text, pictures, and streaming audio and video. It features scores of uncut, full-length (30- to 45-minute) author interviews from Don Swaim's "Book Beat," nationally syndicated by CBS Radio Stations News Service for more than 10 years.

What's the Word? (44) is a radio series sponsored by the MLA since 1997 and broadcast by public radio stations across the United States and abroad. The series is archived annually at MLA's Web site, where listeners can select a program by browsing topics or by participant's name. There is no author or cumulative index, and the site does not support searching. Typically, the programs are thematic discussions about literature based on interviews with contemporary literary scholars.

American Passages: A Literary Survey (45), sponsored by the Annenberg/Corporation for Public Broadcasting video channel, is the companion Web site to a video series available for purchase developed in partnership with Oregon Public Broadcasting, W. W. Norton & Company, and an academic advisory council. The content is organized into 16 units, covering such themes as Native Voices, Utopian Promise, Gothic Undercurrents, Rhythms in Poetry, and Southern Renaissance. The Book Club provides more than 150 author profiles with corresponding suggested classroom activities. The searchable archive of 3,000 items includes visual art, audio files, primary source materials, and additional texts as well as a unique Slideshow tool that allows users to select materials from the archive to create multimedia slideshows. Slideshows can be stored online, e-mailed, or downloaded. Each slide can hold one audio clip and one or two visual elements and allows users to enter their own narrative text.

Scribbling Women (46), carried out by the Public Media Foundation at Northeastern University, dramatizes stories by American women writers for national radio broadcast. Codirected by Lucinda H. MacKethan, Alumni Distinguished Professor of English at North Carolina State University, and James A. Miller, professor of English and American Studies and director of the Africana Studies Program at George Washington University, this Web site features seven women writers (Ellen Glasgow, Zora Neale Hurston, Kate Chopin, Julia Peterkin, Sarah Orne Jewett, Charlotte Perkins Gilman, and Susan Glaspel) with accompanying radio dramatizations of their plays (about 30 minutes in length). Registration is required, but there is free access to teaching tools and lesson plans. In addition to being linked to author profiles, each play is linked to a synopsis, literary interpretation, historical and literary context, further reading, and a biography. General teaching tools offer advice on literary analysis, active listening, and further reading.

The National Council of Teachers of English, in partnership with ExxonMobil Masterpiece Theatre, created the Educator's Site for its American Collection, featuring the work of six authors: *A Death in the Family* by James Agee; *Almost a Woman* by Esmeralda Santiago; *The Song of the Lark* by Willa Cather; *Cora Unashamed* by Langston Hughes; *The American* by Henry James; and *The Ponder Heart* by Eudora Welty (47). Its companion American Writing Gateway provides access to Web resources, contributed and rated by teachers, about 52 American authors. An interactive literary map of the United States, populated by dots, marks the growing compilation of author profiles written by students across the country.

American Writers: Journey through History and American Writers II: The 20th Century (48) comprises the permanent public archives from C-SPAN's 2001 and 2002 special series on American writers. Although the site was developed in consultation with a secondary school curriculum advisory team, there is extensive content of interest to college and university teachers and their students. The site can be navigated by selecting a writer, a work, or a place. The site covers the years 1900 to 1975 and includes almost 50 authors. The video programs can be viewed in their entirety or through a series of clips. For example, users can view a video clip with Arnold Rampersand, editor of *The Life of Langston Hughes*, which includes film of Hughes reading one of his poems.

Mark Twain (49), the companion Web site to Ken Burns's film of the same name, coproduced by WETA, features an interactive scrapbook, video clips about film production, a Twain chronology, selected writings (with links to full text at the University of Virginia), a bibliography, and links to Twain Web sites, including Mark Twain in His Times. Users can also connect to an interview with Stephen Railton, conducted as a special report about Mark Twain on the PBS Online NewsHour. The Classroom Activities are intended for middle and high school students, but the site has valuable information for students at all levels.

The companion Web site to the fourth edition of *The Heath Anthology of American Literature* (50) (Paul Lauter (Trinity College, general editor) offers free access to timelines, more than 100 author profiles, and resources for instructors. "The Internet Research Guide," contributed by Jason Snart (University of Florida) and accessible from the Student Resource Center, covers such topics as the purpose of research, evaluating information, constructing arguments, and plagiarism.

The Norton Anthology of American Literature (51), 6th edition (Nina Baym, University of Illinois, Urbana-Champaign, general editor) offers a publicly accessible ancillary Web site with timelines and maps, self-grading quizzes and overviews by period, author resource pages for 160 of the writers included in the anthology, and a searchable

Explorations section that provides generative questions and projects. Links to full text from the anthology are accessible only to subscribers, but there is a wealth of material about authors freely available.

3.2.5 Resource Links

(1) American Literature Association. Available at http://www.calstatela.edu/academic/english/ala2/.
Directory of Affiliates (American Literature Association) Available at http://www.calstatela.edu/academic/english/ala2/affiliates.html.

(2) The International Theodore Dreiser Society (Keith Newlin, University of North Carolina at Wilmington). Available at http://www.uncwil.edu/dreiser/.

(3) Dreiser on the Web (Roger W. Smith, International Theodore Dreiser Society). Available at http://www.uncwil.edu/dreiser/TDweb.htm.

(4) Stephen Crane Society (Donna M. Campbell, Washington State University). Available at http://www.wsu.edu/~campbelld/crane/index.html.

(5) Edith Wharton Society (Donna M. Campbell, Washington State University). Available at http://www.wsu.edu/~campbelld/wharton/index.html.

(6) William Dean Howells Society (Donna Campbell, Washington State University). Available at http://www.wsu.edu/~campbelld/howells/.

(7) James Fenimore Cooper Society (Hugh MacDougall, founder and secretary, site hosted by the State University of New York College at Oneonta. Available at http://external.oneonta.edu/cooper/.

(8) Cohen, Matt. **Web review: James Fenimore Cooper Society.** April 2004. *JAH*. Available at http://historymatters.gmu.edu/d/5342.

(9) Burnard, Lou, Katherine O'Brien O'Keeffe, and John Unsworth, eds. 2004. *Electronic Textual Editing.* Available at http://www.tei-c.org/Activities/ETE/Preview/. MLA will issue a print version in 2005.

(10) Committee on Scholarly Editions (MLA). Available at http://www.mla.org/resources/committees/comm_publications/comm_scholarly.

(11) TEI Consortium (Oxford University). The TEI is an international and interdisciplinary standard used by libraries, museums, publishers, and academics to represent all kinds of literary and linguistic texts, using an encoding scheme that is maximally expressive and

minimally apt to become obsolescent. Available at http://www.
tei-c.org/.

(12) MLA Committee on Scholarly Editions, **Guidelines for Editors of Scholarly Editions** (August 3, 2005). Available at http://www.
mla.org/cse_guidelines.

(13) MLA Committee on Scholarly Editions, **Guiding Questions for Vetters of Scholarly Editions** (August 3, 2005). Available at http://
www.mla.org/cse_guidelines#d0e354.

(14) Burnard, Lou, et al., eds. 2004. **Principles**. *Electronic Textual Editing*. Available at http://www.tei-c.org/Activities/ETE/Preview/
principles.xml.

(15) Buzzetti, Dino, and Jerome McGann. 2004. **Critical Editing in a Digital Horizon**. *Electronic Textual Editing*. Available at http://www.
tei-c.org/Activities/ETE/Preview/mcgann.xml.

(16) Rosenberg, Bob. 2004. **Documentary Editing**. *Electronic Textual Editing*. Available at http://www.tei-c.org/Activities/ETE/
Preview/rosenberg.xml.

(17) CSE-Approved Editions. 2004. MLA. Available at http://www.
mla.org/resources/documents/rep_scholarly/cse_approved_edition.

(18) Association for Documentary Editing. Available at http://etext.
lib.virginia.edu/ade/.
- ADE Documentary Editing Markup Guidelines
  Available at http://web.archive.org/web/20040206045722/
  http://adh.sc.edu/MepGuide.html
- Projects and Editions by Title, ADE. Available at http://etext.lib.
  virginia.edu/ade/projects/
- Other American literature documentary editions cited by the ADE:
  Frederick Douglass Papers, nineteenth century
  http://www.iupui.edu/~douglass/
  Works of Jonathan Edwards, eighteenth century
  http://www.yale.edu/wje/index.html
  Benjamin Franklin Papers, eighteenth century
  http://www.yale.edu/franklinpapers/index.html
  Santayana edition, nineteenth and twentieth centuries
  http://www.iupui.edu/~santedit/

(19) Model Editions Partnership (site undergoing renovation as of mid-2005). The purpose of the Model Editions Partnership is to explore ways of creating editions of historical documents that meet the standards scholars traditionally use in preparing printed editions. Equally important is to make these materials more widely available through the Web. Nine of the experimental mini-editions are based on full-text searchable document transcriptions; two are based on document images; and one is based on both images and text. Available at http://adh.sc.edu/. **Markup Guidelines for Documentary Editions,** Model Editions Partnership, at http://adh.sc.edu/MepGuide.html.

(20) Modernist Journals Project (Brown University). Available at http://www.modjourn.brown.edu/.

(21) Romantic Circles (University of Maryland). Available at http://www.rc.umd.edu/.

(22) Fraistat, Neil, and Steven Jones. 2004. **The Poem and the Network: Editing Poetry Electronically.** *Electronic Textual Editing.* Available at http://www.tei-c.org/Activities/ETE/Preview/fraistat.xml.

(23) *Poetry Notebooks of Ralph Waldo Emerson* (Mississippi State University Press). See also *The Topical Notebooks of Ralph Waldo Emerson* and *The Complete Sermons of Ralph Waldo Emerson* at http://www.umsystem.edu/upress/otherbooks/orth.htm. *The Collected Works of Ralph Waldo Emerson* (Belknap Press, Harvard University Press) at http://www.hup.harvard.edu/catalog/EMEC01.html.

(24) The Mark Twain Papers and Project (the Bancroft Library and the University of California-Berkeley). Available at http://bancroft.berkeley.edu/MTP/.

(25) The Writings of Henry D. Thoreau (Northern Illinois University). Available at http://www.thoreau.niu.edu/. In June 2003, the Thoreau Edition was designated a National Endowment for the Humanities "We the People" project because of the importance of Thoreau's writings in American history and culture. Published by Princeton University Press, the list of volumes is available at http://www.pupress.princeton.edu/catalogs/series/hdt.html.

(26) Thoreau's Life & Writings (Thoreau Institute at Walden Woods). Available at http://www.walden.org/Institute/thoreau/writings/Writings.htm. **Research Collections** available at http://www.walden.org/Institute/index.htm.

(27) The Willa Cather Archive (Guy Reynolds, University of Nebraska). Available at http://cather.unl.edu/.

(28) The Walt Whitman Archive (Ed Folsom, University of Iowa and Kenneth M. Price, University of Nebraska). Available at http://www.whitmanarchive.org/.

(29) The Classroom Electric: Dickinson, Whitman, and American Culture. Available at http://jefferson.village.virginia.edu/fdw/.

(30) Dickinson Electronic Archives (Martha Nell Smith, University of Maryland). Available at http://www.emilydickinson.org/.

(31) Rotunda (University of Virginia Press). An electronic imprint of the University of Virginia Press, made possible by grants from The Andrew W. Mellon Foundation and the President's Office of the University of Virginia. Available at http://rotunda.upress.virginia.edu.

(32) Dolley Madison Digital Edition (Rotunda, University of Virginia Press). Rotunda's debut publication, this is the first component in the American Founding Era collection. Available at http://rotunda.upress.virginia.edu:8100/dmde/.
　　The Dolley Madison Project. Original project site with publicly accessible resources. Available at http://moderntimes.vcdh.virginia.edu/madison/.

(33) Melville Electronic Library (John Bryant, Hofstra University). Available at http://people.hofstra.edu/faculty/John_l_Bryant/Melville/lib.html.
　　Melville Society. Available at http://people.hofstra.edu/faculty/John_L_Bryant/Melville/.

(34) The Charles Brockden Brown Electronic Archive and Scholarly Edition. Available at http://www.brockdenbrown.ucf.edu/.

(35) RWE.org–The Works of Ralph Waldo Emerson. Available at http://www.rwe.org. **Ralph Waldo Emerson Society papers at Walden Institute**, available at http://www.walden.org/Institute/Collections/Emerson/Emersonsociety.htm.

(36) The Jack London Collection (Berkeley Digital Library SunSITE, University of California-Berkeley). Available at http://sunsite.berkeley.edu/London/.

(37) The Horatio Alger Jr. Digital Repository (Northern Illinois University Libraries). Available at http://www.niulib.niu.edu/rbsc/alger/DigRepos/.

(38) Mark Twain's Mississippi (Northern Illinois University). Available at http://dig.lib.niu.edu/twain/about.html.

(39) Jack Kerouac: The Official Web Site (CSM Worldwide, Inc., for the Estate of Jack Kerouac). Available at http://www.jackkerouac.com/index.php.

(40) Mark Twain in His Times (Stephen Railton, University of Virginia). Available at http://etext.lib.virginia.edu/railton/. Annotated in History Matters and reviewed in *JAH* by Carl Smith. Available at http://www.historymatters.gmu.edu/d/366/.

(41) Uncle Tom's Cabin and American Culture: A Multi-Media Archive (Stephen Railton, University of Virginia). Available at http://jefferson.village.virginia.edu/utc/. Annotated in History Matters and reviewed in *JAH* by Ellen Noonan. Available at http://historymatters.gmu.edu/d/4909.

(42) *Absalom, Absalom!* **Electronic, Interactive! Chronology** (Stephen Railton). Interactive (flash-based) chronology mapping of the complex structure of this work by William Faulkner. Augmented by digital audio files of talks by Faulkner at UVa in 1957 and 1958 and by page images from Faulkner's notes on the chronology, which is housed in UVa Library Special Collections. Available at http://etext.lib.virginia.edu/railton/absalom.

(43) Wired for Books (WOUB Online Radio at Ohio University). Available at http://wiredforbooks.org/.

(44) What's the Word? (Radio program sponsored by the MLA). Available at http://www.mla.org/radio.

(45) American Passages: A Literary Survey. Available at http://www.learner.org/amerpass/index.html. **Book Club** features more than 150 authors with biographies and activities at http://www.learner.org/amerpass/author_list.html.

(46) Scribbling Women (Public Media Foundation at Northeastern University). Available at http://www.scribblingwomen.org.

(47) American Collection. Available at http://www.ncteamericacollection.org/series.htm. **Literary Map** at http://www.ncteamericancollection.org/litmap/amcollectlitmap.htm.

(48) American Writers: Journey through History and American Writers II: The 20th Century. Available at http://www.americanwriters.org.

(49) Mark Twain. A film directed by Ken Burns, coproduced by WETA. Available at http://www.pbs.org/marktwain/.

(50) *The Heath Anthology of American Literature*, 4th edition, Paul Lauter, general editor, Trinity College. Available at http://college.hmco.com/english/lauter/heath/4e/students/index.html. **Internet Research Guide**, Jason Snart (University of Florida). Available at http://college.hmco.com/english/resources/research_guide/1e/students/index.html.

(51) *Norton Anthology of American Literature*, 6th edition, Nina Baym, general editor, University of Illinois, Urbana-Champaign. Available at http://wwnorton.com/college/titles/english/naal6/emedia.htm.

3.3 E-Book Collections and Alternative Publishing Models

3.3.1 Public Domain E-Books

This section considers primarily noncommercial e-book projects and indexes with significant content relevant to the study of American literature. There is no reliable aggregation or comprehensive curated collection of publicly accessible e-books in American literature so users must deploy a variety of strategies for locating and accessing them. In section 3.3.5, five exemplars of alternative publishing communities are explored.

The study commissioned by the United Kingdom's JISC (Joint Information Systems Committee) e-Books Working Group, *An Investigation into Free E-books*, reflects attitudes and concerns that are wholly compatible with those of the scholars surveyed for this report (Berglund et al. 2004). Readers are referred to the JISC report for a more thorough discussion of free e-book collections, text-encoding formats, current levels of usage in higher education, and user needs. It examines attitudes toward free e-books and identifies barriers to as well as opportunities for promoting their adoption in educational settings.

The terms *online books* and *e-books* are often used interchangeably because there are no agreed-on definitions.[33] In practice, *online book* generally refers to a full-text electronic version of a published book that is intended for reading on a computer and does not require a special reader device or viewing software. The NISO (National Information Standards Organization) data dictionary for libraries and information providers that accompanies the standards for e-metrics and statistics defines e-books as "digital documents, licensed or not, where searchable text is prevalent, and which can be seen in analogy to a print book (monograph). The use of e-books is in many cases dependent on a dedicated device and/or a special reader or viewing software"(1).

Principles, philosophies, and the application of technology vary widely among e-book creators. There are differences in the ways in which books are selected and in the methods deployed in converting texts to digital form, including such fundamental considerations as whether the texts are manually transcribed (rekeyed) or scanned (then processed through optical character recognition [OCR] software); the extent of rekeying (single, double, triple) or proofreading; the amount of text editing and encoding; the formats in which the texts are presented; and the ways in which they can be viewed (ASCII text, Web versions), manipulated (searched, copied, down-

---

[33] The trade and standards organization devoted to the development and promotion of electronic publishing, the Open eBook Forum (OeBF), begs the question—What is an electronic book? Noting that "people use this term differently," the OeBF eschews the term *e-book* in its publication structure specification. Instead, it relies on its own "more precise" (and self-referential) term by defining "an OEBPS (Open eBook Publication Structure) Publication" as "the digital content you read (a 'paperless' version of a book, article or other document)." This seems to reflect evolving industry practice, where e-books are increasingly indistinguishable from e-content. See Open eBook Forum 2002.

loaded, e-mailed), and read (plain text, by chapter, entire book).

The JISC *Investigation* describes a variety of file formats and discusses their respective creation and viewing software, portability, file structures, and repurposing characteristics. It draws the following basic conclusions:

- Many of the document formats described above employ a markup scheme that is either a subset of, or a derivation from, HTML.
- A document is easier to repurpose if it adheres to a well-documented standard.
- A complex document is easier to repurpose if it contains explicit structural markup.
- More-complex e-book functionality, such as user annotation and the incorporation of specific fonts with an e-book, tend to be present only in formats that have commercial backing, such as Microsoft's lit and Adobe's PDF (Berglund et al. 2004, 27-28).

It is often difficult for e-book users to determine the source of the base text (not only what edition or editions were used but also their original format) as well as the digitization technologies employed. Free e-book sites created by enthusiasts and commercial entities alike are notorious for failing to provide adequate information about the provenance of texts, editorial practices, and text-conversion accuracy rates. Deegan and Tanner point out "what seem like accurate results (between 95 and 99 percent, for instance) would mean that there would be between 1 and 5 incorrect characters per 100 characters. Assuming there are on average 5 characters per word then a 1 percent character error rate equates to a word error rate of 1 in 20 or higher" (Deegan and Tanner 2004, 495). Almost 10 years ago, LC's National Digital Library Program set a standard for SGML-encoded texts derived from original documents at 99.95 percent to 99.995 percent accuracy. This translates into no more than one wrong character per 20,000 characters keyed, or roughly one wrong character per 10 pages.[34] It bears mentioning, as Deegan and Tanner discuss, that this level of accuracy comes at a high cost of human labor in rekeying texts and thorough professional reading.[35]

Bartleby.com (2), a popular Internet publisher of primarily out-of-copyright reference works, verse, fiction and nonfiction, does provide bibliographic records for all of its titles, but offers no information about its editorial practices, text-conversion methods, or accuracy rates. Because Bartleby.com works in partnership with promi-

---

[34] The Library of Congress National Digital Library Program's 1996 request for proposals for digital images from original documents set a high standard of accuracy for all SGML-encoded texts at 99.95 percent or 99.995 percent. As explained, "Accuracy is based on a character count, including tags, after encoding. For example, an accuracy level of 99.995% means that no more than one (1) wrong character is permitted for any 20,000 characters keyed, roughly one (1) wrong character per ten (10) pages." Available at http://memory.loc.gov/ammem/prpsal/rfp9618e.html.

[35] A discussion of editorial theory is beyond the scope of this report but it affects such factors as what counts as an error, who gets to decide what is an error, and what is corrected. For an introduction, readers may refer to Bryant 2002.

nent university presses and other reputable publishers, the user must trust that the site adopts high standards for converting and editing texts. Some instructors avoid referring their students to any commercial site supported by advertising, such as Bartleby.com, but other instructors rely on this site for free access to a wide range of reference works (e.g., *Roget's II: The New Thesaurus*, *The American Heritage Book of English Usage*, *Bartlett's Familiar Quotations*, Strunk's *Elements of Style*); literary histories and anthologies, including the multivolume *Harvard Classics Shelf of Fiction* and the 18-volume *Cambridge History of English and American Literature*; and titles by American writers and poets. Bartleby.com uses a proprietary back-end database that combines (unspecified) editorial and technical requirements to permit hyperlinked cross-references from biographies to quotations to full-text primary and secondary sources. It has more than 370,000 full-text searchable Web pages categorized by subject and indexed by author (more than 200) and title (more than 300).

3.3.2 Digital Conversion Projects: Overview

The five projects under consideration—Project Gutenberg, Making of America, Wright American Fiction, Early American Fiction, and mass-digitization initiatives (the Million Book Project and Google Print's academic partnerships)—vary in purpose and approach to digital text conversion of materials predominantly in the public domain. It is important that users understand these variables because they affect the integrity of the text, search and navigation functions, and ways in which the text can be read and manipulated. Readers who seek a more thorough introduction to digital-conversion alternatives should refer to the chapters in *A Companion to Digital Humanities* by Perry Willett, "Electronic Texts: Audiences and Purposes"; Marilyn Deegan and Simon Tanner, "Conversion of Primary Sources"; and Allen H. Renear, "Text Encoding" (Schreibman et al. 2004). The projects under discussion also offer documentation about their processes at their respective Web sites.

- Project Gutenberg, with approximately 14,000 digitized books in English as of May 2005, aims "to encourage the creation and distribution of eBooks" for general readers. It relies on a network of volunteers to contribute and proofread scanned and OCRed texts, which are usually presented in ASCII plain text.
- Making of America, carried out at Cornell University and the University of Michigan, is a digital library of primary-source nineteenth-century imprints, with a core concentration on the period from 1850 to 1877. The materials, which are selected from the respective library collections in consultation with library subject specialists and faculty, are scanned, processed by OCR software, and presented as page images with "invisible" unedited text running in the background to facilitate searching.
- The Wright American Fiction project, a collaborative of the Committee on Institutional Cooperation (CIC), used UMI's microfilm collection as its base for digitizing a subset of the books as listed in Lyle Wright's foundational bibliography, *American Fiction, 1851–*

1875. Working from scanned and OCRed microfilm, Wright American Fiction aims to present both page images and fully edited and encoded texts of 2,887 volumes representing 1,450 authors.

- Early American Fiction, a joint project of the University of Virginia's Special Collections Department and Electronic Text Center, presents digitized page images and fully edited and TEI-encoded texts of 886 print volumes by 136 authors, 199 manuscript items, and 124 nontext images. The materials were selected from Virginia's Special Collections, using the physical volume for transcribing and twice rekeying texts. Jointly published by ProQuest/Chadwyck-Healey and the University of Virginia Library, all manuscript items and nontext images are available to the public, but only a subset of the print volumes—158 texts by 52 authors—is publicly accessible.

- Until Google's December 2004 announcement about its mass-digitization initiative with five prominent research institutions, the Million Book Project (an international collaborative led by Carnegie Mellon) represented the most ambitious production goal. Now the Google Print Library Project calls for a redefinition of "mass digitization," eclipsing all other projects with its ambition of digitizing more than 15 million books in the next decade.

3.3.2.1 Distributed Proofreading: Project Gutenberg (3)

Project Gutenberg (PG), founded by Michael Hart in 1971, is probably the best known among free e-book sites. In a 30-day period from early March to early April 2005, more than one million titles were downloaded from PG through its distribution site, ibiblio.org. PG's mission is "to encourage the creation and distribution of eBooks," targeting the "general reader." PG relies on volunteers for its choice of books and their digital conversion. In PG's Mission Statement FAQ, Hart acknowledges that "many of our most popular eBooks started out with huge error levels" and "were done totally without any supervision . . . and only sent to us after the fact," but asserts that now most of its e-books exceed the 99.95 percent level of accuracy recommended by LC. Still, PG adamantly adopts the principles of "minimal regulation" and "non-interference" with its volunteers, one outcome of which is "a lack of a need for perfectionism," stating flatly that it "is not in the business of establishing standards." Instead, PG will accept "eBooks in any format and at any accuracy level" from any volunteer, then ask other "volunteers to convert them to other formats, and to incrementally correct errors" over time. University of Pennsylvania's Digital Librarian John Mark Ockerbloom, who indexes Gutenberg titles at his Online Books Page, reports that PG is now "reasonably responsive" about correcting errors, observing that in his experience "they fix them quickly once they're brought to their attention."[36] Ockerbloom notes other improvements in PG as well, particularly the fact that they now include the specific source edition citation in their texts. (Originally, PG created many e-

---

[36] E-mail correspondence with John Mark Ockerbloom on February 7, 2005.

books from multiple editions.) Moreover, they are beginning to retain their page scans offline, and discussions are under way, according to Ockerbloom, about integrating them online with the transcriptions. Those PG editions would become "research-grade sources," Ockerbloom continues, "since you can always flip from the transcription to the images and back if you're uncertain about the transcription. . . . As they stand now," Ockerbloom concludes, "PG texts are useful for more casual reading, and for quick consultation, and other sources should be consulted when one needs to be sure of a quote and its citation."

PG relies on a Web-based method of distributed proofreading by volunteers, parceling out the work into individual pages so that many proofreaders are working on the same book simultaneously to speed the book-creation process. The scanned images of books are posted for proofreaders on a Web page alongside the text from that image, as produced by OCR software. Proofreaders read the text and correct it to match the page image, fixing OCR errors and marking special text characteristics (such as italic, bold, or footnotes), according to PG's guidelines. In contrast to its initial methodology, two proofreaders now read all pages to minimize errors. As explained at the PG's Distributed Proofreaders Web site, "Once all pages for a particular book have been processed, a post-processor joins the pieces, properly formats them into a Project Gutenberg e-book and submits it to the Project Gutenberg archive." PG initially produced only "plain-vanilla ASCII" texts to make them available in the simplest and easiest-to-use form, but now accepts e-books in all file formats. It prefers formats that are open ("structure is publicly defined and documented, and not burdened with patent or trade secret or copy-protection [a.k.a. 'DRM'] restrictions") and easy to edit.

PG has produced nearly 14,000 English-language titles, of which some 1,500 are classified as American literature (Library of Congress Classification [LoCC], PS). There are various advanced search features to limit queries by author, language, LoCC, or format type; nonetheless, it is difficult to get an overview or speak in terms of a coherent collection. Conducting searches within English-language titles in the PS classification for Poetry retrieves 39 results while Fiction returns 341 results. Among the American authors represented are Horatio Alger, Edward Bellamy, Ambrose Bierce, Stephen Vincent Benét, Charles Brockden Brown, Emily Dickinson, Henry Wadsworth Longfellow, Amy Lowell, Edgar Lee Masters, Edna St. Vincent Millay, James Whitcomb Riley, Sara Teasdale, and Ralph Waldo Emerson. Full-text searching is offered as an "experimental feature."

Despite the potentially valuable content and improvements in its editorial practices, in the minds of many scholars PG has an uphill battle to regain their confidence. It may take only one negative experience with a misassembled novel that scrambles the order of chapters to deter instructors from ever returning to the Web site. Moreover, PG's volunteer-powered, anti-elitist philosophy militates against a consistently reliable, academically viable resource.

Busy scholars do not have the time to play roulette, trying to guess whether or not a particular e-book meets minimal standards. One scholar interviewed denounced PG as nothing short of "disastrous." Still, PG titles are difficult to avoid and often used unwittingly. They populate many other Web sites, such as Blackmask Online, the Million Book Project, the Online Books Page, the Digital Book Index, the Internet Archive, and Alex Catalogue of Electronic Texts. PG titles are also used as the basis for making derivative copies in other formats, including titles in the University of California's Digital Library's Literature at SunSITE (e.g., the Jack London collection), the Humanities Text Initiative at the University of Michigan, and the University of Virginia's Modern English Collection. In this regard, it is important to be able to distinguish derivative copies that were verified against original print editions from those transcriptions that were adopted from PG wholesale without review. PG's titles are also widely retrieved by search engines and subject directories, including Google and Humbul Humanities Hub.

3.3.2.2 Page Images with "Rough OCR": Making of America (4)

Making of America (MoA) began a decade ago as a collaborative project of Cornell University and the University of Michigan, with funding from The Andrew W. Mellon Foundation. MoA's goal is to preserve and make electronically available deteriorating nineteenth-century books and journals deemed of broad scholarly and general interest, focusing on American social history from the antebellum era through reconstruction. MoA was the first to demonstrate the feasibility of a solution that is more scalable than manually transcribing (and double keying) or scanning (and double proofreading) when attempting to reproduce large numbers of digitized books (Shaw and Blumson 1997; Price-Wilkin 1997; Willett 2004). MoA materials are scanned from the original paper source, and conversion to page images is outsourced. According to an explanation of the "Conversion Process" at Michigan's Web site, a minimal amount of document structuring occurs at the point of conversion in order to link image numbers to pagination and to tag self-referencing portions of the text. "Low-level indexing" is added to serials by the partner institutions in the postconversion process. Images are then converted to text through OCR. Michigan's report on measuring the accuracy of the OCR is available at its Web site. To make the project cost-effective and still useful to most researchers, MoA seeks to achieve a "reasonable accuracy standard," set at 99 percent or higher. MoA pioneered the method of displaying digital page images with uncorrected OCR text hidden in the background. This enables users to view digital facsimiles of original pages while performing keyword searches against the unedited text. Scholars seem to prefer the combination of reproduced page images (which they trust) and less-than-precise search results (which they forgive), over viewable, but faulty, text transcriptions without recourse to page images and more-precise searching capabilities.

MoA is organized into two major databases maintained at

separate Web sites. Unfortunately, the plan to make these resources cross-searchable has not come to fruition. Now comprising more than 3.5 million pages and more than 12,000 volumes, the Michigan collection includes 8,500 books and 11 journal titles. Cornell covers 267 monographic volumes, 22 serials, and 2 extensive, multivolume sets (the *Official Records* of the Union and Confederate armies and navies from the Civil War). Because much literary publishing in the nineteenth century appeared exclusively in magazines, both Cornell's and Michigan's collections of journals are of considerable value to the study of American literature, covering such titles as *Appletons' Journal, The Atlantic Monthly, Harper's New Monthly Magazine, Ladies' Repository, Putnam's Monthly Magazine of American Literature, Science and Art, Scribner's Magazine, Southern Literary Magazine, The Southern Quarterly Review*, and *Vanity Fair*. Literary scholars will also find histories and anthologies of American literature such as Evert A. Duyckinck's *Cyclopaedia of American Literature* (1875) and Barrett Wendell's *A Literary History of America* (1900) alongside essays, poems, and letters by notable American writers, including two editions of the *Prose Works of Ralph Waldo Emerson* dating from 1870 and 1875. Both sites support basic and advanced full-text search functions along with browsing by journal title (year and issue) or at the article level by author or title. Results can be printed (one page at a time), e-mailed, or downloaded. MARC records are available for all MoA records, making it possible to create links directly from library online catalogs to the item.

3.3.2.3 Conversion from Microfilm to Fully Encoded Transcriptions: Wright American Fiction (5)

In contrast to the preceding projects, Wright American Fiction (WAF) relies on a foundational bibliography as its basis, namely, Lyle H. Wright's three-volume work *American Fiction*, which constitutes the most comprehensive bibliography of American prose fiction published from 1774 to 1900 and lists 12,000 titles. According to Harner's annotation in *Literary Research Guide*, the bibliography includes "separately published American novels, romances, tall tales, allegories, and fictitious biographies and travels, but excluding juvenile fiction, jestbooks, Indian captivity narratives, periodicals, annuals, gift books, folklore, tracts published by religious societies, dime novels, and subscription series" (Harner 2002, 480–481). Wright American Fiction consists of a subset of the collection, spanning 1851 to 1875, aiming to complement MoA and to extend the coverage of the Early American Fiction project, which covers the years 1774 to 1850, undertaken by the University of Virginia Library in partnership with Chadwyck-Healey. A collaborative within the CIC, the WAF project aims to build expertise among participating partners in digital text production and encoding while bringing to the wider public an important body of American fiction. Participants chose Thomson Gale's microfilm set as the basis for digitization because it was preassembled and virtually 100 percent complete so that it could be digitized relatively quickly and avoid the costs associated with physical copy selection, location, preparation for shipping, insurance, handling and storage requirements during digitization, and postdigitization checking. Conversion to digital page images was outsourced and OCR processing occurred at Indiana University. Editing and encoding the text files to TEI specifications was originally undertaken by participating CIC members but is now outsourced. The TEI encoding guidelines adopted for this project are available at Indiana University's LETRS Web site. As of January 2005, all of the 2,887 volumes, by 1,450 authors, had been scanned and OCRed, and 1,004 volumes had been fully edited and encoded. Completed texts are available as both digital facsimile page images and transcriptions. The project uses the University of Michigan's search and display software. MARC catalog records are available for all titles and they have also been made Open Archival Information System (OAIS)-compliant for harvesting by OAI services such as OAIster.

3.3.2.4 Conversion from Original Print Copy to Fully Encoded Texts: Early American Fiction (6)

The University of Virginia Library's Early American Fiction project began in 1996 when the library received a grant from The Andrew W. Mellon Foundation to digitize several hundred volumes in early American fiction dating from 1789 to 1850. The texts chosen for the project include first printings of works by well-known authors such as James Fenimore Cooper, Edgar Allan Poe, and Nathaniel Hawthorne, as well as more obscure authors such as Rufus Dawes and Hannah Webster Foster. A second phase of funding made possible the digitization of texts from 1851 to 1875, along with related manuscript items held in the library's special collections and images (e.g., engravings, photographs). This added works by 90 authors, including works by Louisa May Alcott, Harriet Beecher Stowe, Herman Melville, and Samuel Clemens. The complete collection, which was selected on the basis of the *Bibliography of American Literature* (see 3.4.3.2) and Lyle Wright's *American Fiction* bibliography, now constitutes 886 volumes, totaling some 230,000 pages and representing 136 authors, in addition to 199 manuscript items and 124 nontext images. Early American Fiction differs from the preceding exemplars in several ways:

- It includes books, manuscripts, and images (engravings and photographs) derived from special collections.
- The texts are digitized, double keyed, and marked up in TEI-conformant XML.
- Full-color images of every page of the first edition texts, including spines and covers, are available online, allowing scholars to explore their illustrations, typography, bindings, design, and construction.
- The texts can be downloaded into various electronic-reader devices.
- The project represents a public/private publishing partnership between the University of Virginia Library and ProQuest/ Chadwyck-Healey.

- A subset of the collection that includes 152 texts by 52 authors, and all the manuscript items and ancillary materials, are publicly available.
- Access to the full collection is licensed through ProQuest.
- Early American Fiction is integral to the University of Virginia Library's Electronic Text Center's Modern English Collection (AD 1500 to present), which makes some 1,800 titles freely available as e-books.
- "Study Resources for Early American Fiction" offers examples of innovative ways in which the texts are used in teaching and research.

3.3.2.5 Mass-Digitization Projects: One Million Books Plus

Before Google's announcement in December 2004, the Million Book Project, or MBP (also known as the Universal Library) (7), which was established in 2001, was the most ambitious mass-digitization project. Designed to address global inequities in the size and accessibility of library collections, to facilitate scholarship and lifelong learning, and to provide a large testbed to support digital library research, the international MBP aims to digitize and provide free-to-read access to a million books by 2005. Under the leadership of Carnegie Mellon University in affiliation with OCLC and the Internet Archive, the MBP collaborative is funded in part by the National Science Foundation with additional support from project partners in China and India. MBP is developing an eclectic, multidisciplinary, multilingual collection of collections that includes materials in the public domain, copyrighted books, and government documents. Of particular interest to American literary scholars is the inclusion of 50,000 titles from *Books for College Libraries* (American Library Association 1988). It is negotiating nonexclusive scanning contracts with several university presses (e.g., University of Texas), think tanks (e.g., Brookings Institution), and scholarly associations (primarily in the sciences). As part of these agreements, participating publishers receive copies of the digital files and relevant metadata. Books selected from participating U.S. university library collections are shipped to international scanning centers, where indigenous materials from India and China are also converted to digital form.

MBP's research objectives include investigation of security issues, copyright laws, digital-rights management, OCR accuracy, image processing, language processing, automatic metadata creation, summarization, intelligent indexing, machine translation, storage formats, and search engines. As the lead institution, Carnegie Mellon University Library is responsible for identifying collections to be sent to international scanning centers, ensuring metadata standards, locating books with permissions given, and identifying the means to sustain the project. It has established the requisite workflow to ensure capture of high-resolution images and essential metadata, to correct problems with page images in postprocessing, and to create searchable ASCII text through OCR processing with 98 percent accuracy. The MBP follows the standards and best practices supported in

"A Framework of Guidance for Building Good Digital Collections," developed by the Institute of Museum and Library Services in 2001 and endorsed by the Digital Library Federation (DLF) in 2002.[37] Since the database is still under development, it is too soon to evaluate its content relevant to American literary scholars. In mid-April 2005, searching the pilot database at the Internet Archive yielded only six hits for American literature and one for Walt Whitman. Users can print, save, or e-mail results one page at a time.

At the writing of this report, details are still sketchy about the Google Print Library Project digitization agreements with five prominent research institutions, but their goal of converting to digital form more than 15 million items dwarfs all other efforts (8). Agreements vary from institution to institution and are subject to nondisclosure clauses. Readers are advised to consult the project Web sites of each institution to obtain the most up-to-date information.[38] The University of Michigan and Stanford University's contracts call for digitizing the entire collection from their major humanities and social science libraries (and eventually from all libraries) at the combined level of an estimated 15 million items, whereas Harvard University, The New York Public Library, and Oxford University's Bodleian Library agreed to lesser portions of their collections. The agreements appear to have three core principles in common: high-quality digital capture (i.e., meeting industry standards of "very good reproductions and preservation-quality files," according to Michigan); nondestructive handling of materials; and, for institutions that include copyrighted materials, appropriate rights management. Participating institutions bear no cost and are protected from damage to their collections. In lieu of payment for the nonexclusive use of their collections, Google provides participants with digital source files that they may use as they wish, but may not offer to other commercial entities. Meanwhile, Google has the unrestricted use of the digital files. Participating institutions plan to build infrastructures for managing sustainable repositories of their digital content and to develop various tools and services for their use. The extent to which participants will share their digital derivatives outside their local environments is not fully known, although it is anticipated that several will make—at the very least—their out-of-copyright materials widely available. OCLC is systematically surveying the Google Five's collections to better understand their characteristics, using WorldCat as a proxy for their holdings. The Google Print Library Project will have a significant impact on any plans to digitize nineteenth-century collections. Library subject specialists estimate that participating libraries hold 75 to 80 percent of the titles listed in Lyle Wright's bibliography of American fiction. Practitioners hope that project participants will develop a registry to track collections as they are proposed, located, and digitized. The scanned content eventually will become integral to Google Print.

---

37 Second edition released in 2004 by the NISO Framework Advisory Group. Available at http://www.niso.org/framework/framework2.html.

38 For an initial skeptical reaction to the Google Print Library Project, refer to Tennant 2005.

3.3.3 Indexes of E-Books

Google Scholar, accessible in beta version at a distinct address, enables users to limit their search to scholarly content, including peer-reviewed papers, theses, books, preprints, abstracts, technical reports, and other forms across all disciplines (9).[39] It retrieves books and articles from a wide variety of academic publishers, professional societies, preprint repositories, and universities as well as scholarly output available across the Web. According to its About page, "Google Scholar uses the same methods of ordering search results as Google, namely by relevance to the search query." It explains that "this relevance ranking takes into account the full text of each article as well as the article's author, the publication in which the article appeared and how often it has been cited in scholarly literature. Google Scholar also automatically analyzes and extracts citations and presents them as separate results, even if the documents to which they refer are not online. This means that search results may include citations of older works and seminal articles that appear only in books or other offline publications." In its present version, results cannot be re-sorted.

A search for scholarship pertaining to Nathaniel Hawthorne's *The Scarlet Letter* (i.e., author:hawthorne scarlet) illustrates the potential strengths and pitfalls of using Google Scholar as currently configured (figure 2). The search retrieved 18 hits: 7 are identified as "citations," another 8 as "books." The remaining three hits, including the top result, are links to a PDF text file created in Korea. When the author attempted to view it, a warning appeared that the file contained Korean fonts and was 4.1 megabytes in size, so the retrieval aborted. Each result offers the following additional link options, when available: View as HTML, Cited by [#], Library Search, and Web Search. The first hit's "View as HTML" really links to the Korean PDF file. "Cited by" links to an eclectic mix of 26 references but not necessarily to this particular text. "Library Search" links to the audio book version of *The Scarlet Letter*. Finally, "Web Search" retrieved 125,000 results that include both citations to and online versions of book. In the example below, the Library Search page connects to Seymour Lee Gross's 1988, not 1978, edition. The Web Search retrieved 4,160 hits, which link to various editions of the "authoritative text."

Fig. 2. Sample Google Scholar result for author:hawthorne scarlet

[BOOK] The scarlet letter
N Hawthorne, WA Dwiggins - 1980 - hawthorne.or.kr
Page 1. 7 / 2000 ( ) : The Scarlet Letter "A" 5 Hawthorne The House of the Seven Gables 29 51 The Scarlet Letter 77 Hawthorne 97 Hawthorne Updike 117 ...
Cited by 42 - View as HTML - Web Search - Library Search

---

[39] See Martin Myhill's December 2004 review of *Google Scholar* freely available from *The Charleston Advisor* at http://www.charlestonco.com/.

As a demonstration project, Google Scholar shows great potential, but it is too soon to know how it will function alongside Google Print once this service contains the scanned content from its research library partners. Until then, Google Scholar will need to improve its search precision and recall to become an effective tool for educational use.

3.3.3.1 A Master Index: Digital Book Index (10)

A review of five indexes to online books and electronic texts illustrates other approaches to making online books accessible. These indexes vary in purpose, coverage, and functionality, as shown in Appendix 3. At one end of the spectrum, the Digital Book Index (DBI) is a multidisciplinary metasite that identifies and links to both commercial and noncommercial e-books, indexing some 105,000 titles. At the other, the Oxford Text Archive, currently comprising an estimated 2,500 texts, serves as a depository of electronic texts in the humanities with the aim of cataloging and preserving digital source files and making them available for redistribution.

DBI is the best starting point for general readers because it indexes titles from a wide array of publishers covering popular sites such as Bartleby.com and Project Gutenberg; academic sites such as Making of America, Wright American Fiction, and Documenting the American South; digital library collections such as the Library of Congress's American Memory, Tufts University's Perseus Project, and the University of Virginia's and University of California-Berkeley's digital e-book collection. DBI also covers hundreds of university presses and commercial publishers, including about 25,000 NetLibrary titles and 49,000 Questia titles (7,000 indexed thus far). According to DBI developer Tom Franklin, when publishers cooperate, he is able to index their lists comprehensively. It is the only publicly accessible e-book index to feature browsing by publisher; Franklin reports a backlog of 40,000 to 50,000 titles.[40] Although DBI requires (free) registration with each use, the site is well organized, easy to navigate, and clearly identifies the provider of each title. It includes an estimated 12,000 texts in English and American literature and claims "the most comprehensive, openly accessible collection of nineteenth-century American Literature available on the Internet." American literature and texts can be browsed by century or special categories (e.g., Harlem Renaissance). In addition, readers can browse authors and titles categorized by genre: fiction, folklore, myth, legend, fable, and drama/theatre. Annotated entries present the following information: author, title, date of edition, format, price (where applicable), and publishing organization. Finally, DBI links to helpful information about downloading texts into assorted e-book reader devices. To cite one example, F. Scott Fitzgerald's *This Side of Paradise* has five entries: two HTML versions of the 1920 edition from Bartleby and the University of Virginia's American Studies Web site; one ASCII text entry from Project Gutenberg; and two Simon & Schuster editions downloadable in Adobe MsR Palm available for purchase at $4.50 and $3.38, respectively.

---

40 E-mail correspondence from Tom Franklin on April 12, 2005.

3.3.3.2 An Archival and Distribution Management Service: Oxford Text Archive (11)

The Oxford Text Archive (OTA), founded by noted researcher and TEI European Editor Lou Burnard, has almost 30 years of experience in collecting, preserving, and redistributing electronic texts to the academic community. The OTA offers archival and distribution-management services for data creators and depositors. According to the Web site's FAQ, data resources that are offered for deposit to the OTA will be evaluated to assess:

- how appropriate the content of the resource is for inclusion in the OTA collection;
- their intellectual content and thus the level of potential interest in their reuse;
- how (even whether) they may viably be managed, preserved, and distributed to potential secondary users; and
- the level and quality of documentation. The OTA will be looking for material that is accompanied by a high level of documentation. The documentation should relate to both the content and the technical format of the resource. The better the level of documentation, the quicker that the resource will be properly deposited and appear in the OTA online catalog. Documentation accompanying the text for deposit should be TEI-compliant SGML format.

Depositors are required to grant the OTA a nonexclusive license to distribute their texts. This does not mean that they must hand over the rights of their resource to the OTA; instead, the depositor grants OTA the right to make copies of its resource and make it available for redistribution. In the interest of the academic community as a whole, the OTA encourages depositors to make their textual data available to the broadest-possible spectrum of users. It is possible, however, to restrict access to different classes of use.

The OTA may serve as the first port of call for digital text developers who seek advice about how to digitize texts or who need reliable, well-documented raw source files. The Electronic Text Center at the University of Virginia, for example, credits the OTA for providing most of the publicly accessible texts in its Middle English Collection. Moreover, the OTA has a collection policy that articulates the scope, data types, and evaluation criteria for texts they accept as well as documentation standards, preservation, access and use, and rights management.[41] International and multilingual in scope, an estimated 950 texts are in English, including texts by major American literary authors such as Louisa May Alcott, Horatio Alger, Nathaniel Hawthorne, Henry James, Sinclair Lewis, Herman Melville, Thomas Paine, Edgar Allan Poe, Sylvia Plath, Mark Twain, and Walt Whitman.

---

[41] Although texts are documented, some practitioners report that at least early OTA texts were flawed, indicating that no one had checked the accuracy of the texts accepted for deposit.

3.3.3.3 Online Books Page (12), A Celebration of Women Writers (13), and the Alex Catalogue of Electronic Texts (14)

The territory between the DBI and the OTA is represented by the Online Books Page (OBP), A Celebration of Women Writers (CWW), and the Alex Catalogue of Electronic Texts. Of the three, Alex has the narrowest subject focus (classics of American and English literature as well as Western philosophy) and corresponding smallest size—only 650 texts. Without secure funding, Alex serves primarily as a prototype for cataloging and storing electronic texts locally, which lends greater stability. The public domain source texts were derived primarily from Project Gutenberg and a now-defunct site at Virginia Tech. On an experimental basis, developer Eric Lease Morgan is creating TEI-compliant XML versions of some texts to enable full-text searches and to facilitate downloading into various e-book reader devices.

The OBP, an index to about 20,000 free books on the Web, was founded and is edited by John Mark Ockerbloom, a digital library planner and researcher at the University of Pennsylvania Libraries. Its counterpart CWW is edited by Mary Mark Ockerbloom and features access to online books by and about women authors. The OBP exclusively indexes texts created elsewhere, whereas CWW has produced about 250 new digital texts. These can be searched separately as "local editions." The titles indexed in OBP are based largely on reader interest, according to John Ockerbloom, who estimates that it includes more than 5,000 Project Gutenberg titles, more than 500 titles from the University of Virginia, and virtually all of Bartleby.com's 300 titles. He hopes to update his indexing using OAI harvesting for such sites as Making of America. Both sites also solicit digitized texts from individual contributors, with preference given to ASCII plain text and HTML formats. Although OBP has a collection statement, it features an eclectic and uneven mix of titles. It is difficult for readers to know what they may or may not find reliably at this site.

3.3.4 Scholars' Concerns: Ensuring Quality and Sustainability

The attitudes and concerns of scholars interviewed about online books are consistent with the findings of *An Investigation into Free eBooks*, conducted on behalf of the United Kingdom's JISC e-Books Working Group. In summary, the barriers to e-book adoption reported by JISC include the following:

- lack of availability of a complete range of titles for any given course
- doubts about quality assurance
- lack of confidence in the persistent availability of resources
- costs involved in the cataloging, archiving, and management of resources
- costs involved in computing support for users
- poor design of free e-books and poor ergonomics of reading on screen (Berglund et al. 2004, 5)

With the exception of a relatively small number of nationally prominent, well-documented projects, most free online book Web sites lack quality control and textual integrity. A multitude of these so-called enthusiast sites are considered largely worthless by academics, who lament the idiosyncratic selection of titles and editions, owing in part to reliance on out-of-copyright materials. They are baffled by the absence of bibliographic information about the editions used. The Fiction collection hosted at the EServer (English Server) Web site, sponsored by the English Department at Iowa State University, for example, is a hodgepodge of "works of and about fiction collected from our members, contributing authors worldwide, and texts in the public domain." There are not only numerous instances of broken links within this relatively small collection but also no notes about who digitized the texts or from what source editions. Such is the case, for example, with Cather's *My Ántonia*, Chopin's *The Awakening*, Dreiser's *Sister Carrie*, and Wharton's *Summer*. In sharp contrast, the now-defunct Eldritch Press—whose titles remain accessible through the OBP—was careful to document the source text thoroughly. To illustrate the complexity of the choices involved, the note accompanying Eldritch Press's digital edition of *The Scarlet Letter* is reproduced below.

> **We use the first edition as copy-text.** The first American edition of *The Scarlet Letter* was published in Boston by Ticknor and Fields in 1850 and is thus now in the public domain. (See the legal notice if you plan to use these pages in any way other than as you would a copyrighted book from a library). We checked our OCR against the Norton Critical Edition text [Brad78]. The manuscript of the book has been lost, probably burned by Hawthorne after it was used to set the type. The second American version, set from new type, introduced many new errors, and was not proofread by Hawthorne, so cannot be used as copy-text (except the added preface). Another online edition, at Project Gutenberg (sl10), is an ASCII version, scanned at Dartmouth College from the first (pirated) English edition, and therefore has Anglicised spelling and punctuation (and also subtle as well as obvious errors)–scrlt11.txt has a very short introduction and some corrections. The New Bartleby Library edition is quite attractive and has paragraphs numbered in the right margin.
>
> **There are minor differences between our text and the now-standard text.** The authoritative text of *The Scarlet Letter* is the edition published by (and newly copyrighted by) the Ohio State University Press in 1962 as volume I of the 23-volume Centenary Edition of the Works of Nathaniel Hawthorne [Ce0162] (and as corrected in 1963 and any later editions). The Modern Language Association approves it for teaching purposes. The $60 cloth edition has definitive notes on the text and the methodology of bibliography used. (The Library of America

ISBN 0-949450-08-9 as well as several paperback editions license the Centenary Edition text.) In our notes to each chapter we note differences between our online edition and the Centenary Edition. Specifically: we have supplied the missing verb "form" in paragraph 52 of "The Custom-House", in accordance with the Centenary Edition page 279 (others have agreed with that reasonable guess); but we have not regularized the spelling of "die" or "elfish", nor changed the "sobre-hued" adjective in Chapter 24, though we agree it should be "sombre-hued" [Ce0162p275].

Unlike most other e-book sites, the annotation goes on to explain how to refer to page numbers, how to link to paragraph numbers, and the spelling conventions (15).

The U.K.-based Arts and Humanities Data Service's *Creating and Documenting Electronic Texts: A Guide to Good Practice* outlines the advantages and disadvantages to various approaches of creating electronic texts and emphasizes the importance of documenting the process in order to provide bibliographic information appropriate to the needs of teachers and researchers (Morrison et al. [n.d.]).

What can be done to improve the quality of e-book production and facilitate more-widespread adoption? Once again, the JISC report recommendations are germane to the higher education community in the United States.

- Take measures to offer more-comprehensive ranges of titles in specific areas.
- Support efforts to migrate existing collections to common formats.
- Institute a system of quality assurance (of text integrity and metadata).
- Ensure the permanence of collections.
- Support the professional, standardized cataloging of electronic resources.
- Offer support for users in the basic ICT (Information and Communication Technologies) dimension of the use of e-books.
- Offer help with integration into VLEs (Virtual Learning Environments) (Berglund et al. 2004, 5).

In view of the importance given to quality assurance by potential users, the JISC study developed some ad hoc procedures to evaluate free e-books. Their checklist, fully reproduced in Appendix 4, assesses e-books according to five criteria:

1. Is it what it says it is?
2. Fitness for purpose
3. Text integrity
4. Text format and encoding
5. Factors external to the text

These assessment factors should prove useful to digital library developers and data curators in determining appropriate uses and the sustainability of electronic texts.

3.3.5 Postscript to the Future: Alternative Publishing Communities

There are no nationally prominent e-book publishing initiatives devoted to American literature equivalent to the History E-Book Project (16), sponsored by the American Council of Learned Societies (ACLS) in collaboration with eight learned societies, sixty contributing publishers and librarians at the University of Michigan Scholarly Publishing office, or Gutenberg-e (17), led by the American Historical Association (AHA) and Columbia University Press. Both initiatives received support from The Andrew W. Mellon Foundation and have generated useful reports, such as Nancy Lin's (2003) ACLS white paper on technology development and production workflow for XML-encoded e-books, and candid reviews, such as Patrick Manning's (2004) evaluation of the Gutenberg-e project published in the *American Historical Review*. American literary scholars, who lack a national forum for public debate about digital scholarship, also have much to gain from the prominent deliberations engendered by the AHA (e.g., Darnton 1999; Darnton 2000; Manning 2004; Thomas and Ayers 2003; Townsend 2001; Townsend 2004).

Five examples illustrate the types of community building and alternative publishing activities under way that involve scholars of American literature. They include EServer, the Electronic Literature Organization, NINES, eScholarship Editions, and the Rotunda Electronic Imprint of the University of Virginia Press. While these initiatives all support experimentation in the production, dissemination, and preservation of digital scholarship, they vary considerably in purpose, content, and quality control. Appendix 5 summarizes their main characteristics.

3.3.5.1 EServer (18)

EServer, originally developed at Carnegie Mellon University in 1990, is sponsored by the English Department at Iowa State University. EServer describes itself as "a growing online community where hundreds of writers, artists, editors, and scholars gather to publish and discuss their works." It has more than 200 active members, including editors of an eclectic mix of 45 discrete "collections" (Web sites), which "publish" more than 32,000 works. Contributors agree to conform to EServer's acceptable-use policy, but are otherwise given complete control over the content. Some collections, including most of the genre-based Web sites, consist primarily of links to digitized texts (of varying origin and quality). In other instances, EServer serves primarily as a group work space for projects such as Arizona State University's Anti-Slavery Literature or publishing space for author societies such as the Thoreau Society's Thoreau Reader or the David Mamet's Society's review journal. EServer also serves as a forum where members give and receive advice about project development.

3.3.5.2 Electronic Literature Organization (19)

The Electronic Literature Organization (ELO), established in 1999, aims "to promote and facilitate the writing, publishing, and reading of literature in electronic media." It is headquartered at the University of California-Los Angeles under the direction of N. Katherine Hayles, a leading scholar in humanities and technology and author of *How We Became Posthuman: Virtual Bodies in Cybernetics, Literature, and Informatics* (1999). ELO serves as a forum for the international electronic literature community and focuses on "new forms of literature that utilize the capabilities [of] emerging technologies to advance the state of the art for the benefit of present and future generations of readers." The ELO maintains a database of electronic literature, including poetry, fiction, drama, and nonfiction. To qualify for inclusion in the ELO Directory, works must meet certain criteria, demonstrating that they make "significant use of electronic techniques or enhancements," such as "new forms of writing hypertexts and other interactive pieces, kinetic or animated poems, multimedia works, generated texts, and works that allow reader collaboration." It excludes works that make only "minimal use of graphics," feature "nonvariable text," or "incorporate the symbols or syntax of computer code, the jargon of chat room discussion, or other types of textual content associated with computers." It further excludes texts with "standard e-book features," identified as

- hypertext index or table of contents
- links to footnotes
- full-text search capability
- electronic bookmarks

The ELO Directory includes links to more than 2,000 works, representing more than 1,150 authors and nearly 200 publishers of electronic literature. It includes a large number of self-published works. The directory can be browsed by genre, technique, title, author, or publisher and searched by these parameters as well as by language (from Afrikaans to Turkish). Through its preservation, archiving, and dissemination research project, the ELO also "seeks to identify threatened and endangered electronic literature and to maintain accessibility, encourage stability, and ensure availability of electronic works for readers, institutions, and scholars."

3.3.5.3 NINES: A Networked Interface for Nineteenth-Century Electronic Scholarship (20)

The first initiative of its kind, NINES was established as a scholarly collective in 2004 "to protect, sustain, and enhance digital scholarship and criticism in nineteenth-century English-language studies." Under the leadership of Jerome McGann, University of Virginia, Department of English, and creator of the Rossetti Archive, NINES has assembled an impressive steering committee and three editorial boards to oversee its Americanist, Romantic, and Victorian scholarship. Further, it has procured as sponsors four major scholarly associations (American Studies Association, American Literature

Association, North American Society for the Study of Romanticism, and North American Victorian Studies Association), along with other major digital projects and initiatives (e.g., the Institute for Advanced Technology in the Humanities, the Maryland Institute for Technology in the Humanities, and the TEI Consortium). NINES aims to develop an aggregated body of peer-reviewed scholarly resources accessible through a common interface, along with standards-based tools and markup schemes. As stated on its About page, NINES expects to make a significant impact in the following areas:

- It will create a robust framework to support the authority of digital scholarship and its relevance in tenure and other scholarly assessment procedures.
- It will help establish a real, practical publishing alternative to the paper-based academic publishing system, which is in an accelerating state of crisis.
- It will address in a coordinated and practical way the question of how to sustain scholarly and educational projects that have been built in digital forms.
- It will establish a base for promoting new modes of criticism and scholarship promised by digital tools.

Under the auspices of Applied Research in Patacriticism and its research affiliate at the University of Virginia, the Speculative Computing Laboratory, NINES will develop standards-compliant, open-source tools, markup schemes, and interfaces to facilitate tasks essential to digital scholarship (arranging, comparing, transforming, discussing, commenting on, and collecting texts and images). To ensure interoperability with NINES, the project supports both the conversion of existing resources, such as Romantic Circles, and the production of new ones, such as The Poetess Archive. It has instituted a summer fellowship program for professional development and training of project directors and editors. NINES is funded in part through McGann's 2002 Distinguished Achievement Award from The Andrew W. Mellon Foundation.

3.3.5.4 eScholarship Program (21)

The California Digital Library at the University of California (UC) initiated the eScholarship program in 1999. It "is designed to facilitate innovation and support experimentation in the production and dissemination of scholarship. Through the use of innovative technology, the program seeks to develop a financially sustainable model and improve all areas of scholarly communication, including its creation, peer review, management, dissemination, and preservation." It features the following three components:

1. An eScholarship Repository supports the full range of scholarly output from prepublication materials to journals and peer-reviewed series by offering UC departments direct control of publishing within a free, open-access repository infrastructure.
2. eScholarship Editions provide access to a growing collection of digital texts and monographs from academic presses, including

more than 1,400 UC Press titles. Access is open to members of the UC academic community, and a "significant number" of titles are also freely available to the public.

3. eScholarship Publications include journals and peer-reviewed series from the repository, digital monograph collections produced by UC departments, experimental interactive publications, and legacy content.

Launched in 2002, the eScholarship Repository comprises nearly 7,000 individual digital objects (e.g., working papers, postprints, peer-reviewed submissions) selected and placed on deposit by UC units, departments, and programs, thus far representing predominantly the sciences and social sciences, including linguistics. Early in 2005, full-text downloads (PDF downloads by individuals) hit a record high with more than 35,000 downloads in a single week, bringing the total to more than 1.3 million.

eScholarship Editions released its first 500 UC Press titles in January 2003 and continues to add titles as they are TEI encoded and become available. It has nearly 1,500 titles and expects to post another 400 soon. As of April 2005, there were 37 eScholarship Editions in American literature with imprint dates ranging from 1987 to 2000, all from the UC Press; 13 were available to the public. American studies was represented by 145 titles, of which 27 were freely available. eScholarship Editions supports browsing by subject, author, or titles, as well as basic and advanced search options.

3.3.5.5 Rotunda Electronic Imprint (22)

The mission of Rotunda, the University of Virginia Press's electronic imprint, "is to combine the traditional roles of university press publishing with technological innovation in order to disseminate peer-reviewed work comparable in its originality, intellectual rigor, and scholarly value to the books issued by the print side of the press."[42] Made possible by grants from The Andrew W. Mellon Foundation and the President's Office of the University of Virginia, Rotunda hopes to promote new business models for the distribution of scholarly works as part of a nonprofit press. To date, Rotunda has announced two collections: the American Founding Era, which debuted in August 2004 with the release of the Dolley Madison Digital Edition, and Nineteenth-Century Literature and Culture, which will publish *Emily Dickinson's Correspondences* in fall 2005. According to information posted at Rotunda's Web site, the Dolley Madison Digital Edition is purchased as a licensed product with tiered pricing based on the type of institution, ranging from $145 for high schools to $545 for Association of Research Libraries members. Consortial pricing is also available. Each Rotunda publication carries an annual $50 maintenance and update fee, which is waived for high schools

---

42 Refer to the Association of American University Presses' Web site for a list of "Electronic Publishing at University Presses." Available at http://aaupnet.org/resources/electronic.html.

and independent scholars and may be discounted for other types of institutions when they purchase multiple Rotunda products.

The American Founding Era is also developing a fully searchable online edition of the multivolume *Papers of George Washington*. Meanwhile, the Nineteenth-Century Collection has announced its intention to publish John Bryant's *Herman Melville's "Typee": A Fluid-Text Edition* and to create fully searchable online editions of five previously published titles from the University of Virginia Press's backlist.

3.3.6 Resource Links

(1) NISO Z39.7-2004 Information Services and Use: Metrics and Statistics for Libraries and Information Providers–Data Dictionary. Entry 4.10.5, eBooks, available at http://www.niso.org/emetrics/current/subcategory4.10.5.html.

(2) Bartleby.com. Available at http://www.bartleby.com.

(3) Project Gutenberg (PG). Available at http://www.gutenberg.org. PG's Mission Statement and FAQ-0 discusses prior error rates and current standards at http://www.gutenberg.org/about/faq0.
> **PG's Principle of Minimal Regulation/Administration**
> http://www.gutenberg.org/about/faq3
> **Project Gutenberg's Distributed Proofreaders**
> http://www.pgdp.net/c/default.php
> **PG's Distributed Proofreaders, FAQ Central**
> http://www.pgdp.net/c/faq/faq_central.php
> **Beginning Proofreaders' FAQ**
> http://www.pgdp.net/c/faq/ProoferFAQ.php
> **PG's Distributed Proofreading Guidelines, Version 1.7 (August 31, 2004)**
> http://www.pgdp.net/c/faq/document.php
> **PG's Distributed Proofreaders General Workflow Diagram**
> http://www.pgdp.net/c/faq/DPflow.php
> **PG's FAQ: Format FAQ**
> http://www.gutenberg.org/faq/gutfaq.htm#F.1

(4) Making of America. Cornell site at http://cdl.library.cornell.edu/moa/. **Michigan site** at http://www.hti.umich.edu/m/moagrp/.
> **Conversion Process**
> http://www.hti.umich.edu/m/moagrp/moa_conversion.html
> **Measuring the Accuracy of the OCR in *Making of America***
> http://www.hti.umich.edu/m/moagrp/moaocr.html
> **MOA4 Workflow**
> http://www.umdl.umich.edu/moa4/workflow.html

(5) Wright American Fiction (CIC institutions led by Indiana University). Available at http://www.letrs.indiana.edu/web/w/wright2/.

Explanation about status of collection until encoding is complete
http://www.letrs.indiana.edu/web/w/wright2/explain.html
TEI encoding guidelines adopted by CIC for use in this project
http://www.letrs.indiana.edu/web/w/wrightmrc/guidelines.html

(6) Early American Fiction (EAF) (University of Virginia with Chadwyck-Healey). Publicly accessible collection at http://etext.virginia.edu/eaf/pubindex.html.

About EAF at http://etext.virginia.edu/eaf/overview.html
EAF Workflow at http://etext.virginia.edu/eaf/work.html
"The Electronic Text Center Introduction to TEI and Guide to Document Preparation," by David Seaman, at http://etext.lib.virginia.edu/tei/uvatei.html
Study Resources for EAF at http://etext.virginia.edu/eaf/eaf study.html
1,800 publicly available e-books from the University of Virginia Library E-text Center
http://etext.virginia.edu/ebooks/
The Modern English Collection
http://etext.lib.virginia.edu/modeng/modeng0.browse.html

(7) Million Book Project (Internet Archive). Available at http://www.archive.org/details/millionbooks.

Million Book FAQ, Carnegie Mellon University Libraries
http://www.library.cmu.edu/Libraries/MBP_FAQ.html
"Understanding and Assessing the Million Book Project," by Denise Troll Covey
http://www.library.cmu.edu/Libraries/MBPfinalNO_PICTS.ppt
"Google Print, Million Book and Google Scholar," by Gloriana St. Clair
http://www.library.cmu.edu/Libraries/FIDArchive.html#MBPnews
The Universal Library, U.S. site
http://www.ulib.org/html/index.html
The Universal Library, China site
http://www.ulib.org.cn
The Digital Library of India
http://www.dli.ernet.in/aui

(8) Google Print. Available at http://print.google.com/googleprint/about.html.

Google Print Library Project
http://print.google.com/googleprint/library.html#4
Harvard University Library FAQ: The University's Pilot Project with Google
http://hul.harvard.edu/publications/041213faq.html
NYPL Partners with Google to Make Books Available Online
http://www.nypl.org/press/google.cfm
Oxford University, Google Checks Out Bodleian Library Books
http://www.admin.ox.ac.uk/po/041214a.shtml

Stanford University and Google Mass Digitization Project
http://library.stanford.edu/about_sulair/special_projects/
google_sulair_project.html
University of Michigan's Press Release and FAQ
http://www.umich.edu/news/?Releases/2004/Dec04/library/
index

(9) Google Scholar. Available at http://www.scholar.google.com.

(10) Digital Book Index. Available at http://www.digitalbookindex.
com/.

(11) Oxford Text Archive. Available at http://ota.ahds.ac.uk/.
See FAQ for information about depositing and using texts.

(12) Online Books Page (John Mark Ockerbloom, University of
Pennsylvania Digital Library). Available at http://digital.library.
upenn.edu/books/. **Archives** (listing of other e-book sites and
sources) at http://onlinebooks.library.upenn.edu/archives.html.

(13) A Celebration of Women Writers (Mary Mark Ockerbloom,
University of Pennsylvania Digital Library). Available at http://
digital.library.upenn.edu/women/.

(14) Alex Catalogue of Electronic Texts. Available at http://www.
infomotions.com/alex/. **Pilot Newer Version** available at
http://www.infomotions.com/alex2/.

(15) Eldritch Press. Available at http://eldritchpress.org/.
    Nathaniel Hawthorne
    http://eldritchpress.org/nh/hawthorne.html
    Scarlet Letter: **A Note on the Text**
    http://www.eldritchpress.org/nh/sl.html#thetext

(16) History E-Book Project (ACLS). Available at http://www.his-
toryebook.org/. **Reviews and Notices** at http://www.historyebook.
org/hebnews.html#reviews. See especially: Nancy Lin's 2003 "Report on Technology Development and Production Workflow for XML
Encoded E-Books."

(17) Gutenberg-e (AHA and Columbia University Press). Available at
http://www.gutenberg-e.org. **Gutenberg-e and the Press** at
http://www.gutenberg-e.org/aboutframe.html. See especially Patrick Manning's December 2004 article "Gutenberg-e: Electronic Entry
to the Historical Professoriate" *American Historical Review.*

(18) Eserver, Iowa State University. Available at www.eserver.org.

(19) Electronic Literature Organization. Available at http://
eliterature.org.

ELO Directory
http://directory.eliterature.org/index.php
Inclusion Criteria: ELO Directory
http://directory.eliterature.org/html/criteria.shtml.en
PAD (Preservation, Archiving and Dissemination project)
http://www.eliterature.org/pad/

(20) NINES: A Networked Interface for Nineteenth-Century Electronic Scholarship. Available at www.nines.org.
    Romantic Circles. General editors: Neil Fraistat and Steven E. Jones
    http://www.rc.umd.edu/
    The Poetess Archive. General editors: Paula Feldman, Katherine Harris, Laura Mandell, Eliza Richards
    http://www.orgs.muohio.edu/womenpoets/poetess/

(21) eScholarship Program (California Digital Library). Available at http://www.cdlib.org/programs/escholarship.html.
    eScholarship Repository
    http://repositories.cdlib.org/escholarship/
    eScholarship Editions
    http://texts.cdlib.org/escholarship/

(22) Rotunda Electronic Imprint (University of Virginia Press). Available at http://rotunda.upress.virginia.edu/.

3.4 Reference Resources and Full-Text Primary Source Collections

3.4.1 Quality Proprietary Products

Commercial vendors, typically in consultation with librarian and faculty advisory boards, have produced a reliable set of digital reference tools and full-text databases that provide access to a large body of primary resources in British and American literature. Scholars seem satisfied—even enthusiastic—about the quality, quantity, and ready availability of these materials. Suddenly, they and their students can view and read primary sources that are fragile, rare, or held in distant repositories. Having desktop online access is more than a matter of convenience, although few miss long hours crouched over a microform reader. These large-scale databases inspire ideas, permitting scholars to ask different questions and see new relationships of meaning. The ability to navigate through large bodies of text enhances productivity, making it feasible to trace the use of terms, identify concepts, or recognize patterns within a single author's work or across a corpus much more quickly.

Not intended as a comprehensive list, the reference tools and full-text collections annotated in this section are produced primarily by four major vendors: Alexander Street Press,[43] Newsbank/Readex,

---

[43] Some Alexander Street Press products are also covered in section 3.4.3 of this report.

ProQuest/Chadwyck-Healey, and Thomson Gale. There are also examples of large-scale noncommercial resources developed by research libraries and collections produced in partnership by libraries and publishers. Together, they represent a combination of imprint- or period-based collections derived from the conversion of large microform sets (e.g., all the corpora projects) and "crafted" thematic collections based on materials selected by specialists (e.g., Alexander Street Press products). These full-text collections and corpora also represent a mix of image-based products with searchable ASCII text and related metadata and double-keyed, fully encoded SGML/XML transcriptions.

Many of the vendors describe fully their digitization processes and goals for textual accuracy. For example, Chadwyck-Healey (according to Literature Online's Information Centre on Text Conversion) aims for textual accuracy of between 99.970 and 99.995 percent. It asserts spending more than 50 million pounds on digitization in the past decade to achieve this level of quality. As explained at the product Web site, an editorial team marks up copies of original documents for encoding in SGML. Then "texts are either double-keyed by two different operators and the resulting versions compared by computer programs for differences, or they are re-keyed once and compared to a version of the text generated by optical character recognition (OCR) software." ProQuest continues: "The next stage in the text-conversion process is thorough proofreading of the converted texts against the original source material by our editorial teams. All SGML coding is also checked manually and by computer programs. Data is then passed to our software team for building into a searchable database and extensive product testing before being loaded online."[44]

In the case of image-based products that rely on OCR-generated text for searching, vendors have developed specialized search functions to help overcome "false hits" that result from the vagaries of spellings or misinterpretations of text. Readex, for example, gives special instructions about how use the wild card (?) and truncation (*) symbols to search Early American Imprints, effectively taking into account colonial English variant spellings. For its Eighteenth Century Collections Online product, Thomson Gale has devised "fuzzy search" settings to enhance full-text searches by retrieving near matches on a term. With three levels (low, medium, and high), users can fine-tune a search of Harbor to include close matches with a low fuzzy search setting (e.g., harbor and harbour) or broad matches with the search set on high (e.g., harbor, harbour, Harper, and Harben).

Alexander Street Press uses controlled vocabularies and its signature "semantic indexing" to facilitate refined searches. Instead of traditional indexing by elements such as series, volume, chapter, page, or word, semantic indexing facilitates richer "who, what, when, where" retrievals. Thus, it is possible, for example, to locate productions of *Uncle Tom's Cabin* by George L. Aiken staged in New York in

---

[44] Literature Online Information Centre Text Conversion guidelines available at http://lion.chadwyck.com/marketing/academics/textconv.jsp.

the 1800s. Alexander Street Press also features "conductor search" technology that permits users to access external content in its original context through linking and indexing selected relevant Web sites.

3.4.1.1 Evaluated

Unlike many of the resources discussed elsewhere in this report, these proprietary products are the subject of evaluative reviews. The most authoritative source of information about reference tools for English literary studies is James L. Harner's *Literary Research Guide* (*LRG*), 4th edition (MLA 2002). Harner's thorough descriptions and critical appraisals are invaluable. He not only provides the bibliographic history of the resource but also comments on how its coverage and functionality have changed over time. In preparing revisions for the fifth edition, Harner reports that he is "finding a major problem with electronic resources that are digital clones of print/microform ancestors," because, he continues, "the electronic resources do not explain the scope, limitations, and editorial policies of the print sources; consequently, users who are unfamiliar with the print originals are at a substantial disadvantage in using the electronic versions." Noting that "this problem is going to be exacerbated as we move forward in the use of electronic resources," Harner is concerned that "the collective memory of the print originals will be lost."[45] For example, in discussing Readex's new Evans Digital Edition, Harner advises users, "While Early American Imprints vastly improves access to information hidden away in Evans (especially anonymous works), it replicates silently many of the limitations and quirks of its progenitor." "Thus," he concludes, "a thorough familiarity with American Bibliography is a prerequisite for informed use of the digital archive."[46] All available *LRG* annotation entry numbers are provided for resources covered in this section of the report and readers are advised to consult Harner's continuing, online Addenda for updates. The checklist he uses to evaluate resources for inclusion in *LRG* appears in Appendix 6 of this report.

Although the MLA is not yet certain what form a digital *LRG* may take, Executive Director Rosemary Fcal hopes that an electronic version with regular electronic updates will be released with the fifth edition by the summer of 2007. Harner elaborates that it would be more than electronic text with OpenURL linking. It might become a portal, offering guided-search queries to direct users to primary sources, novels, or American print resources covering a particular period. This would be a boon to the academic community. In particular, representatives of ACRL's Literatures in English Section note that if *LRG* were widely available in digital form, it would relieve library subject specialists around the country from developing redundant annotated research guides and Web site resource listings. If optimally designed, it would permit them to select relevant entries and

---

[45] E-mail correspondence from James Harner on April 22, 2005.

[46] See the ongoing addenda to *LRG* that Harner maintains at http://www-english.tamu.edu/pubs/lrg/addenda.html.

incorporate them directly into customized local guides. If Harner's conceptualization is realized, *LRG* would provide the equivalent of personalized online tutorials in research methodologies.

Meanwhile, the academic community relies on the knowledge and expertise of local library subject specialists to develop guides to electronic resources. There are many fine examples across the country with extensive, qualitative listings. Using Northwestern University Library as one example, library users have access to an outstanding suite of Web pages for electronic resources in support of literatures in English; a bibliography for a senior honors seminar in English; a workshop guide to "ECCO and Other Electronic Resources for the Study of the 18th Century at Northwestern University"; and an overview of the Evans Digital Edition.[47]

3.4.1.2 At a Price

The Charleston Advisor: Critical Reviews of Web Products for Information professionals (not widely known outside librarianship) offers thorough assessments and gives resources a composite score based on separate ratings of content, searchability, price, and contract options. In its online version, *The Charleston Advisor*, which is available only on a subscription basis ($295/year for academic libraries), can be searched or browsed by title, vendor, reviewer, or journal issue. Librarians might only hope that more products were reviewed and with greater regularity. Among the resources discussed here, 11 have been reviewed by *The Charleston Advisor*—including three major corpora: EEBO (Early English Books Online), Early American Imprints (Evans Digital Edition), and ECCO (Eighteenth Century Collections Online). Citations to *The Charleston Advisor* reviews are included in the resource annotations in this section of the report.

As is the case with Harner's guide, *The Charleston Advisor* reviewers provide readers with in-depth analysis about the scope of reborn-digital resources. For example, in his October 2004 review of Eighteenth Century Collections Online, Dennis Brunning (Arizona State University) alerts readers to these important lacunae:

> Of the 334,000 eighteenth century records in the English Short Title Catalog (the comprehensive cataloging of sixteenth, seventeenth, and eighteenth century English imprints), many relate to straight reissues published outside Great Britain or are straight reprints. These did not qualify for inclusion in the Eighteenth Century film project from which ECCO derives. In addition, as soon as Gale Group became aware of the Readex/ Newsbank Evans project, Gale Group decided to omit the purely American imprints that are part of the Evans project.

---

[47] Available at

http://www.library.northwestern.edu/collections/english/reference.html;

http://www.library.northwestern.edu/reference/instructional_services/class_pages/thompson.htm;

http://www.library.northwestern.edu/collections/english/18thcenturyonline.pdf;

http://2east.northwestern.edu/2003_12/_article_1.html.

The Charleston Advisor distinguishes itself by ferreting out and rating otherwise difficult-to-obtain pricing and contract options. Potential buyers can learn the basic parameters, if not the full details. For example, Thomson Gale's list pricing for all seven modules in ECCO begins at $500,000, Brunning informs readers, but varies according to an institution's microfilm set holdings. Readers are referred to Gale for customized quotes. Brunning further notes, "Each module can be purchased separately. A library that buys a module receives all content included in that module up to that point. Gale Group grants perpetual access to information in the module when it is purchased, but it will not automatically include titles added later." Turning to Early American Imprints (Evans Digital Edition), reviewer Norman Desmorais tells readers that Readex's "initial fee is determined by the type and size of the institution, ranging from a high of $107,500 for a Ph.D.-granting university to as little as $14,000 for a small college with 1,000 students." Desmorais elaborates: "Readex also offers prepublication discounts during the production period, a microform trade-in allowance, and consortia discounts; in addition, institutions that acquire more than one digital Archive of Americana collection receive additional discounts. Upon payment of an annual maintenance fee, libraries will have access rights in perpetuity."

Although it is beyond the scope of this report to investigate the cost of this "breadbasket" of goods, scholars and librarians alike express great concern about its high price. The scholars interviewed repeatedly expressed misgivings about the growing inequities in access to essential resources. They worry about the future of their former graduate students, who are trained at research universities with a rich array of electronic resources but enter into the professoriate at a diverse set of institutions—many of which are unable to afford these tools. They must learn to "do literature on the cheap," to rephrase Christopher Hanlon's tactic at Eastern Illinois University, where he "makes historicists out of undergraduates" by relying on digital archives in the public domain such as Making of America or American Memory (Hanlon 2005). Meanwhile, librarians wonder how many times they will have to find the money to purchase or, more aptly, repurchase content in new forms. Many of these large-scale digital resources are derived from microform sets for which libraries have already paid—or continue to pay dearly, since production of the microfilm keeps pace. Of course, most publishers reward repeat customers with discounts. Nonetheless, research libraries that have paid $1 million or more for Thomson Gale's Primary Source Microfilm collection *The Eighteenth Century* may find acquisition of the digital version—at any price—difficult to accept.

3.4.2 Scholar-Publisher-Librarian Partnerships
Despite accelerating budget pressures and concerns about growing licensed (rather than owned) content, relations between humanists and publishers are amicable. Librarians credit publishers with developing large-scale products that would be otherwise impracticable. As one library practitioner noted ruefully, the academy—acting on its

own—has not been very successful at harnessing the volunteer ethos of the Internet to build sustainable digital resources without substantial grant support or public-private partnerships. Virtually all the resources discussed in this report bear out this statement. And one notable exception, Wright American Fiction—the project to produce fully edited and encoded transcriptions of 3,000 novels undertaken by members of the CIC—has taken much longer to complete and cost far more ($475,000) than originally planned.

The primary publishers of full-text digital collections have developed their products in consultation with librarians and scholars. Through the establishment of advisory boards and participation in professional conferences, they have encouraged a productive exchange of ideas. To cite two examples: Readex is producing its Archive of Americana in consultation with the American Antiquarian Society, and the University of Virginia's E-text Center partnered with Chadwyck-Healey to create a suite of Early American Fiction titles—a subset of which is freely available to the public.

Aside from price, scholars' criticisms of these new digital resources are few, and responsive publishers are rapidly addressing many of the criticisms that do exist. The scholars' needs include the following:

- They want improved Help screens and basic tips about how to navigate the site.
- They would like keywords highlighted in retrievals.
- They lament the conceptual restrictions of browsing categories, which may overlook important rubrics.
- They would like more fully searchable texts accompanying page images.[48]

However, another problem looms on the horizon: How will vendors meet the demand for unified search interfaces across databases (e.g., as EEBO becomes cross-searchable through Literature Online; Evans Digital Edition is integrated into the Archive of Americana; or Thomson Gale launches its PowerSearch—single-search technology) while still providing nuanced search strategies appropriate to unique content in the component databases?[49] Regular communication among publishers, scholars, and librarians is necessary as these products and technologies evolve to ensure that the competing needs of different constituents are met.

3.4.2.1 Text Creation Partnership

The Text Creation Partnership (TCP)—an international cooperative headquartered at the University of Michigan—is the premier model of publisher and research library collaboration. It provides a viable way to work effectively with the commercial sector, whose support

[48] Based on telephone interviews and faculty reviews of the Evans Digital Edition available at http://www.readex.com/scholarl/eai_digi.html.

[49] For information about Thomson Gale's PowerSearch, refer to http://www.gale.com/Technical/index.htm and the PDF fact sheet available at http://www.gale.com/Technical/PowerSearch.pdf.

libraries need, while helping establish new business models that are profitable for commercial publishers yet attractive to libraries' long-term goals of interoperability and an open-access environment. The TCP supports the creation of accurately keyboarded and encoded editions of thousands of works across all fields of scholarly endeavor. Three major projects are under way, with a fourth in planning (Shaw-Shoemaker), representing three vendors in partnership with hundreds of libraries worldwide. Once complete, coverage will extend from 1473 through 1819 for American imprints and authors:

- 1473–1700 Early English Books Online with ProQuest
- 1639–1800 Evans Digital Edition: Early American Imprints I with Readex
- 1701–1800 Eighteenth Century Collections Online with Thomson Gale
- 1801–1819 Shaw-Shoemaker Digital Edition: Early American Imprints II with Readex

In consultation with librarians and scholars, a subset of texts is selected for transcription and encoding, thereby giving the TCP community access to accurate transcriptions (faithful to the spellings and organization of the original works) alongside digital page images. The TCP protects the public domain rights of the larger society to access out-of-copyright materials through its agreement with publishers: TCP partners have rights to the texts five years after the projects are completed. As a result, over the next decade more than 50,000 texts associated with these projects will come under the nonexclusive purview of the TCP, making it possible for partners to distribute them freely. In short, the TCP corpus could form the foundation of a distributed digital collection of British and American imprints.

The cost for Evans TCP works out to about two dollars per text for a research library and less for a smaller library. The question of OCR accuracy in reading early texts aside, why should libraries support full-text conversion? TCP's lead proponent, Mark Sandler, collection development officer at the University of Michigan Library, gives the following reasons:

- Accurate or not, commercial companies won't reveal their OCR—hence you cannot retrieve keywords in context, can't read the ASCII text, cannot manipulate it (e.g., cut-and-paste, edit), and cannot print from it.
- The TCP texts (considered to be some of the most useful and valuable from the overall corpus) are fully owned by the library community and can be incorporated into local collections as new editions.
- The accurate text can be read as well as searched, so is a benefit for undergraduates who struggle to decipher old fonts.
- The encoding of TCP texts allows for refined searching for scholars—e.g., a scholar can limit a search to notes or search within a chapter of a particular work.
- Scholars can use the keyboarded texts as a basis for creating new scholarly editions.

- The Evans texts can be crossed-searched with the EEBO (and eventually ECCO) texts.
- The TCP texts will support the public domain: They will be broadly distributed by 2014.[50]

Advocates seek leadership from national organizations such as DLF and the MLA to adopt the TCP as a strategic initiative and to start discussing how they might leverage these texts to develop new tools and resources. Could experimentation begin with a subset of texts in linguistics or literature to create a more robust search engine? Should a network of sites showcase teaching tools and demonstrate applications to the curriculum? By sharing their expertise, TCP members might encourage smaller teaching colleges to adapt EEBO, Evans, and ECCO for classroom use. Coordinated national leadership, with participation by front-line librarians, is needed for the TCP to achieve its full potential.

3.4.3 Resource Descriptions

This annotated listing of resources covers the following categories: catalogs; bibliography of printed works; indexes; bibliographies of scholarship; corpora; and full-text periodicals, newspapers, fiction, poetry, and drama; as well as selected integrative platforms. It excludes dictionaries, encyclopedias, single-author resources, literary histories, works pertaining to theory and criticism, predominantly British sources (e.g., Women Writers Online and Victorian Women Writers Project), and most global resources with broad (although relevant) coverage, such as OCLC's WorldCat, RLG's Eureka, JSTOR, and Project Muse. Each entry is annotated with a link to the provider's Web site. Resources that have been reviewed in *The Charleston Advisor* are so indicated with a bullet point. In addition, if the resource is included in the *Literary Research Guide* (Harner 2002) or Harner's online addenda, the "*LRG* annotation" entry number is provided.

Descriptions of these products are quoted in full or extracted from the vendors' Web sites. They are not intended as original, evaluative critiques. Readers should consult Harner 2002 for qualitative reviews of reference sources and databases.

3.4.3.1 Catalogs

English Short Title Catalogue (1473–1800) (ESTC) is a growing database and union catalog of 468,000 bibliographic records for items published anywhere in Great Britain or its colonies or in English anywhere from printing's beginnings through the eighteenth century. All recorded English monographs printed between 1473 and 1800 are represented in the database, as are 80 percent of the recorded serials titles for the period 1620–1800. Previously known as the Eighteenth-Century Short Title Catalogue, ESTC was enhanced and renamed in

---

[50] From e-mail correspondence with Mark Sandler on February 7, 2005. See also Sandler 2003 and 2004.

1994, with the addition of nearly 75,000 records for works published before 1701. ESTC's extensive indexing and regular additions and corrections make it "an essential source for identifying extant works by an author, about a topic, or in a genre and for locating copies" (Harner online Addenda).

- Available from RLG at http://www.rlg.org/en/page.php?Page_ID=179.
- *LRG* annotation: M1377 with Addenda update at http://www-english.tamu.edu/pubs/lrg/addenda.html.

Nineteenth-Century Short Title Catalogue (1801–1919), established in 1983, is an exhaustive bibliography, with more than 1.2 million records from the nineteenth-century holdings of the Bodleian Library, British Library, Cambridge University Library, Trinity College (Dublin), National Library of Scotland, and Newcastle University Library, plus LC and Harvard University Library holdings from 1816 to 1919. It covers virtually all printed materials published in the United States and the British Empire from 1801 to 1919. Bibliographic records include author and author epithet, imprint (including date and place), library location, subject classification, and reference number. Users can group records of special interest and download the entries electronically.

- Available from Chadwyck-Healey: http://www.umi.com/products/pd-product-19thstc.shtml.
- *LRG* annotation: M2475.

3.4.3.2 Bibliography of Printed Works

Bibliography of American Literature (Revolutionary era to 1930) originally appeared in nine volumes, published for the Bibliographical Society of America by Yale University Press between 1955 and 1991. This fully searchable database contains nearly 40,000 bibliographical descriptions for the original book publications of nearly 300 authors "'who, in their own time at least, were known and read' and who primarily published belles lettres" (Harner 2002, 379). Listings for each author include Primary Works, Reprints, and References for Primary Works; information includes a title-page transcription, details on pagination, collation and binding, publication history, and the location of at least one copy.

- Available from Chadwyck-Healey at http://www.proquest.com/products/pd-product-BAL.shtml.
- *LRG* annotation: Q3250.

3.4.3.3 Indexes

Nineteenth Century Masterfile (1774–1920) is an Anglo-American master index providing access to more than 60 indexes to periodicals, books, newspapers, patents, and U.S./U.K. government documents. It comprises the following five series:

Series I: Multi-Title Periodical Indexes
Poole's *Index to Periodical Literature, Index to Legal Periodical Literature* (Jones and Chipman), *Catalogue of Scientific Papers*, the *Religion Index*, and more.

Series II: Indexes to Books
ALA Index to General Literature, nineteenth-century bibliographic
database, and others.

Series III: Indexes to Newspapers
New York Times Index, New York Daily Tribune Index, Palmer's Index,
and others.

Series IV: Indexes to Individual Periodicals
Harper's Weekly, Atlantic Monthly, North American Reviews (with
free links to full text).

Series V: U.S. and U.K. Government Documents Indexes and U.S.
Patent Index
Congressional Record, Papers of the President, Hansard's Parlia-
mentary Indexes, and others.

- Available from Paratext at http://www.paratext.com/19cm_intro.
  htm.
- *LRG* annotation: Q4150 (Poole's Index to Periodical Literature and
  Poole's Plus).

Periodical Contents Index Full Text (1770–1995) (PCI) provides access to the contents pages of more than 4,500 humanities and social
sciences periodicals published primarily in North America and Western Europe from their inception to 1995. It includes separate records
for approximately 14 million journal articles, covering 37 key subject
areas and 40 languages and dialects. New journals are added regularly, and the index will grow to encompass more than 5,000 journals
and 20 million articles. PCI indexes such journals as *American Literary History, American Literature, Appleton's Magazine, Early American
Literature*, and *Emerson Society Quarterly*. PCI has article-level linking
to the full image of articles from 160 titles held in the JSTOR archive.
PCI Full Text draws on the strength of the index records in PCI to
make a growing number of the back files of periodicals that are already indexed in PCI available electronically. PCI Full Text contains
the contents of 368 journal runs, providing access to more than 6.5
million article pages—representing over 1 million articles. These are
drawn from the 15.3 million article citation records in the PCI. PCI
Full Text will expand to more than 375 full-text journals by the end of
2005.
- Available from Chadwyck-Healey at http://pcift.chadwyck.com.
- *LRG* annotation: G397.

3.4.3.4 Bibliographies of Scholarship
Annual Bibliography of English Language and Literature (ABELL)
(1892–present), compiled under the auspices of the Modern Humanities Research Association by an international team of editors, contributors, and academic advisers, lists monographs, periodical articles,
critical editions of literary works, book reviews, collections of essays,

and doctoral dissertations published anywhere in the world. This international bibliography contains more than 860,000 records from 1892 through 2003 (current records from ABELL are available with monthly updates through LION, described below). ABELL is linked to more than 120 full-text journals through LION with corresponding subscriptions. It covers more than 6,785 titles and adds 30,000 records annually.

- Available from Chadwyck-Healey at http://www.proquest.com/ products/pd-product-ABELL.shtml.
- *LRG* annotation: G340.

MLA International Bibliography of Books and Articles on the Modern Languages and Literatures (1963 to present, with some earlier coverage) (MLAIB) provides a classified listing and subject index for books and articles published on modern languages, literatures, folklore, and linguistics. It is compiled by the staff of the MLA Office of Bibliographic Information Services with the cooperation of more than 100 bibliographers in the United States and abroad. It includes citations from more than 3,000 journals (including e-journals) and series published worldwide as well as monographs, working papers, and conference proceedings. There is no geographical limitation to coverage; the bibliography represents all national literatures and annually indexes more than 66,000 books and articles. The MLA began to include JSTOR indexing and links in its electronic bibliography products in April 2003. In libraries that subscribe to JSTOR, users can seamlessly go from citations in the electronic bibliography to the electronic full text. The MLA is also linking 88 previously indexed titles not included in the language and literature collection. According to Harner, data from the print volumes of the bibliography for the years 1926 to 1962 will eventually be added to the database, and with the inclusion of JSTOR titles, the bibliography already covers earlier materials.

- Available from a multitude of vendors. See MLA's chart comparing the features offered by seven different distributors at http://www.mla.org/bib_dist_comparison.
- Information about JSTOR and MLAIB, including the journal title list, is available at http://www.mla.org/bib_jstor_project.
- *The Charleston Advisor* review by Jody Condit Fagan (July 2003), comparing EBSCO, InfoTrac, and OVID.
- *LRG* annotation: G335 with Addenda update: http://www-english.tamu.edu/pubs/lrg/addenda.html.

3.4.3.5 Corpora

Sabin Collection Online (1492–1850s), Thomson Gale's digital version of Primary Source Microfilm's set based on Joseph Sabin's *Bibliotheca Americana: A Dictionary of Books Relating to America from its Discovery to the Present Time*, is scheduled for release in 2005. The collection includes books, pamphlets, broadsides, and other documents written or published in the United States, as well as items printed elsewhere, that provide insights into the attitudes and opinions of

Europeans and others toward the course of history in the Americas. The Sabin materials are selected by the Huntington Library, San Marino, and comprise more than 22,000 works (6 million pages), with new releases annually.

- Forthcoming from Thomson Gale.[51] Information about the original microfilm set available at http://www.gale.com.
- *LRG* annotation for Sabin's 29-volume bibliography: Q4015.

Early English Books Online (1473–1700) (EEBO), when complete, will contain all the works—more than 22 million pages—represented in the microfilm series Early English Books I and II, which include the titles listed in these comprehensive bibliographic records of English literature: *The Short-Title Catalogue I* (Pollard and Redgrave, 1475–1640); *The Short-Title Catalogue II* (Wing, 1641–1700); *The Thomason Tracts*, a compendium of broadsides on the English Civil War printed between 1640 and 1661; and *The Early English Books Tract Supplements*. More than 100,000 of 125,000 titles are finished: STC I (units 1–66) and STC II (units 1–113). The remaining STC I and II titles will be scanned between 2005 and 2007; scanning of the Tract Supplements will begin in 2006. The database offers complete citation information and digital facsimile page images with searchable, OCRed ASCII text. TCP partners will have access to 25,000 accurately edited and SGML/XML-encoded text editions.

- Available from ProQuest at http://www.proquest.com/products/ pd-product-EEBO.shtml.
- Notable features: EEBO is a target for inbound OpenURL linking, allowing users to link from outbound compatible sources such as the ESTC to items available in EEBO. It is also Z39.50 compliant. MARC records are provided gratis for EEBO and the *Thomason Tracts* collection. Later in 2005, EEBO authors covered in LION (see 3.4.3.11) will be linked, giving EEBO users access to LION biographies and other keyed texts or to different editions of works by those authors.
- Text Creation Partnership goal: 25,000 texts selected from the 125,000 titles in EEBO http://www.lib.umich.edu/tcp/eebo/.
- TCP title selection criteria: http://www.lib.umich.edu/tcp/eebo/ proj_stat/ps_text.html.
- Number of TCP participants: About 150 institutions, including the recent addition of 13 colleges from the Oberlin Group.
- Currently completed TCP editions: 8,700 texts (as of 4/15/2005). About 500 added bimonthly.
- Probable completion date: 2009.
- Available for release to TCP "owners": 2014.
- TCP local downloads: University of Chicago loaded EEBO and is running it behind its PhiloLogic interface (http://www.lib.uchicago.edu/e/ets/efts/ARTFL.html); Oxford University has it running behind DLXS. Also run locally at Washington University (St. Louis), the University of Pennsylvania, the University of Victoria (Canada) and Northwestern University.

---

[51] E-mail correspondence with Jeffrey Moyer, April 22, 2005.

- EEBO reviews: http://www.lib.umich.edu/tcp/eebo/archive/archive_reviews.html. See also a more critical review: William Proctor Williams and William Baker. 2001. "*Caveat Lector*, English Books 1475–1700 and the Electronic Age," *Analytical and Enumerative Bibliography* ns 12:1–29.
- Annual Undergraduate Essay Prize: http://www.lib.umich.edu/tcp/eebo/edu/edu_essay.html.
- *The Charleston Advisor* review by John P. Schmitt (April 2003).
- *LRG* annotations: Pollard and Redgrave M1990. Wing, M1995. Addenda update available at http://www-english.tamu.edu/pubs/lrg/addenda.html.

Early American Imprints, Series I (1639–1800) (Evans Digital Edition) covers almost every aspect of life in seventeenth- and eighteenth-century America, from agriculture and auctions through foreign affairs, diplomacy, literature, music, religion, the Revolutionary War, temperance, and witchcraft. It consists of digital facsimile page images and searchable OCR, ASCII text from the microform set *Early American Imprints, Series I*, based on Charles Evans's *American Bibliography: A Chronological Dictionary of All Books, Pamphlets, and Periodical Publications Printed in the United States of America from the Genesis of Printing in 1639 down to and Including the Year 1820* [i.e., 1800] and enhanced by Roger P. Bristol's *Supplement to Evans' American Bibliography*. Ultimately, it will include all titles contained in Evans microform editions—more than 36,000 items and more than 2.3 million images; a database enriched by more than 1,200 cataloged new items; and integrated bibliographic records from the American Antiquarian Society.

- Available from Readex: http://www.readex.com/scholarl/eai_digi.html.
- Notable features: The "History of Printing" tab provides browsing by name of bookseller, printer, and publisher. Images may be downloaded in GIF, PDF, and TIFF formats. Multiple-page bundling limits printing and downloading to 25 pages. Supports OpenURL and federated searches. Catalog records available for purchase.
- TCP goal: 6,000 texts of the 36,000 titles in Evans selected in consultation with the American Antiquarian Society: http://www.lib.umich.edu/tcp/evans/.
- Number of TCP participants: About 50, including the Appalachian College Association (representing more than 30 colleges).
- Currently completed TCP editions: 750 (as of April 15, 2005). About 150 added bimonthly.
- Probable completion date: December 2007 (contract written with five-year window to join: 2002–2007).
- Available for release to TCP partners: December 2012.
- Evans Digital Edition Reviews: http://www.readex.com/scholarl/eai_digi.html.
- A Most Un-Digital Man: Charles Evans and the Evans Digital Edition, by Seth A. Cotlar, Willamette University.

- American Originals, by Katherine Stebbins McCaffrey, Boston University.
- An MRI of Early America, by Jay Fliegelman, Stanford University.
- From Movable Type to Searchable Text, by Cathy N. Davidson, Duke University.
- *The Charleston Advisor* review, by Norman Desmarais (October 2004).
- *LRG* annotation: Q4005. Addenda update for the electronic edition available: http://www-english.tamu.edu/pubs/lrg/addenda. html.
- Evans forms part of Readex's Archive of Americana suite of products, along with Shaw-Shoemaker (see below), Early American Newspapers (see below), and the U.S. Serial Set. http://www. readex.com/digital/digcoll.html.

Early American Imprints, Series II (1801–1819) (Shaw-Shoemaker Digital Edition) starts where Evans ends, covering Ralph R. Shaw and Richard H. Shoemaker's *American Bibliography: A Preliminary Checklist for 1801–1819* and Shoemaker's *A Checklist of American Imprints for 1820–1829*. It will include all titles from the Shaw-Shoemaker microform editions—more than 36,000 American books, pamphlets, and broadsides, and more than 4 million images; the database is enriched by more than 3,600 cataloged new items and integrated bibliographic records from the American Antiquarian Society. It contains many state papers and early government materials that chronicle the political and geographic growth of the developing American nation. As with Evans Digital Edition, searchable, OCR-generated ASCII text will be associated with each image. There are currently more than one million pages available with new releases planned monthly through 2007. TCP partners will have access to a subset of accurately edited and SGML/XML-encoded texts.

- Available from Readex at http://www.readex.com/scholarl/ earlamim.html.
- Text Creation Partnership goal: Under development.
- *LRG* annotation: Shaw: Q4125; Shoemaker: Q4130. Addenda update for the electronic edition available at http://www-english. tamu.edu/pubs/lrg/addenda.html.
- Shaw-Shoemaker forms part of Readex's Archive of Americana suite of products along with Evans (see above), *Early American Newspapers* (see 3.4.3.7), and the *U.S. Serial Set*. Available at http://www.readex.com/digital/digcoll.html.

Eighteenth Century Collections Online (1701–1800) features 150,000 printed works and editions comprising more than 30 million pages, covering English-language and foreign-language titles printed in Great Britain and thousands of works from the Americas. The collection is an ongoing project based on *The English Short Title Catalogue*. A variety of materials is included—from books and broadsides, Bibles, tract books, and sermons to printed ephemera—with works by many well-known and lesser-known authors. ECCO is presented in seven subject areas, one of which is Literature and Language. A center-piece of this collection is the complete works of 28 major (primarily British) eighteenth-century authors, including Thomas Paine and Benjamin Franklin. ECCO consists of digital facsimile page images with OCRed ASCII text. TCP partners will have access to a subset of 10,000 accurately edited and SGML/XML-encoded texts.

- Current status: 24,000 books completed.
- Available from Thomson Gale at http://www.gale.com/ EighteenthCentury/find.htm.
- Notable features: "Fuzzy search" functions to retrieve variant spellings. Ability to rotate page images and navigate by list of illustrations. The About file includes information about ESTC metadata and how it is mapped to various search paths and page features. InfoMarks are persistent URLs (such as predefined searches) that can be bookmarked for future reference or copied into an e-mail message or onto a Web page.
- TCP goal: 10,000 texts of the 150,000 titles http://www.lib.umich. edu/tcp/ecco/.
- Number of TCP participants: Estimated 30 partners as of May 2005.
- Currently completed TCP texts: In production, with demonstration anticipated in summer 2005.
- Probable completion date: five-year window to join, i.e., 2005–2010.
- Available for release to TCP "owners": 2015.
- ECCO reviews at http://www.gale.com/EighteenthCentury/ reviews.htm (excerpts and accolades).
- *The Charleston Advisor* review by Dennis Brunning (April 2004).
- *LRG* annotation: Consult Harner's Addenda online for future annotations and updates at http://www-english.tamu.edu/pubs/ lrg/addenda.html.

Nineteenth-Century Collections Online is being developed by Thomson Gale as a counterpart to ECCO covering the nineteenth century (loosely defined). Three collections have been released: *The Times* (London) Digital Archive (1785–1985); Making of Modern Law: Legal Treatises, 1800–1926; and Making of the Modern Economy, 1450–1850. Later in 2005, it is scheduled to release Making of Modern Law: Supreme Court Records and Briefs (1832–1978); Nineteenth-Century U.S. Newspapers (see below); and the Sabin Collection Online (see above). In addition, it is planning—but has no firm delivery date for—Nineteenth-Century U.K. Periodicals and American Prose Fiction.

- Available from Thomson Gale.[52] Search its catalog at http://www. gale.com.

---

[52] E-mail correspondence with Jeffrey Moyer on April 21, 2005.

3.4.3.6 Full-Text Periodicals

American Periodicals Series (1741–1900) consists of digitized images of 1,200 periodicals first published between 1741 and 1900, including special interest and general magazines, literary and professional journals, children's magazines, and many other historically significant periodicals. Titles range from Benjamin Franklin's *General Magazine* to *Appleton's*, *Putnam's*, *Vanity Fair*, *Ladies' Home Journal*, *The Dial*, *Puck*, and *McClure's*. Issues can be browsed from the journal title list (many scattered runs) and searches conducted within a publication. The entire database can be cross-searched with ProQuest's Historical Newspapers.

- Available at ProQuest, http://www.proquest.com/products/pt-product-APSOnline.shtml.

Making of America (1851–1875) is two separate databases, as described more fully in section 3.3.2.2. It was conceived as a collaborative between the University of Michigan, focusing on monographs, and Cornell, focusing on periodicals of the nineteenth century that document American social history from the antebellum period through reconstruction. Now comprising more than 3.5 million pages and more than 12,000 volumes, the Michigan collection includes 8,500 books and 11 journal titles, while Cornell covers 267 monographic volumes, 22 serials, and 2 multivolume sets.

- Michigan site: http://www.hti.umich.edu/m/moagrp/.
- Cornell site: http://moa.cit.cornell.edu/moa/.
- A subset is available as The Nineteenth Century in Print: Books and Periodicals as part of American Memory, Library of Congress. Twenty-three periodical titles can be browsed or searched from http://memory.loc.gov/ammem/ndlpcoop/moahtml/snctitles.html.
- *The Charleston Advisor* review by Stefanie Dennis Hunker (April 2001).

Godey's Lady's Book (1830–1885) includes searchable full text of all issues from the magazine, comprising more than 50,000 pages and more than 18,000 plates and illustrations.

- Britannica Online entry has a brief history of the magazine at http://search.eb.com/women/articles/Godey's_Lady's_Book.html.
- Available from Accessible Archives at http://www.accessible.com/wnew/glb3.htm.

3.4.3.7 Full-Text Newspapers

Early American Newspapers (1690–1876). While assembling the original collection for the microform set, Readex began its publishing efforts with Clarence Brigham's *History and Bibliography of American Newspapers, 1690–1820* (American Antiquarian Society, 1947). The core of the Readex collection is formed by Isaiah Thomas's own collection of Colonial- and early national-period newspapers and supplemented by nearly two million issues added by Thomas's successors at the American Antiquarian Society. Numerous other institutions and historical societies have contributed to the collection, including the Boston Athenaeum, the Connecticut Historical Society, the Connecticut State Library, the Library Company of Philadelphia, the Library of Congress, the libraries of universities such as Brown and Harvard, and private collections. Page images are formatted for easy viewing, magnification, printing, and saving. Searchable, OCR-generated ASCII text will be provided with each image. As of mid-April 2005, there were 125 titles available, constituting 109,259 issues and 495,439 pages.

- Available from Readex at http://www.readex.com/scholarl/earlamnp.html.
- Product developed in consultation with an editorial advisory board: http://www.readex.com/americana/ean_avboard.html.
- *LRG* annotation of Brigham's bibliography: Q4035.
- Early American Newspapers forms part of Readex's Archive of Americana suite of products, along with Evans, Shaw-Shoemaker, and the *U.S. Serial Set* at http://www.readex.com/digital/digcoll.html.

African-American Newspapers: The Nineteenth Century (1827–1902) starts with *Freedom's Journal* in 1827 and continues in chronological order with the addition of 10 to 12 million words of new text each year (downloaded monthly). The database will ultimately contain the complete text of the major African-American newspapers published in the United States during the nineteenth century. As of April 2005, five of the seven newspapers are complete—*Freedom's Journal, The Colored American* (*Weekly Advocate*), *The North Star, The National Era*, and *Provincial Freeman*. The remaining two, *Frederick Douglass Papers* (1851–1859) and *The Christian Recorder* (1861–1902), are not yet finished.

- Available from Accessible Archives at http://www.accessible.com/about/aboutAA.htm.
- Also available from Accessible Archives: *Godey's Lady's Book; The Liberator* (1831–1865); *The Pennsylvania Gazette* (1728–1800); The Civil War: A Newspaper Perspective (November 1860–April 1865), a database of articles from *The Charleston Mercury, The New York Herald*, and *Richmond Enquirer; American County Histories to 1900* (various titles); The Pennsylvania Genealogical Catalogue: Chester County (1809–1870); and The Pennsylvania Newspaper Record: Delaware County (1819–1870). More information is available at http://www.accessible.com/about.htm.
- *The Charleston Advisor* review by Nancy M. Godleski (April 2000).

National Digital Newspaper Program (NDNP) (1836–1922) is a long-term effort (estimated at 20 years), funded by NEH in partnership with LC to develop a national digital resource of historically significant newspapers from all the states and U.S. territories published between 1836 and 1922. Maintained by LC and freely accessible through the Internet, this searchable database will have an accompanying national newspaper directory of bibliographic and holdings information (with links to digitized titles) as well as an Encyclopedia of Newspaper History, with brief essays about the digitized titles. In its first phase, NDNP is developing a testbed of newspapers published from 1900 through 1910 that will be converted primarily from microfilm. The first awards were announced in April 2005, going to the University of California, Riverside; the University of Florida Libraries, Gainesville; the University of Kentucky Research Foundation, Lexington; The New York Public Library; the University of Utah; and the Library of Virginia, Richmond. The first release is anticipated in September 2006. According to the digital-asset specifications, NDNP will provide full text of content within visual newspaper layout. American Memory's "Stars and Stripes" World War I newspaper project serves as the prototype. NDNP builds on the foundation established by an earlier NEH initiative: the United States Newspaper Program.

- Information about NDNP is available at http://www.neh.fed. us/projects/ndnp.html.
- NDNP Guidelines: http://www.neh.fed.us/grants/guidelines/ ndnp.html.
- Press release about 2005 awards: http://www.loc.gov/today/ pr/2005/05-082.html.
- Information about the U.S. Newspaper Program at http://www. neh.fed.us/projects/usnp.html.
- Prototype: American Memory's "Stars and Stripes": http:// memory.loc.gov/ammem/sgphtml/sashtml/sashome.html.

HarpWeek (1857–1912) has created searchable full text of *Harper's Weekly* through complete rekeying of every word (including advertisements) using a double-keying system to produce a database of 99.995 percent accuracy. *Harper's Weekly* features the first American-run serialized novels by Charles Dickens, George Eliot, Thomas Hardy, Wilkie Collins, and Anthony Trollope, as well as short fiction and poetry of many other writers. With more than 1,000 synopses, HarpWeek provides summaries of every piece of prose in *Harper's Weekly*. The thesaurus-based index provides access to the literature by author, title, publisher, and format. A literary-genre index allows the user to find such items as Humorous Tales or Patriotic Verse. Searches can be limited to 1 of 17 features, including fiction, poetry, biographical sketches/obituaries, cartoons, travel narratives, publishers' notices (more than 1,000 book reviews), illustrations, and portraits.

- Available from HarpWeek at http://www.harpweek.com/.

Historical Newspapers (1851–2001) offers digital page images of articles from newspapers dating back to the nineteenth century. For most titles, the collection includes digital reproductions of every page from every issue in downloadable PDF files. Current coverage includes *Atlanta Constitution* (1868–1925), *Boston Globe* (1872–1901), *Chicago Tribune* (1890–1969), *Christian Science Monitor* (1908–1991),

Los Angeles Times (1881–1969), *The New York Times* (1851–2001), *The Wall Street Journal* (1889–1987), and *The Washington Post* (1877–1988). Marked documents can be printed, e-mailed, or exported into bibliographic-management software (e.g., Endnote). Users can create a Web page with links to articles, searches, and publications.

* Available from ProQuest at http://www.proquest.com/products/pt-product-HistNews.shtml.
* *The Charleston Advisor* review of *The New York Times* access by Tom Gilson (January 2004).

Nineteenth-Century Newspapers (circa 1850–1900). Thomson Gale has announced its intention to build a collection of digital newspapers that will focus on the second half of the nineteenth century (extending the Readex collection of Early American Newspapers). An advisory board of scholars will select an estimated 200 titles (1.5 million pages) that will include a mix of urban and rural newspapers, representing a variety of political and social views.[53]

3.4.3.8 Full-Text Fiction

Early American Fiction (1789–1875). The University of Virginia, with financial support from The Andrew W. Mellon Foundation and in partnership with Chadwyck-Healey, released Early American Fiction (EAF) in two phases. It now consists of 886 first-edition texts by 136 authors in addition to 199 manuscript items and 124 images.

A subset of 158 volumes by 52 authors plus the manuscripts and images is freely accessible to the public. As discussed more fully in section 3.3.2.4, each text exists as a full set of color page images and a searchable, TEI-conformant XML text. Two standard bibliographies, *Bibliography of American Literature* (see 3.4.3.2) and Lyle H. Wright's *American Fiction* (described below), were used to define the project.

* Available from Chadwyck-Healey at http://www.proquest.com/products/pd-product-EarlyAmFiction.shtml. (Description does not include full product, which now extends to 1875.)
* Product review by Cheryl LaGuardia and Laura Farwell Blake from *Library Journal* (August 2003) is available at http://www.proquest.com/division/docs/american-fic.html.

American Prose Fiction (1774–1920). Thomson Gale has announced its intention to create a digital product based on Primary Source Microfilm's set *American Fiction*. This covers all three volumes of Lyle H. Wright's *American Fiction: A Contribution Towards a Bibliography* (1774–1910), its supplement by Geoffrey D. Smith, *American Fiction, 1901-1925: A Bibliography*, and the "Library of Congress Shelf List of American Adult Fiction." Altogether, this would comprise nearly 14,000 novels, or approximately three-quarters of all American fiction published in the United States.

* Forthcoming (no date set) from Thomson Gale.[54] A description of the microfilm set is available at http://www.gale.com.

---

[53] E-mail correspondence with Jeffrey Moyer on April 22, 2005.

[54] E-mail correspondence with Jeffrey Moyer on April 21 and 22, 2005.

Wright American Fiction (1851–1875), described more fully in section 3.3.2.3 of this report, Wright American Fiction consists of accurately edited and fully encoded transcriptions along with digital page images of the novels listed in Lyle Wright's bibliography *American Fiction, 1851–1875*, produced by libraries in the CIC. Encompassing the second volume of Wright's bibliography, this project contains 2,832 titles in adult fiction, including novels, novelettes, romances, and short stories. MARC catalog records for all titles are also freely available.

- Description of the Thomson Gale microfiche collection on which this project is based: http://www.gale.com/servlet/BrowseSeries Servlet?region=9&imprint=000&titleCode=PSM408&edition.
- Freely available from Indiana University Library on behalf of CIC members at http://www.letrs.indiana.edu/web/w/wright2/.
- *LRG* annotation for all three volumes of Lyle Wright's *American Fiction*: Q4180.

Black Short Fiction is available from Alexander Street Press (see section 3.5.4.1).

3.4.3.9 Full-Text Poetry

American Poetry (1600–1900) provides 40,000 works from more than 200 poets, selected by an editorial advisory board. Its principal bibliographic source is the *Bibliography of American Literature*, supplemented with additional poets to provide a more thorough and rounded collection. The complete text of each poem is included. Any accompanying text written by the original author and forming an integral part of the work, such as notes, dedications, and prefaces to individual poems, is also generally included.

- Available from Chadwyck-Healey at http://www.proquest.com/ products/pd-product-AmPoetry.shtml.

African-American Poetry (1760–1900) has 3,000 poems by African-American poets among those listed by William P. French et al., *African-American Poetry and Drama, 1760–1975: A Guide to Information Sources* (Detroit: Gale, 1979).

- Available from Chadwyck-Healey at http://www.proquest.com/ products/pd-product-AfAmPoetry.shtml.
- *LRG* annotation of French's guide: Q3845.

Twentieth-Century American Poetry has more than 52,000 poems from more than 300 twentieth-century American poets.

- Available from Chadwyck-Healey at http://www.proquest. co.uk/products/tcap.html.

Twentieth-Century African-American Poetry has 12,000 poems by more than 100 African-American poets.

- Available from Chadwyck-Healey at http://www.proquest. co.uk/products/a-a_poetry.html.

3.4.3.10 Full-Text Drama

American Drama (1714–1915) has more than 1,500 dramatic works from the Colonial period to the beginning of the twentieth century, including many rare or unique items from major research library collections that are available for the first time as searchable electronic texts.

- Available from Chadwyck-Healey at http://www.proquest.com/products/pd-product-AmDrama.shtml.

Twentieth-Century Drama offers 2,500 plays in English from around the world from the 1890s to 2003. Features mostly copyrighted texts, including many out-of-print works. Available through LION (described below) for an additional charge because of the royalties paid on its contents.

- Available from Chadwyck-Healey at http://www.proquest.com/products/pd-product-20thcenturydrama.shtml.

Asian American Drama brings together more than 250 full-text plays (at least half of which have never been published), along with related biographical, production, and theatrical information.

- Available from Alexander Street Press at http://alexanderstreet.com/products/aadr.htm.

Black Drama has 1,200 plays by more than 300 writers from North America, Africa, Europe, the Caribbean, and the rest of the African diaspora. The works from early twentieth-century America include key writings of the Harlem Renaissance, works performed for the Federal Theatre Project, and plays by critically acclaimed dramatists through the 1940s. American works from the later twentieth century cover the Black Arts movement of the sixties and seventies, works performed by the Black Arts Repertory Theatre/School, the Negro Ensemble Company, and others.

- Available from Alexander Street Press at http://alexanderstreet.com/products/bldr.htm.
- *The Charleston Advisor* review of various Alexander Street Press products, including *Black Drama* by Lois Kuyper-Rushing (April 2002).

Latino Literature: Poetry, Drama, Fiction is available from Alexander Street Press (see section 3.5.4.1).

North American Women's Drama includes the full text of 1,500 plays written from Colonial times to the present by more than 100 writers from the United States and Canada, including 300 previously unpublished works.

- Available from Alexander Street Press at http://alexanderstreet.com/products/wodr.htm.

Twentieth-Century North American Drama, when complete, will contain the full text of 1,500 plays by more than 100 playwrights from North America and written from the late 1800s to the present.

Many of the works are rare, hard to find, or out-of-print; nearly one-quarter of the collection consists of previously unpublished plays. The database includes accompanying reference materials, ancillary information, a performance database, and images. It also includes links to related media resources, including flyers, postcards, play-bills, set designs, and other promotional materials. As of mid-April 2005, this product comprised 319 plays by 53 playwrights, 25 of which were previously unpublished. The database uses the University of Chicago's PhiloLogic software to enable in-depth browsing and searching of both bibliographic and full-text elements. It offers access by author, character, production, company, theater, year, play, scene, and subject.

- Available from Alexander Street Press at http://www.alexander-street2.com/nadrlive/.

3.4.3.11 Integrative Platforms

Literature Online (600 AD to the present)[55] is a fully searchable database of English and American poetry, drama and prose, 153 full-text literature journals, and other key criticism and reference resources, constituting more than 350,000 works altogether. Most of the Chadwyck-Healey individual literature collections described above are available in LION, permitting users to search across them. (Refer to the full product description for a list of all standard and premium modules.) A cross-searchable reference shelf incorporates dictionaries and literary encyclopedias and provides a comprehensive indexing of Web sites, bibliographic information, and background information on authors and their works. "Poets on screen" comprises more than 840 clips of poets reading their own or other poets' work.

- Available from ProQuest at http://www.proquest.com/products/pd-product-Lion.shtml.
- Notable features: LION supports marked lists so that users can save citations for printing or e-mailing (complete with durable URLs linking to the full record); export citations (to bibliographic-management software, e.g., EndNote); and link from citations to locally held copy (e.g., SFX) through OpenURL linking. LION is Z39.50-compliant.
- ProQuest asserts textual accuracy of between 99.97 and 99.995 percent. Late in 2005, LION searches will extend to metadata for all 100,000 works as well as the TCP full text of EEBO (accessible to partners).
- In April 2005, ProQuest announced a new annual prize in association with the e-journal *Early Modern Literary Studies* for the best article published in *EMLS* in the preceding 12 months, in the judgment of a committee appointed by the editor and including a representative from Literature Online.
- LION's Resources for Teaching and Research provides case studies and testimonials as well as details about the text-conversion

---

[55] For a discussion by the publisher about the early development of LION, refer to Hall 1998.

process, and an author e-mail alerts service. See http://lion.
chadwyck.com/marketing/academics/ac_contents.jsp.
- *The Charleston Advisor* review by Claire T. Dygert (July 2000).

LitFinder and Literature Resource Center (LRC) are international in
scope; LitFinder has more than 126,500 full-text poems and 850,000
poem citations and excerpts, along with 10,000 essays, speeches,
plays, and stories spanning from antiquity to the present day. Basic and advanced search features are supplemented by numerous
browsing options by genre, subject, contemporary works, or children's titles.

The Literature Resource Center provides access to biographies,
bibliographies, and critical analysis of authors from all time periods
in many genres drawing from *Contemporary Authors*, the *Dictionary
of Literary Biography*, and *Contemporary Literary Criticism*. It includes
more than 415,000 full-text journal articles from more than 250 literary journals. LRC is integrated with the MLA *International Bibliography*.
- Available from Thomson Gale. LitFinder product description
  is available at http://www.gale.com/pdf/facts/LitFinder.pdf;
  Literature Resource Center product description: http://www.gale.
  com/pdf/facts/lrc.pdf.
- *The Charleston Advisor* review of PoemFinder (precursor to Lit-
  Finder) by Freddie Bush Siler and of Literature Resource Center
  by Susan Gordan Herzog (January 2001).

North American Theatre Online, launched in April 2005, is a comprehensive reference work covering all aspects of Canadian and
American theater. It has some 40,000 pages of major reference materials, together with records to more than 25,000 plays and screenplays,
more than 20,000 authors, 3,000 theatres, 15,000 productions, 15,000
characters within plays, and 2,500 production companies. The database also includes some 5,000 images, playbills, postcards, scrapbooks, and other resources. Subscribers to Alexander Street Press's
five full-text drama databases can search across the content of more
than 3,150 plays with an additional 2,000 plays anticipated in the
near future. Among the reference works featured in North American Theatre Online are Durham's three volumes of *American Theatre
Companies* covering 1749–1986 (*LRG* annotation Q3505); Odell's
15-volume *Annals of the New York Stage* covering 1699–1894 (*LRG* annotation Q3510), complemented by *American Theatre: A Chronicle of
Comedy and Drama* by Bordman and others, covering 1869–2000 (*LRG*
annotation Q3510a); and Bordman's (2004) *The Oxford Companion to
the American Theatre* (*LRG* annotation for 1992 edition, Q3500). It also
includes many early public domain sources and indexes more than
a dozen publicly accessible Web sites such as collections from LC's
American Memory. Relevant Alexander Street Press literary collections are integral to North American Theatre Online.
- Available from Alexander Street Press at http://alexanderstreet.
  com/products/atho.htm.

- Notable features: extensive semantic indexing. Expects to add 20,000 records annually. Offers examples of the types of questions that can be answered with this database. Makes MARC records available for every play and reference book.
- Unique contract option: "Texts produced for North American Theatre Online are considered research materials and receive the same level of stewardship as books, paper documents, and photographs. Once complete, copies of the database will be given to all purchasing institutions, so ensuring that the materials are available to subsequent generations." http://www.alexanderstreet6.com/atho/atho.about.html.

3.5 Collections by Design[56]

This section first considers several broad issues relevant to digitizing and discovering collections and then highlights collections designed around particular topics, genres, or themes. After discussing reasons for digitizing and the importance of metadata to discovery, it identifies alternative entry points to digital resources. These digital collection directories or aggregations are usually created and managed by large organizations involved in exploring and setting standards in the areas of metadata, preservation and access, harvesting and aggregating, and delivery. These agencies are tackling the challenges of digital collections and scholarship by testing varied ways of ensuring that digital assets, regardless of format, are discoverable and versatile in the areas of interoperability, integration, and preservation. The existence and use of these repositories are encouraging individual projects to think carefully about issues of metadata and harvesting that are shaping the ways in which materials are processed, made accessible, manipulated, and preserved. Particular attention is given to resources derived from archives and special collections along with the role of EAD finding aids and exhibits on the Web.

"Collections by Design" are resources that are crafted by careful selection of materials related to a particular area of interest. Categories include genre (e.g., novels, short stories, poetry, fiction, drama, diaries); topics and themes (e.g., women's writings about cooking, the pioneer experience, Broadway); and time periods (e.g., early American, Victorian, Civil War). As with the other types of resources covered in this report, there are overlaps in these categorizations. The important point is that there are many collections of materials related to American literature that are not necessarily described as such, and not all these resources are equally searchable or versatile. Some are in the form of databases, some in the form of digital exhibits. Many of these collections, because they are drawn from libraries, archives, special collections, and even personal collections, contain previously unpublished material. All the collections, however, serve the same ethos: Users want to be able to find collections organized

---

56 Daphnée Rentfrow is the lead author of this section, adding substantially to Martha Brogan's preliminary report, which concentrated primarily on special collections and archives, finding aids, and topical collections.

around themes and genres and to search or browse within them.

3.5.1 Why Digitize?

Before materials are digitized and cataloged in these collections, whether the end product is commercial or freely available, they are first selected for inclusion. While issues of item selection, quality, and processing are beyond the scope of this report, it is worthwhile to consider *why* some of these materials should be made available digitally in the first place. In their chapter "Conversion of Primary Sources" in *A Companion to Digital Humanities*, Marilyn Deegan and Simon Tanner identify the different data forms that primary sources for humanists can take, including documents, visual materials, three-dimensional objects, and time-based media (Deegan and Tanner 2004). Many of the projects identified in this report include several if not all of these forms. Because digital conversion is a time-consuming and costly endeavor, the advantages of digitization should be clearly understood and appreciated by both creators and users of digital materials. Deegan and Tanner provide the following list of advantages of digitization for humanists:

- the ability to republish out-of-print materials
- rapid access to materials held remotely
- potential to display materials that are in inaccessible formats, for instance, large volumes or maps
- "virtual reunification"—allowing dispersed collections to be brought together
- the ability to enhance digital images in terms of size, sharpness, color contrast, noise reduction, etc.
- the potential for integration into teaching materials
- enhanced searchability, including full text
- integration of different media (e.g., images, sounds, video)
- the potential for presenting a critical mass of materials for analysis or comparison (Deegan and Tanner 2004, 491).

Once the advantages are clear, other questions arise, one of the most important being, "What, exactly, is being digitized?" Is the aim to create a digital facsimile of the original, that is, a stand-in that can be printed at will by users? If so, what about nontextual artifacts included in the collection? If the canvas reproduced as an image file is not meant to be printed out as a facsimile, then what is its purpose and its relationship to the text? Is the most important thing to be captured the *content* of an object or the *form*? For text, this brings in questions of edition and manuscript details; for painting, the type of brush or canvas used; for audio, the type of equipment used in recording and playback. What is gained in the digital and what is lost? These questions must be considered before projects begin production and throughout their evolution, especially as technology and practices advance. These questions will help shape the face of a project as well as help structure the metadata that is critical at all stages of creation and management of the resource.

3.5.2 Metadata

Metadata, or data about data, includes the structured information that describes, contextualizes, locates, and explains an information object.[57] Metadata makes it possible to retrieve, use, manage, and link information resources. While the term is used differently in different communities and is not limited to digital objects, it has particular importance for the latter. Certainly, the fact that metadata facilitates discovery of digital information objects is its greatest selling point, but it is as important in its ability to help organize these resources, facilitating interoperability while supporting archiving and preservation. Good metadata of digital objects allows for the following opportunities critical to the discovery and use of electronic resources:

- *Increased accessibility*: Metadata makes it possible to search across multiple collections, create collections from materials located in different repositories, search at the item and collection levels across systems, and distinguish dissimilar resources.
- *Retention of context*: Metadata documents and maintains the relationships among objects in a collection as well as their associations with other relevant information, reducing the decontextualization of the object.
- *Expanding use*: Metadata facilitates different ways to search for information, present results, aggregate objects, and manipulate objects across networks without compromising the integrity of the object.
- *Multiversioning*: Metadata allows multiple versions of an object to be linked, defined, and distinguished from each other.
- *Legal issues*: Metadata makes it possible for repositories to document and track rights issues for the objects and their variants.
- *Preservation*: Metadata that describes the ways in which a digital object was created and maintained makes it possible for the object to survive multiple migrations from different generations of hardware and software.
- *System improvement and economics*: Technical data, often computer generated, is necessary in evaluating and refining systems and planning for new ones (Gilliland-Swetland 2000).

There are three main types of metadata:

1. *Descriptive*, which refers to the attributes of the material being described and can include elements such as title, abstract, author, keywords, and subject. Descriptive metadata tends to be the one most often considered by creators of digital resources and is the category for which scholars and specialists in a particular field

---

[57] Metadata is too complex a topic to treat thoroughly in these pages. This overview is intended as an introduction for the nonexpert who is beginning to consider the ways in which digital resources are described and cataloged, and who is interested in some of the behind-the-scenes details of the digital collections described here. There are many sources for more information about metadata, two of them cited here. Thanks to Matthew Beacom, metadata librarian at Yale University Library, for his helpful suggestions regarding this topic.

are most valuable, as they are the ones best qualified to describe a given object.
2. *Structural*, which encompasses information about how objects are put together, such as how pages are ordered to form chapters.
3. *Administrative*, which refers to how and when a resource was created, e.g., file type, location information, and selection criteria.

Other types of metadata include preservation, technical, and rights management (though the latter is sometimes included as a subset of administrative metadata). Each type of metadata has different types of characteristics, from being machine generated to being static or dynamic, long-term or short-term.

There are many metadata schemes, or sets of metadata elements designed for a specific purpose, available to creators of digital projects. While each scheme has different semantics of how the elements should be encoded, most current schemes use SGML or XML. The most common metadata schemes are the following:[58]

- Dublin Core
- TEI
- Metadata Encoding and Transmission Standard (METS)
- Metadata Object Description Scheme (MODS)
- EAD
- Visual Resource Association (VRA) Core
- IEEE Learning Object Metadata (LOM)
- MPEG Multimedia Metadata
- Categories for the Descriptions of Works of Art (CDWA)
- Content Standard for Digital Geospatial Metadata (CSDGM)

In addition to metadata schemes, there are metadata crosswalks, which further facilitate the mapping of elements and semantics from one metadata scheme to another. These crosswalks are especially important for virtual collections in which resources are drawn from a variety of sources but which are expected to act as a whole (e.g., with one search engine).

A metadata record is a composite of different types and different schemes that work together to provide information to the user and to the computer aggregators and harvesters that collect the information and make it searchable. While users of a digital collection may feel that the most important feature of well-structured metadata is its ability to make objects discoverable, they should also be aware of the importance of the other information provided by metadata—documentation of rights management, preservation, technical information, ability for objects to interoperate, and so forth. Creators of digital collections especially should be well informed about the importance of metadata and its role in the success and longevity of a digital resource.

---

58 For a full description of these metadata schemes and others, see NISO 2004.

3.5.3 Discovery

The greatest challenge for the user of digital projects that are not commercially produced or maintained may simply be to discover what is available. While scholars tend to be familiar with the most successful projects in their fields (successful projects are usually defined as ones that have survived for relatively long periods, whose names are widely recognized, and that have already made significant scholarly and pedagogical contributions to their discipline), they are largely unaware of smaller, more-localized ventures. Most scholars in the humanities have at least heard of, if not used, American Memory, Making of America, Women Writers Project, and The Valley of the Shadow, but few will have heard of the various dime-novel projects or the smaller poetry archives. This, of course, is also true of analog collections: Scholars tend to know where the largest and most accessible collections in their disciplines are located, while smaller, less-renowned collections languish in obscurity in the libraries and archives of various institutions around the world. Archivists themselves do not always know what resides in the hundreds of boxes in their collections. Until an item is processed, it remains largely undiscoverable, and items in a backlog are often not processed until a user requests to see them. In many ways, then, digitization is prompting librarians, archivists, and curators to think differently about their collections and their backlogs and to imagine new ways of making their materials accessible. While there is some concern expressed by these professionals that digitization will both increase the handling of fragile materials and decrease the onsite use of the originals, it seems clear that the costs of digitizing material thoughtfully and thoroughly, in light of the sheer volume of material waiting to be processed, will prevent archivists and librarians from digitizing themselves out of business. Rather, digitization endeavors will spur archivists, librarians, and curators to think differently about their collections, their integration into curricula, their status in scholarship, and their appeal to general users.

Because metadata schemes have evolved over time, and since many projects (especially independent ones) were not considering issues of metadata when they began production, many digital resources remain invisible to the user; without metadata available for harvesting, repositories and aggregators simply do not detect the materials. Until metadata standards and discovery tools are more widely used by every organization creating digital objects, it is unlikely, and perhaps even undesirable, that one single repository will be able to catalog and make accessible all digital collections. Additionally, because so much material crosses disciplinary boundaries, and because terms such as *digital archive*, *electronic collection*, and *digital/electronic resource* are used interchangeably and to describe significantly different material, it appears certain that users will need to search a variety of repositories and collections to find relevant objects. Most scholars say that they discover digital collections either by accident or by word of mouth; this pattern does not seem likely to change in the near future. Metadata schemes and crosswalks, however, are enabling greater discovery of material and increased collaboration and sharing among repositories. The following descriptions of projects, collections, and repositories will make clear the importance of metadata and the challenges presented when metadata is not judiciously created and applied to information objects. Similarly, the list is meant as a representative sample of the ways in which collections can be discovered, organized, aggregated, and harvested. Resource and product descriptions are drawn primarily from the producers' Web sites with little or no editing.

3.5.3.1 Directories of Digital Collections or Aggregations

Earlier in this report, quality-controlled subject gateways were discussed as a way to facilitate access to Web resources in American literature. The author noted that while there are several resources serving as entry points to material of interest in the field, for the most part these gateways are labors of love, often maintained by scholars with the help of graduate students, and few with the continuity of a resource such as History Matters. Similarly, reliable and publicly accessible directories of digital collections exist, but almost all are limited in some way. These directories, unlike the previously cited gateways, are maintained by organizations.

DLF, for example, has a directory of Public Access Collections (1). This is a searchable database of nearly 300 publicly accessible online digital collections (616 bibliographic records of collections) published by DLF members and allied institutions, including RLG. So far, 35 institutions appear to have submitted records of their digital collections. Keyword-searchable and browsable by record and by institution, the database has no controlled vocabulary and appears to rely on the descriptions that its providers include. This explains why a search yielded only one return for "American literature" and only three results for "American Studies," while a search for "American" yielded 142 results, several of which would be of interest to scholars in American literature but whose descriptions did not contain the word *literature*—for example, the project African American Women Writers of the 19th Century of The New York Public Library.

The Institute of Museum and Library Services (IMLS) Digital Collections Registry, built and maintained by the University of Illinois Urbana-Champaign, is restricted to projects funded through the IMLS, in this case, those funded through the IMLS National Leadership Grant (NLG) Program (2). The current database of more than 130 projects is browsable by subject, object, place, title of the collection, NLG project, and institution. A search for "American literature" yielded only one result, while a search for "American" returned 48 results, many of which are collections that, while not specifically about America literature, contain material of interest for the field.

Also at the University of Illinois Urbana-Champaign is the Digital Gateway to Cultural Heritage Materials (3). This Open Archives Initiative (OAI)–based service focuses on cultural heritage materials and provides access to records with and without directly corresponding digital content. A May 2005 search of "American literature" retrieved 1,223 results (with an unknown extent of duplication), of which 314 were images and videos and 69 were derived from museums and archives collections. Text, sheet music, and Web sites accounted for 295 hits and "all types of materials" for 678.

OAIster, a project of the University of Michigan Digital Library Production Service, is aiming to provide access to freely available, academically oriented digital resources. It is named for the OAI Protocol for Metadata Harvesting (PMH), which was developed to make it easier for institutions to share metadata (4).[59] OAI-PMH–compliant metadata would contain the URLs of actual digital objects themselves, thereby offering a link within the metadata record to the full text, image, or video. The exchange among host institutions that provide the protocol and requesting institutions that use software to harvest the metadata allows the latter to receive metadata linked to digital objects from all over the world. Launched in 2003, OAIster searches through nearly five million records from almost 500 digital repositories, half of which are from outside North America. A search for "American literature" produced 904 results, although some of these may be duplicates if more than one institution is providing records of the same object.

Alternately, proprietary software such as CONTENTdm promises to manage an institution's digital material in its various forms while offering metadata standards such as OAI, Dublin Core, and VRA Core to ensure the material's discoverability. OCLC's WorldCat, for example, is now harvesting metadata from selected collections that use CONTENTdm. Additionally, CONTENTdm maintains a Customer Collections page with links to the different collections using the software to manage their material (5). Though not searchable, the list is browsable by category or by organization. Because relevant collections with American literature material may be organized under Art and Drama, Documents and Books, History and Culture, and other such categories, searching is not as easy as one would like. However, it is possible to search the site; a search for "American literature" produced 26 results, though not all results were relevant. Arguably, this service is best appreciated as a way to envision how the software can manage different types of collections (which is, of course, why it is offered).

DLF Aquifer is an initiative designed to enable teaching, learning, and scholarship through "scalable solutions" to managing and leveraging digital library content (6). Beginning with content in the area of American culture and life, Aquifer plans to develop testbed tools for a wide range of digital library work, including collection development of quality digital content. Additionally, Aquifer aims to promote collaboration among its partners to build and test repositories, content-management systems, metadata and information architecture standards, interoperability, and related practices and solutions. Its first interinstitutional project is to build a virtual collec-

---

[59] For more information about OAIster, see Hagedorn 2005.

tion in American Studies by leveraging the work of two multi-institutional initiatives: AmericanSouth (based at Emory University) and American West (based at the California Digital Library). The former is a collaboration among a large number of Southern research libraries that harvests metadata from library and museum archives into a central location for aggregation, indexing, search, and discovery. AmericanSouth has nearly 30,000 records from 27 archives indexed. American West is assembling a virtual collection drawing from the resources of major research institutions. In using these two multi-institutional projects, Aquifer will be able to build a cross-disciplinary, cross-media collection for the support of innovation in teaching, learning, and research in American history, society, culture, environment, geography, and art. It will look to AmericanSouth and American West "to define collection development paths and processes for collections of cultural materials bearing on American history and society. It will commission collection development strategies for American literature and American music" (Greenstein 2004). It remains to be seen how successful Aquifer will be, though it already promises to be a leader in the areas of ensuring interoperability and metadata standards.

3.5.3.2 Finding Special Collections and Archives

Manuscripts, objects, photographs, posters, postcards, and other media in varying formats all happily coexist in archival collections, but this heterogeneity and surplus of nonprocessed material can mean that collections are not ready for digitization. The extensive Web directory Repositories of Primary Sources, maintained by Terry Abraham at the University of Idaho, excludes virtual collections in favor of a list, organized by geographic region, of more than 5,000 Web sites describing holdings of manuscripts, archives, rare books, historical photographs, and other primary sources (7). The size and scope of this list make it apparent that it will be many years before materials in these collections are available digitally.

Alternately, access to aggregated directory information about special collections and archives is available through proprietary products such as the fee-based ArchivesUSA (Chadwyck-Healey), a directory of approximately 5,500 repositories and more than 140,000 collections of primary source material in the United States (8). As described at its Web site, ArchivesUSA integrates collection and repository information including the following:

- The entire collection of National Union Catalog of Manuscript Collections (NUCMC) from 1959 to the present. NUCMC includes information gathered and indexed by LC and covering more than 98,600 collections (see below).
- Names and detailed subject indexing of more than 61,000 collections whose finding aids have been published separately in ProQuest UMI's microfiche series *National Inventory of Documentary Sources in the United States.*
- Collection descriptions submitted directly to us from repositories.
- A growing number of more than 5,000 links to online finding aids.

The Library of Congress provides free searching access to archival and manuscript collections available in the RLG and OCLC catalogs through gateways to the NUCMC (9). In this way, users can locate the name of the repository holding the collection.

Discovery of material in archives and special collections is enabled by finding aids or by inventories, indexes, and guides that are created by archival and manuscript repositories to provide detailed descriptions of the content and intellectual organization of collections. The development and widespread adoption of the standards of the Encoded Archival Description Document Type Definition (EAD DTD) has allowed many libraries and museums to digitize their existing finding aids. The EAD DTD for encoding archival finding aids using XML is maintained by LC in partnership with the Society of American Archivists. These online finding aids may have links to digital representations of the material, or may be simply searchable versions of the analog. Unfortunately, many repositories lack the requisite staff and training to produce EAD finding aids. The Archivists' Toolkit, a suite of open-source software tools for processing and managing archival information, promises to mitigate this challenge. EAD guidelines and selected tools are annotated below.

3.5.3.3 EAD Tools

The Archivists' Toolkit is a suite of open-source software tools for processing and managing archival information. Its objective is to decrease the time and cost associated with archival processing and to promote the standardization of archival information. Early implementation of the toolkit will focus on small- to medium-size repositories for which resources and staffing are comparatively limited.

The toolkit will provide archives with tools for more easily establishing their presence on the Web and for sharing information on their holdings with other repositories and union catalogs. This is a collaboration of the University of California-San Diego, New York University, and Five Colleges, Inc., with support from The Andrew W. Mellon Foundation. Available at http://euterpe.bobst.nyu.edu/toolkit/index.html.

RLG's EAD Best-Practice Guidelines, which can be applied both to retrospective conversion of legacy finding aids and the creation of new finding aids, were developed to
- facilitate interoperability of resource discovery by imposing a basic degree of uniformity on the creation of valid EAD-encoded documents
- encourage the inclusion of particular elements
- develop a set of core data elements
Available at http://www.rlg.org/en/page.php?Page_ID=450.

The LEADERS Toolkit is a generic tool set that will link EAD to electronically retrievable resources. The LEADERS project aims to enhance remote-user access to archives by providing the means to present archival source materials within their context. This is being achieved by linking encoded transcripts and digitized images of paper-based archival materials (content) to encoded finding aids and authority records (context). A demonstrator application is available through the LEADERS home page. This site includes background material on the XML applications used by LEADERS on related projects and on research into the needs of archive users. Available at http://www.ucl.ac.uk/leaders-project/.

3.5.3.4 Consolidated Access to Finding Aids

With the more-widespread use of EAD standards, institutions are aggregating finding aids into publicly accessible databases. Some examples with material relevant to American literature follow.

Archival Resources is a subscription-based product that provides centralized searching and retrieval of a rich set of finding aids. Archival Resources also includes the RLG's Archival and Mixed Collections descriptive records, which are timely, high-level summaries for more than 700,000 collections of manuscripts and archives. In both the extensive finding aids and brief descriptive records, users may also find links to actual digitized archival materials. Available at http://www.rlg.org/en/page.php?Page_ID=120&dataGoo.x=16&dataGo.y=9.

Integrated Finding Guide to Walt Whitman's Poetry Manuscripts demonstrates effective scholar and archivist collaboration with an innovative way to integrate dispersed collections and create item-level access through the EAD finding guide. Available at http://www.whitmanarchive.org/manuscripts/.

Library of Congress Finding Aids enables users to search and browse by subject (including literature categories), name, collection title, collection date, or collection by repository. Available at http://lcweb2.loc.gov/faid/.

OASIS at Harvard University allows users to search by word or phrase within different categories (e.g., name, place, title, subject/genre) with year delimiters. They may search for names as keywords. An "American literature" search by subject/genre retrieved 28 finding aids. It is possible to search within the finding aid for particular words. Available at http://oasis.harvard.edu/.

Archival Finding Aids at Duke University includes search and browse functions. It is possible to retrieve scores of finding aids related to "American literature" and to link from the finding aid to the local catalog record. Available at http://scriptorium.lib.duke.edu/findaids/. See **American and British Literary Materials** at http://scriptorium.lib.duke.edu/literary/.

Finding Aids Database at Yale University retrieved 338 "documents," or finding aids, in response to a search of "American" near "literature." There are links from the finding aid to the local catalog record and further search capability to locate digital images within the collection. Available at http://webtext.library.yale.edu/finddocs/fadsear.htm.

UCSD Finding Aids (University of California-San Diego). Available at http://orpheus.ucsd.edu/speccoll/testing/mscl-fa1.html. See **Archive for New Poetry: Manuscript Collections** at http://orpheus.ucsd.edu/speccoll/testing/fa_anp.html.

Virginia Heritage: Guide to Manuscript and Archival Collections in Virginia. Available at http://www.lib.virginia.edu/vhp/.

Archival Research Catalog is the online catalog of the National Archives and Records Administration's nationwide holdings in the Washington, D.C., area, and in regional archives and Presidential libraries. The Archival Research Catalog allows users to perform a keyword, digitized image, and location search. Advanced functionalities permit searches by organization, person, or topic. The bibliographic record links to electronic finding aids, which link to archival materials that have been digitized. Available at http://www.archives.gov/research_room/arc/index.html.

Online Archive of California has the potential to provide integrated access to distributed, digitized primary source material. It includes a searchable database of finding aids to primary sources and digital facsimiles from more than 100 repositories across California, including libraries, museums, and archives. Source materials include letters, diaries, and manuscripts as well as photographs, maps, oral histories, artifacts, and ephemera. It also provides access to thematically based digital collections of images and texts such as California Cultures, California Heritage, or the Free Speech Movement. Although the Online Archive of California focuses on cultural heritage and history, it demonstrates the potential for a broad-based literary-oriented archive. Available at http://oac.cdlib.org/about/.

    List of finding aids: http://oac.cdlib.org/titles/

    Contributing institutions: http://oac.cdlib.org/institutions/

3.5.3.5 Exhibitions on the Web

Resources from special collections and archival collections are often presented as exhibits on the Web, or as digital versions of local, on-site exhibits. The Smithsonian Institution libraries maintain Library and Archival Exhibitions on the Web (10), a growing collection of more than 3,000 online exhibits created by libraries, archives, historical societies, and museums that can be browsed by title or searched by exhibition name, institution, or subject term. A subject search of "American literature" retrieved scores of exhibits. A few stellar examples are provided below.

Women's Literary Salons Archive, 1975–1985: New York, Cerridwen, Paris, Los Angeles offers ephemera from the collection of Gloria Orenstein, professor of Gender Studies and Comparative Literature, University of Southern California. Inspired by the historic examples of salon women such as Mme. de Rambouillet, Mme. Geoffrin, Mme. de Staël, Gertrude Stein, five feminist writers of the 1970s, Natalie Clifford Barney, Marilyn Coffey, Erika Duncan, Karen Malpede, Gloria Orenstein, and Carole Rosenthal, decided to create a forum for intellectual discussion and for the presentation of feminist writings that would serve a new generation of women writers in the ways that the salons of the past had served the male intellectuals and writers of their times. The Women's Salon for Literature was established in New York and flourished from 1975 until 1985. Sections of the archive, particularly the newsletters, publicity statements, and fliers, have been converted into HTML format. Available at http://www.usc.edu/isd/archives/womens_salons/.

Household Words: Women Write from and for the Kitchen is an exhibition from the Esther B. Aresty Collection of Rare Books in the Culinary Arts, University of Pennsylvania. The Aresty Collection spans five centuries and represents cultures from nearly every part of the world. The books provide material for culinary and social histories from many points of view. Titles include

- *Esther Bradford Aresty: Her Booke*
- *A Book of Her Owne*
- *The Delights for Ladies*
- *The Communal Kitchen*
- *Social Reform in the United States*
- *British and American Public Voices & The Culinary Canon*
- *A Curriculum for Ladies*
- *The Handmaidens of Industry*

Available at http://www.library.upenn.edu/exhibits/rbm/aresty/aresty8.html.

Rave Reviews: Bestselling Fiction in America (University of Virginia) celebrates the fiction Americans actually read. The books displayed are significant both as physical objects and as reminders of great stories. They provide an index of American interests and reading tastes over past 250 years. The exhibition stems from the collecting efforts of Lillian Gary Taylor, who assembled more than 1,900 literary bestsellers. Her handwritten notebooks provide a portrait of a collector who loved to read and who understood that literary merit is not the only measure of a book's importance. Available at http://www.lib.virginia.edu/small/exhibits/rave_reviews/.

"Agents Wanted": Subscription Publishing in America (University of Pennsylvania) explores a relatively unknown and inadequately documented aspect of the American publishing industry in the nineteenth century. The resources of the Zinman Collection, a small portion of which is seen here, will assist scholars in reassessing the story of this industry's growth and of its significance in American life. Available at http://www.library.upenn.edu/exhibits/rbm/agents/.

National Archives and Records Administration: Exhibit Hall is a digital collection of some of the many exhibits held at NARA. These multimedia collections include the following areas of interest, each with several galleries:
- The Charters of Freedom
- American Originals
- Picturing the Century: One Hundred Years of Photography from the National Archives
- A New Deal for the Arts
- When Nixon Met Elvis
- Treasures of Congress
- Panorama
- Portrait of Black Chicago
- Powers of Persuasion
- Designs for Democracy
- Tokens and Treasures: Gifts to Twelve Presidents
- Featured Documents

Available at http://www.archives.gov/exhibit_hall/index.html.

NYPL Digital Gallery (The New York Public Library) provides access to more than 300,000 images digitized from primary sources and printed rarities in the collections of the NYPL, including illuminated manuscripts, historical maps, vintage posters, rare prints and photographs, illustrated books, printed ephemera, and more. There are 37 collections categorized as Arts and Literature. American literary scholars will find a wealth of resources, including hundreds of portraits picturing more than 120 authors writing in English from the 1860s to 1920s from the Henry W. and Albert A. Berg Collection of English and American Literature, the Cabinet Card Portraits in the collection of radical publisher Benjamin R. Tucker, more than 2,000 dust jackets from American and European books (1926–1947), and more than 200 photographs by Carl Van Vechten from *Gertrude Stein: Part of a Life in Pictures*. Available at http://digitalgallery.nypl.org/nypldigital/index.cfm.

3.5.4 Genre Collections

Online directories, repositories, and other aggregating systems such as OAIster, along with EAD finding aids and Web exhibits, offer ways to discover digital material or digital pointers to analog material. In sections 3.2 through 3.4 of this report, collections are categorized as author studies, e-book collections, and reference resources. Other collections are organized more broadly around topics and genres, including fiction, drama, poetry, primary sources, letters and diaries, and popular culture. Such categorizations, like all such systems, are for convenience more than for instruction. Materials in each category could easily fit into another, and many digital collections are interdisciplinary and multimedia in scope, making it nearly impossible to sustain any divisions. Yet it makes sense to indicate a few of the exemplary projects within those categories, especially since some of the projects define themselves within those parameters. This list is not exhaustive; rather, it is meant to be representative of the types of thematic, topical, or generic projects, archives, collections, and other repositories that are available digitally with material relevant to American literature. It is the author's hope that in providing subscription-based products (e.g., Alexander Street Press) alongside free ones, readers will become more attuned to the ways in which each provides a scholarly service, why each must be supported, and what can happen when they are not. One case in point: Women and Social Movements in the United States, 1600–2000 (11). Started in 1997 as a course assignment for a senior seminar taught by SUNY-Binghamton professor Kathryn Kish Sklar, the Web site, with the collaboration of her colleague Thomas Dublin, rapidly expanded into a successful scholarly resource funded by a series of grants. Despite its success (or perhaps because of it), the project proved unsustainable in terms of labor and cost. By 2002, Dublin and Sklar were in conversation with Alexander Street Press, which eventually became the primary publisher of the site, with Sklar and Dublin as coeditors. While they have been able to greatly expand the numbers of materials included on the site and in the collection, the resource is now subscription based. In the absence of other business models, many projects begun years ago and now struggling to maintain production and visibility may look to commercial producers to sustain their efforts.[60]

Collections may contain scholarly essays and commentaries or simply provide access to the source material. The texts, images, and other resources are collected by curators, scholars, librarians, and archivists, and are designed into a coherent whole with databases, search functions, and display options that vary from project to project. Some of the collections are created by gathering related materials already digitized by other institutions and bringing them together as a thematic collection. (This is the case with many of the American Memory collections.) Because of these and other differences, it is important to emphasize that the projects listed below are offered neither as models of standards and best practices nor as models of leading projects; rather, they are a representative sample of the different types of organized collections that are available to scholars of American literature.

3.5.4.1 Fiction

The Beadle and Adams Dime Novel Digitization Project (Northern Illinois University) is a multiyear initiative by the Northern Illinois University (NIU) Libraries to further research on the topic of early American literature and dime novels. Concentration is on *The House*

---

[60] For more information on Women and Social Movements, see http://womhist.binghamton.edu/and the project notes available at http://womhist.binghamton.edu/notes.htm.

of Beadle & Adams and Its Dime and Nickel Novels, the landmark bibliography by Albert Johannsen. The digitized bibliography will provide a framework for the digitization of Beadle's publications held in the NIU Libraries. The NIU Libraries hold Albert Johannsen's own collection of Beadle and Adams's dime novels and other popular literature of the late-nineteenth and early-twentieth centuries. Available at http://www.niulib.niu.edu/badndp/index.html.

Black Short Fiction (Alexander Street Press) brings together 100,000 pages and an estimated 8,000 works of short fiction produced by writers from Africa and the African diaspora from the earliest times to the present. North American coverage targets early Southern Blacks, the Harlem Renaissance, post-Harlem, and contemporary writers. The materials have been compiled from early literary magazines, archives, and the personal collections of the authors. Some 30 percent of the collection is fugitive or ephemeral or has never been published before. Forms include fables, parables, ballads, folktales, short story cycles, and novellas. Available at http://www.alexander-streetpress.com/products/blfi.htm.

Dime Novels and Penny Dreadfuls (Stanford University) consists of more than 8,000 items and includes long runs of the major dime novel series (e.g., Frank Leslie's *Boys of America*, *Happy Days*, Beadle's *New York Dime Library*) and equally strong holdings of story papers such as the *New York Ledger* and *Saturday Night*. Available at http://www-sul.stanford.edu/depts/dp/pennies/home.html.

Emory Women Writers Resource Project (Emory University) is a collection of edited and unedited texts by women writing in English from the seventeenth through the nineteenth century. It is used as a pedagogical tool to offer graduate and undergraduate students in various disciplines the opportunity to edit their own texts. Available at http://chaucer.library.emory.edu/wwrp/.

George Kelley and Paperback Pulp Fiction Collection (University of Buffalo) comprises more than 25,000 pulp-fiction books and magazines, the earliest dating from the 1940s. The collection contains hundreds of paperbacks from this period, and thousands from the 1950s and 1960s. Many of these never appeared in hardcover; the remainder are paperback originals published in the 1970s and 1980s. Detective and mystery stories make up the largest part of the collection, followed by science fiction paperbacks and magazines. Catalog records for the collection may be searched in BISON, the online catalog of the University at Buffalo Libraries, and in WorldCat. As available through copy cataloging, topical headings from the Library of Congress Subject Headings have been applied, and authors' names conform to the Library of Congress Name Authority File. Available at http://ublib.buffalo.edu/libraries/units/lml/kelley/.

Latino Literature: Poetry, Drama, Fiction (Alexander Street Press) delivers approximately 200 novels and many hundreds of short stories, 20,000 pages of poetry, and 400 plays. Most of the collection is in English, with selected works of particular importance (approximately 25 percent of the collection) presented in Spanish. The collection begins with the works of writers from the Southwest who became citizens of the United States in 1850. It covers the body of Chicano writers such as Maria Amparo Ruiz de Burton, Maria Cristina Mena, Josefina Niggli, and Daniel Venegas, who began to create a distinctive literature in the early nineteenth century. Much of this work has long been out of print and unavailable. The collection includes major writers from the Chicano renaissance and current writers as well. The works of some *teatros* created in the late 1960s and early 1970s are targeted for inclusion; these include *El Teatro Campesino* and *El Teatro de la Esperanza*. Available at http://www.alexanderstreetpress. com/products/lali.htm.

Library of Southern Literature (University of North Carolina) documents the diversity of Southern experience as presented in 100 of its most important literary works. The bibliography was compiled by the late Robert Bain, based on suggestions from colleagues in Southern studies around the country. Available at http://docsouth.unc. edu/southlit/southlit.html.

North Carolina History and Fiction Digital Library (University of North Carolina-Charlotte) comprises approximately 200 digital texts and maps pertaining to the history of 29 counties in eastern North Carolina and works of fiction that relate to some of those counties. The materials were selected from the North Carolina Collection and the Snow L. and B. W. C. Roberts Collection of more than 1,100 works of fiction set in North Carolina and dating from 1734. Full-text searchable. Available at http://www.lib.ecu.edu/ncc/historyfiction/.

3.5.4.2 Poetry
American Verse Project (University of Michigan) is an electronic archive of volumes of American poetry dating primarily from the nineteenth century, although a few eighteenth- and early twentieth-century texts are included. The archive includes books of poetry by a number of African-American and women poets. In many cases, the texts are the only existing editions of the author's work. Titles were selected in consultation with faculty but do not necessarily derive from a special collection. Available at http://www.hti.umich.edu/a/ amverse/.

Langston Hughes National Poetry Project (NEH and the University of Kansas) began as part of the centennial celebration of Langston Hughes's life and work. It involves a series of public poetry and book discussion programs and an accompanying Web site. Targeting diverse audiences and populations, "Speaking of Rivers" proposes to increase interest in and exposure to poetry as a spoken and written art, a form of participatory democratic activity, and a means of advancing human understanding. Available at http://www.kuce. org/hughes/.

Online Journal and Multimedia Companion to Anthology of Modern American Poetry (Oxford University Press, 2000) (Department of English, University of Illinois at Urbana-Champaign) is a comprehensive learning environment and scholarly forum for the study of modern American poetry. It includes syllabi, 161 companion sites for poets, and links to publishers of poetry. Available at http://www. english.uiuc.edu/maps/.

The Poetess Archive (Miami University of Ohio and NINES) includes poetry by women and men, British and American, writing in the poetess tradition, 1785–1900, and comprising peer-reviewed, TEI-encoded works. Available at http://www.orgs.muohio.edu/women-poets/poetess/.

Poetry Cybercasts (Library of Congress) comprises two series: Poet Vision and Poet and the Poem. Poet Vision features great poets reading and talking about their work. Originally filmed and broadcast in Philadelphia from 1988–1990, the episodes capture for posterity insights from and about Lucille Clifton, Rita Dove, Allen Ginsberg, Louise Glück, Sam Hamill, Michael Harper, Stanley Kunitz, Denise Levertov, and Robert Penn Warren. The Poet and the Poem is an ongoing series of live poetry evenings at the Library of Congress with distinguished artists. Webcasts are now available of recent events, including the appearances of two U.S. poets laureate. Available at http://www.loc.gov/poetry/cyberpoet.html.

Poetry Here and Then (University of Michigan) is a sampling of the papers of Michigan poets from various collections housed at the Bentley Historical Library, featuring handwritten and typed manuscripts, letters, and essays as well as photographs, sketches, certificates, and other personal items. Available at http://images.umdl. umich.edu/b/bhlpoetry/.

The Poetry Magazine Archives Project/ Modern Poetry Collection (University of Chicago) comprises issues from the first decade (1912–1922) of *Poetry: A Magazine of Verse* digitized and converted for full-text searching. The site was created as part of a project that aims to conserve, stabilize, reformat, and digitize materials from the archives of *Poetry*. Selected materials from the archive for which permissions can be obtained will be digitized, and a Web site will be created to provide a historical and cultural context for the material. Available at http://www.lib.uchicago.edu/e/spcl/mopo.html.

Poets.org (Academy of American Poets) is one of the many programs sponsored by the Academy of American Poets. The academy was founded in 1934 to support American poets and to foster the appreciation of contemporary poetry. The site includes the Poetry Audio Archive, a collection of nearly 500 recordings dating to the 1960s, Poetry Exhibits, and a searchable database of more than 1,200 poems. Available at http://www.poets.org.

3.5.4.3 Manuscripts, Documents, Archival Ephemera

Avalon Project (Yale University Law Library) is a collaboration between the Yale Law School and Yale Law Library to make historical and present-day legal documents available online. This international collection focuses primarily on modern documents but contains some documents from before the eighteenth century. There are currently 3,500 documents available in full text with supporting documentation linked where appropriate. Available at http://www.yale.edu/lawweb/avalon/avalon.htm.

Early Americas Digital Archive (EADA) (University of Maryland) is a collection of electronic texts and links to texts originally written in or about the Americas from 1492 to about 1820. Available to the public for research and teaching purposes, EADA is published and supported by the Maryland Institute for Technology in the Humanities (MITH) under the general editorship of Ralph Bauer, a professor of English at the University of Maryland at College Park. Intended as a long-term and interdisciplinary project committed to exploring the intersections between traditional humanities research and digital technologies, it invites scholars from all disciplines to submit their editions of early American texts for publication (Bauer 2003). EADA consists of two basic components: the EADA Database and the Gateway to Early American Authors on the Web. In the EADA Database, users can find texts that are housed at EADA and that have been encoded using TEI, which makes it possible for them to search for specific terms such as author, title, and subject, within and across the texts. EADA vouches for the accuracy of the header information as well as for the authenticity and quality of the texts contained in its database, which is continually expanding. Gateway to Early American Authors on the Web allows users to browse a list of early American authors whose texts are available both at EADA and on sites that others have posted on the Web. Materials include poetry, works of fiction, and various nonfiction texts. Available at http://www.mith2.umd.edu:8080/eada/index.jsp.

Early Encounters in North America: Peoples, Cultures and the Environment (Alexander Street Press) documents the relationship among various European, Indian, African, Caribbean, and other cultures. The resource is accessible, indexed, and cross-searchable, including *The Jesuit Relations* in French and Latin with English translations. It currently contains 1,482 authors and more than 100,000 pages of letters, diaries, memoirs, and accounts of early encounters. Particular care has been taken to index the material so that it can be used in new ways; for example, users can identify all encounters between the French and the Huron between 1650 and 1700. It also includes more than 1,200 color images, including many works by George Catlin and John James Audubon. Available at http://www.alexanderstreetpress.com/products/eena.htm.

In Their Own Words (Dickinson College) is a digital collection of books, pamphlets, letters, and diaries dating from the latter eighteenth through the early twentieth century that reflects the history of the United States. This collection contains more than 23,500 pages of text and corresponding transcriptions covering a variety of topics, including colonial American politics; U.S. politics, government, and foreign relations; historical biography and autobiography; slavery and abolition; the American Civil War; the temperance movement; foreign travel; economics; medicine; philosophy; and theology. Available at http://deila.dickinson.edu/theirownwords/.

North American Slave Narratives (University of North Carolina at Chapel Hill) is part of Documenting the American South. North American Slave Narratives documents the individual and collective story of the African American struggle for freedom and human rights in the eighteenth, nineteenth, and early-twentieth centuries. The goal is to digitize all known narratives written by fugitive and former slaves and published as broadsides, pamphlets, or books in English up to 1920 as well as many of the biographies of fugitive and former slaves published in English before 1920. Available at http://docsouth.unc.edu/neh/index.html.

The Salem Witch Trials Documentary Archive and Transcription Project (University of Virginia) consists of an electronic collection of primary source materials relating to the Salem witch trials of 1692 and a new transcription of the court records. The documentary archive was created under the supervision of Benjamin C. Ray, a professor at the University of Virginia. Bernard Rosenthal, a professor at the University of Binghamton, supervises the transcription project. Together with a team of scholars, Professor Rosenthal is undertaking a new transcription of the original court records, titled "Records of the Salem Witch Hunt," to be published by Cambridge University Press. Available at http://etext.virginia.edu/salem/witchcraft/home.html.

Samuel May Anti-Slavery Collection (Cornell University) gathers together more than 8,500 pamphlets and leaflets relating to the anti-slavery struggle at the local, regional, and national levels. Many are the original copies held in the personal libraries of the movement's leaders. Sermons, position papers, offprints, local Anti-Slavery Society newsletters, poetry anthologies, freedmen's testimonies, broadsides, and Anti-Slavery Fair keepsakes all document in an intimate manner the social and political implications of the movement. With the support of the federal Save America's Treasures program, Cornell has cataloged and digitized all items (300,000 pages) in a manner that protects the originals while ensuring full capture of the text, illustrations, annotations, markings, and embossments. Full conservation treatment is restoring these items to a usable state for current and future scholars requiring access to the original artifacts. Available at http://www.library.cornell.edu/mayantislavery/.

3.5.4.4 Letters, Diaries, and Oral Histories

American Civil War Collections (Electronic Text Center at the University of Virginia) presents a variety of primary source material on the American Civil War, including letters, diaries, and newspapers. Letter collections include searchable transcriptions as well as digital images of the manuscripts. Available at http://etext.lib.virginia.edu/civilwar/.

The American Civil War: Letters and Diaries (Alexander Street Press) contains 2,009 authors and approximately 100,000 pages of diaries, letters, and memoirs. Each source has been carefully chosen using leading bibliographies. The product includes 4,000 pages of previously unpublished manuscripts, such as the letters of Amos Wood and his wife and the diary of Maryland planter William Claytor. The collection also includes biographies, an extensive bibliography of the sources in the database, and material licensed from *The Civil War Day-by-Day* by E. B. Long. Available at http://www.alexanderstreet2.com/cwldlive/.

I Remain: A Digital Archive of Letters, Manuscripts, and Ephemera (Lehigh University) represents a range of lives—from ordinary citizens to presidents, literary luminaries, movie stars, soldiers, and politicians. The digital archive offers the opportunity to study the evolution of communication, trace the development of social networks, examine material culture, and gain insight into the way working writers and scientists shaped their ideas and shared their thoughts. Available at http://digital.lib.lehigh.edu/remain/.

North American Immigrant Letters, Diaries and Oral Histories (Alexander Street Press) is composed of contemporaneous letters and diaries, oral histories, interviews, and other personal narratives. The series includes works by 2,162 authors and approximately 100,000 pages of information, providing a unique and personal view of what it meant to immigrate to America and Canada between 1800 and 1950. In selected cases, users can hear the actual audio voices of the immigrants. Available at http://www.alexanderstreet2.com/imldlive/.

Open Collections Project (Harvard University), when complete, will contain more than 2,200 books and pamphlets, 1,000 photographs, and 10,000 manuscript pages from the Harvard libraries. The first collection to be released is entitled Working Women, 1870–1930, and includes autobiographies, letters, and other documents relevant to American literature. Available at http://ocp.hul.harvard.edu/ww/.

Oral History Online (Alexander Street Press) is a major initiative that aims to index all the important oral histories in English, available either on the Web or in archives, from around the world. The index points to thousands of collections that represent millions of pages of histories. Tens of thousands of pages are full text, many with associated audio and video files. It directly links users to repositories with materials that are live on the Web. There are detailed bibliographic records for every interview, collection, and repository. New collections are added regularly. Available at http://www.alexanderstreetpress.com/products/orhi.htm.

A companion feature, **Oral History Directory**, is a permanent, free resource that indexes major oral history collections in English around the world. It features the "Oral History Top 100," a ranking of the most popular collections, based on the number of times each collection link is used. Available at http://alexanderstreet2.com/oralhist/.

North American Women's Letters and Diaries (Alexander Street Press) is an electronic collection of women's diaries and correspondences spanning more than 300 years that presents the personal experiences of hundreds of women. The collection includes approximately 150,000 pages of letters and diaries from Colonial times to 1950, including 7,000 pages of previously unpublished manuscripts in electronic format for the first time. The material is drawn from more than 1,000 sources, including journal articles, pamphlets, newsletters, monographs, and conference proceedings. Much of it is in copyright. Represented are all age groups and life stages, a wide range of ethnicities, many geographical regions, the famous, and the not so famous. More than 1,500 biographies enhance the use of the database. Available at http://www.alexanderstreetpress.com/products/nwld.htm.

Trails of Hope: Overland Diaries and Letters, 1846–1869 (Utah Academic Library Consortium) is a collection of the original writings of 49 voyagers on the Mormon, California, Oregon, and Montana trails. Some diarists tell their stories with eloquence and others with maddening brevity, while telling stories of persistence and pain, birth and death, God and gold, dust and debris, bugs and buffalo, love and laughter, and trail tedium. Accompanying the original diary images and their searchable transcripts are 43 contemporary maps; 7 trail guides; 82 photographs, watercolors and art sketches; and 4 essays on the Mormon and California trails, maps, and trail guides. Offers suggested readings for further discovery and brief biographies of 45 of the 49 diarists. Available at http://overlandtrails.lib.byu.edu/index.html.

Wisconsin Pioneer Experience (University of Wisconsin Digital Collections) is a digital collection of diaries, letters, reminiscences, speeches, and other writings of people who settled and built Wisconsin during the nineteenth century. Available at http://digicoll.library.wisc.edu/wipionexp/.

3.5.4.5 Drama

Al Hirschfeld, Beyond Broadway (Exhibition, Library of Congress) celebrates the gift to the nation of original drawings given by the artist in honor of LC's bicentennial. The exhibition features 25 works drawn from the gift and from LC's collections, spanning Hirschfeld's career and offering a look back at the origins of his wondrous, unaccountable line. Available at http://www.loc.gov/rr/print/swann/hirschfeld/.

The American Variety Stage (Library of Congress/American Memory) is a multimedia anthology selected from various LC holdings. The collection illustrates the vibrant and diverse forms of popular entertainment, especially vaudeville, that thrived from 1870 until 1920. Included are 334 English- and Yiddish-language play scripts, 146 theater playbills and programs, 61 motion pictures, 10 sound recordings, 143 photographs, and 29 memorabilia items documenting the life and career of Harry Houdini. Theater posters and additional sound recordings will be added to this anthology. Available at http://lcweb2.loc.gov/ammem/vshtml/vshome.html.

Black Drama (Alexander Street Press) is described in section 3.4.3.10, as are descriptions of other Alexander Street Press products related to drama. Available at http://www.alexanderstreet.com/products/bldr.htm.

J. Willis Sayre Collection: Photographs (University of Washington, Seattle) consists of a selection of 9,856 images from more than 24,000 photographs of theatrical and vaudeville performers, musicians, and entertainers who played in Seattle between about 1900 and 1955 (some of the materials date back to the 1870s). The collector was J. Willis Sayre, a drama critic, journalist, and promoter. The collection is strongest for the little-studied period when Seattle had a prominent place in the development of vaudeville between 1905 and 1914. John Cort, Alexander Pantages, and Sullivan & Considine all operated out of Seattle, and the Sayre Collection includes not only the expected thousands of publicity photographs from New York photographers but also hundreds done in Seattle, Portland, and San Francisco. Available at http://content.lib.washington.edu/sayrepublicweb/index.html.

Joseph Urban Theatre Collection (Columbia University), a product of The Joseph Urban Stage Design Models and Documents Stabilization and Access Project, funded by NEH, will preserve 240 three-dimensional stage models created by Joseph Urban for New York theaters between 1914 and 1933. They include productions for the Ziegfeld Follies, the Metropolitan Opera, and a variety of Broadway theaters. The project will also create and link digital images of related stage design documents and drawings to the existing online finding aid. Available at http://www.columbia.edu/cu/libraries/inside/projects/urban/.

The New Deal Stage: Selections from the Federal Theatre Project, 1935–1939 (Library of Congress/American Memory) includes more than 13,000 images of items selected from the Federal Theatre Project Collection at LC. Featured are stage and costume designs, still photographs, posters, and scripts for productions of *Macbeth* and *The Tragical History of Dr. Faustus* as staged by Orson Welles, and for *Power*, a topical drama of the period (more than 3,000 images). Also included are 68 other play scripts (6,500 images) and 168 documents selected from the Federal Theatre Project administrative records (3,700 images). Available at http://memory.loc.gov/ammem/fedtp/fthome.html.

Performing Arts in America, 1875–1923 (The New York Public Library) consists of visual and audio images drawn from the extensive archival collections at NYPL. The site features an authentic look at this past, from the Broadway theater and Tin Pan Alley to the art of dancer Loie Fuller and composer Charles Griffes. The overall richness of these collections is demonstrated by the variety of complementary original resources that, studied together, can inform and further an understanding of one artist, an entire production, or a whole era. Included are clippings from a broad range of newspapers; composite photographs, or "keysheets," that contain large numbers of reduced-size promotional shots; music sheet samples featuring popular music, show tunes, jazz, and dance music; photographs of theater, dance, and popular performance; and publicity posters and lobby cards, the latter produced in the early years of the film industry and used in theater lobbies to promote films. Available at http://digital.nypl.org/lpa/nypl/lpa_home4.html.

The Printed Ephemera Collection (Library of Congress/American Memory) comprises 28,000 primary-source items of Americana dating from the seventeenth century to the present and encompassing key events and eras in American history. The first release of the digitized Printed Ephemera Collection presented more than 7,000 items. The next release presented more than 10,000 items. While the broadside format represents the bulk of the collection, there is a significant number of leaflets and some pamphlets. Rich in variety, the collection includes proclamations, advertisements, blank forms, programs, election tickets, catalogs, clippings, timetables, and menus. They capture the everyday activities of ordinary people who participated in the events of nation building and experienced the growth of the nation from the American Revolution through the Industrial Revolution up to present day. A future final release will include thousands of oversize items in the collection. Available at http://memory.loc.gov/ammem/rbpehtml/pehome.html.

Ringling Theatre Collection (University of Florida) is a vast collection of source material and memorabilia relating to all aspects of circus life. In the course of bringing the material to the Internet, the collection's index, linking individuals to images, was converted from a card file to an SQL database. The database's information was subsequently updated with full names, birth and death dates, and information about the sex and nationality of those depicted. In addition, keywords—a shortened list of terms taken from LC's *Thesaurus of Graphic Materials*—were assigned to images, allowing them to be searched by subject for the first time. Searching is handled by passing queries to the SQL database through Active Server Pages. Retrieved records are subsequently rendered for display using HTML templates. Available at http://web.uflib.ufl.edu/digital/collections/theatre/ringling/.

Touring West: 19th-Century Performing Artists on the Overland Trails (Exhibition, The New York Public Library) celebrates the creators, promoters, and performers of professional theater, music, and dance who toured the American continent. The time frame is defined at one end by the Louisiana Purchase in 1803, and at the other by the Columbian Exposition in Chicago in 1893. Performances are documented through promotional ephemera such as broadsides, programs, flyers, handbills, souvenirs, postcards, and, after 1848, photographs. Through scores and prompt scripts, annotated by musicians and stage managers, users can learn what the audience experienced at the events. Business records, ship or train schedules, and shipping manifestos speak to the realities of the tour. Available at http://www.nypl.org/west/tw_subhome.shtml.

The Vault at Pfaff's: An Archive of Art and Literature by New York City's Nineteenth-Century Bohemians (Lehigh University). Charles Pfaff's beer cellar in lower Manhattan was a magnet for some of the most unconventional and creative individuals of nineteenth-century New York City, including Walt Whitman, poet and actress Adah Issacs Mencken, social critic Henry Clapp, playwright John Brougham, and artist Elihu Vedder. This collection brings together the poetry, drama, art, fiction, and social commentary that the Pfaff's bohemians produced, including the *New York Saturday Press*, the weekly periodical that served as the group's literary organ. Available at http://digital.lib.lehigh.edu/pfaffs/.

The Zora Neale Hurston Plays (Library of Congress/American Memory) is a selection of 10 plays by Hurston (1891–1960), author, anthropologist, and folklorist. Deposited in the U.S. Copyright Office between 1925 and 1944, most of the plays were unpublished until they were rediscovered in the Copyright Deposit Drama Collection in 1997. The plays reflect Hurston's life experience, travels, and research, especially her study of folklore in the African-American South. Totaling 1,068,000 images, the scripts are housed in LC's Manuscript, Music, and Rare Books and Special Collections Divisions. Available at http://lcweb2.loc.gov/ammem/znhhtml/znhhome.html.

3.5.5 Resource Links

(1) Public Access Collections (Digital Library Federation). Available at http://www.hti.umich.edu/cgi/b/bib/bib-idx?c=dlfcoll.

(2) IMLS Digital Collections Registry (Institute of Museum and Library Services). Available at http://imlsdcc.grainger.uiuc.edu/collections/.

(3) UIUC Digital Gateway to Cultural Materials (University of Illinois, Urbana-Champaign). Available at http://nergal.grainger.uiuc.edu/cgi/b/bib/bib-idx.

(4) OAIster (University of Michigan). Available at http://oaister.umdl.umich.edu/o/oaister/.

(5) CONTENTdm: Customer Collections. Available at http://contentdm.com/customers/index.html.

(6) DLF Aquifer (Digital Library Federation). Available at http://www.diglib.org/aquifer/.
    AmericanSouth (Emory University and others)
    http://americansouth.org/
    American West (California Digital Library)
    http://dla.ucop.edu/inside/projects/amwest/

(7) Repositories of Primary Sources (Terry Abraham, University of Idaho). Available at http://www.uidaho.edu/special-collections/Other.Repositories.html.

(8) ArchivesUSA (Chadwyck-Healey). Available at http://archives.chadwyck.com/.

(9) National Union Catalog of Manuscript Collections (Library of Congress). Available at http://www.loc.gov/coll/nucmc/.
    Free Search of the RLG Union Catalog: http://www.loc.gov/coll/nucmc/rlinsearch.html
    Free Search of the OCLC Catalog: http://www.loc.gov/coll/nucmc/oclcsearch.html

(10) Library and Archival Exhibitions on the Web (Smithsonian Institution Libraries). Available at http://www.sil.si.edu/SILPublications/Online-Exhibitions/.

(11) Women and Social Movements in the United States (Alexander Street Press)
    Product Description
    http://www.alexanderstreetpress.com/products/wasm.htm
    Project Notes
    http://womhist.binghamton.edu/notes.htm

3.6 Teaching Applications

3.6.1 A Profusion of Resources

Faculty, English departments, government agencies, textbook publishers, course management software developers, scholarly associations, librarians, database providers, digital content managers, instructional technologists, public media organizations, and even students themselves are all actively involved in developing digital resources for teaching and learning. Acting singly or in concert, they are responsible for a profusion of resources ranging from online syllabi to interactive learning environments. This section samples a small portion of the growing array of digital teaching resources and highlights trends in pedagogy.

In undergraduate teaching, at a basic level, instructors are providing links to relevant online resources through their syllabi, referring students to Bartleby.com for ready reference when the most recent edition is not paramount, exploiting Project Gutenberg for quick look-up of passages or easy classroom projection, and using the electronic companions to standard print anthologies of American literature (1). American literature instructors are also using freely available large text collections such as Making of America and American Memory to "make historicists out of undergraduates" (Hanlon 2005). They are also exploiting the National Archives and Records Administration's Digital Classroom, which makes valuable primary documents accessible and gives ideas about how to use them in the classroom (2).

Scholars at well-resourced institutions are delighted, if somewhat bewildered, by the variety and sophistication of new proprietary full-text databases available to them. They are asking students to gather evidence in new ways while rapidly revising course assignments (3).[61] Institutions with learning management systems (LMS) are struggling to resolve issues of interoperability that will enable faculty to integrate open-access and proprietary databases into structured learning environments. Meanwhile, digital content management software, such as CONTENTdm, can be used with WebCT and Blackboard to integrate digital content into online courses (4). Similarly, textbook companies such as Houghton Mifflin and Heath are working closely with course management-system developers to facilitate the integration of digital content into traditional, hybrid, and online classrooms (5).[62]

3.6.2 From "Dynamic Syllabi" to Digital Learning Environments

Intrepid faculty are creating "dynamic syllabi"[63] (6); developing annotated gateways to American literature (7); substituting hand-craft-

---

[61] For a recent report on using EEBO in teaching and research, see Beer 2005.

[62] Refer to Bass 2001 for a discussion about the interplay between new media and the textbook anthology.

[63] The American Studies Association's Crossroad Web site offers a definition of dynamic syllabi and has an (outdated) annotated directory of examples. Available at http://www.georgetown.edu/crossroads/webcourses.html.

ed online anthologies for print editions (8); scanning, transcribing, and editing digital texts (9); and creating digital collections so that students can explore primary sources outside the archives (10). Stephen Railton's premier Web project, Mark Twain in His Times, along with Uncle Tom's Cabin & American Culture, and *Absalom, Absalom!* Electronic, Interactive! Chronology, are the leading examples of sophisticated, multidimensional digital collections, offering texts and contexts for in-depth exploration and interpretation (11). Pointing the way to the future, the California Digital Library, in consultation with a faculty advisory board, has launched American West, which aims to create a digital learning environment, building on its eScholarship Editions and the Online Archive of California to leverage diverse and distributed resources, targeting different constituents in various educational settings (12).

The creators of the thematic research collections have all developed companion teaching resources. For example, the Women Writers Project (Brown University) provides selected syllabi and teaching support (13). The Classroom Electric: Dickinson, Whitman and American Culture is a "constellation of Web sites," including the Dickinson Electronic Archives and the Walt Whitman Electronic Archive, drawing on the work of 15 scholars and making it possible to search their resources by site, keyword, poet, creator, or theme (14).

3.6.3 Taking a Closer Look: Syllabus Finder

Catching more than one million syllabi in its net, Syllabus Finder, an experimental tool under development at George Mason University's Center for History and New Media, holds great promise to inform the curious about who is teaching what, where, for whom, and, to some extent, how—that is, with what assignments and resources (15). A March 2005 search of "American literature" and "Web" retrieved more than 2,460 results, far too many to peruse productively until the tool is refined (as planned), so results can be processed, manipulated, and stored in various ways. On the other hand, searching to find references to "Wright American Fiction" retrieved a manageable 32 results.

Wonder if courses in bibliography and research methods are ghosts of the past? Not at more than a dozen institutions, including Louisiana State University, where the English Department's graduate seminar description reads:

> The visionary world of literary scholarship turns on the greasy axle of the print media and their various successors. This course will introduce students to the physical history, indeed archaeology of learning, beginning with early manuscripts and hand-press imprints and climaxing with futuristic digital archives. Canons, attributions, authorship, editions, evidence, the history of research, research resources, obscurantia, and the nature of a scholarly career will be but a few of the topics considered by the professor and by a whizzing carousel of exciting and often erudite guest speakers. Occasional off-site excursions will add to the adventure (16).

The potential to use Syllabus Finder in trend analysis will grow
as more and more institutions worldwide make their syllabi available to the public through the Web, adding to our knowledge, for
example, about the adoption of digital resources.[64]

3.6.4 Intentional Change: The Visible Knowledge Project (17)

As a participant in the Visible Knowledge Project (VKP), Professor Edward J. Gallagher of Lehigh University thoughtfully engages
new media.[65] VKP is a five-year, multiagency, national initiative,
directed by Randy Bass, associate provost for teaching and learning
at Georgetown University. Now in its final year of "synthesis and
findings," the VKP aims to improve college and university teaching in American Studies "through a focus on both student learning
and faculty development in technology-enhanced environments." In
an article entitled "History and the New Technology: The Missing
Link," Gallagher, a VKP independent investigator, describes how he
uses technology to meet three pedagogical objectives: investigation,
collaboration, and publication (Gallagher 2004a).

To support "investigation," Gallagher has created two teaching
"archives"—The Enola Gay Controversy and The Vietnam Wall—for
his "inquiry-driven first-year writing courses." These highly structured archives of annotated primary source material are fertile
ground for students to confront how the past is interpreted through
the lens of a war that "we won" and one that "we lost." Gallagher
also describes a "completely different kind of investigative archival
experience" in a team-taught "Virtual Americana" course that relies
on five collections from the Library of Congress's American Memory
in lieu of a textbook (18).

To support "collaboration," Gallagher seeks to improve the un-
glamorous "discussion board," which he views as "the most under-
valued of the new technologies." His basic premise is that "discussion boards have an enormous potential to enhance critical thinking
and the sense of community." Gallagher uses his lower-level undergraduate course "American Literature: The Essentials" as the testing
ground to strengthen the discussion board as a pedagogical tool.
By the end of the course, his students describe the main goal of the
discussion board as "facilitating interaction leading to better understanding" with half of them feeling that it ultimately added value to
their learning and the other half expressing "strong mixed or negative responses," Gallagher discloses in his project report. The framework that Gallagher developed for his students to start a discussion
in the online environment, which he calls "The Five Eyes," proved so
successful that he is considering applying it to writing assignments,
replacing full-length essays with paragraph-level writing structured

---

[64] Syllabus Finder was developed by Daniel J. Cohen, assistant professor of
history and art history, and director of research projects at the Center for History
and New Media at George Mason University. He used it as the basis for an
analysis of textbook adoption in U.S. history survey courses. See Cohen 2005.

[65] For more details, refer to the citations by Hatch et al. 2004, Gallagher 2004a and
2004b, Gallagher et. al 2004, and Bass et al. 1998.

by the "eyes." Described more fully in his report about the course, the "Five Eyes" are

1. hypothesize: what is the film or story about?
2. analyze: how does it work?
3. synthesize: how does it compare with others?
4. internalize: how does it relate to me?
5. criticize: what is your evaluation of it? (19)

Finally, in support of "publication" Gallagher's Reel American History is an "archive built by novices" that serves as a cumulative virtual performance or workspace for graduate and undergraduate student projects on films about American history. He not only testifies that students "do better work when they are publicly accountable," as suggested by Bass (Bass et al. 1998), but also extols the continuous nature of the site that engenders a fluid, evolving, multilayered perspective reflecting multiple generations of students, and even permitting the original student creators to add "layers" in the future (20).

Fulfilling the promise of its name, the VKP has involved more than 70 faculty members from 21 campuses; some of their work is prominently displayed in the VKP Gallery (21). Here one will find valuable case studies organized around three major themes: critical reading, multimedia authoring, and online discussion.

Active and critical reading addresses the question: How do both novices and experts read texts and images, especially as new technologies transform reading practices? To cite two examples: Randy Bass's project, "An Inquiry into Student Reading Practices in a 19th-Century American Literature Course," charts the evolution of his pedagogic objectives over a seven-year period. Meanwhile, Wyn Kelley, senior lecturer in the Department of Literature at Massachusetts Institute of Technology, explores the use of multimedia annotation for close reading and analytical writing in her project, "Midnight Forecastle: A Classroom Database" (22).

The other two themes receive similar close attention and evaluation. The VKP is the best example of a large-scale professional development strategy, involving numerous faculty members in American literature, to construct a pedagogic framework at the intersection of teaching and new media. It further distinguishes itself as a collaborative effort bringing together key organizations that hold a stake in the scholarship of teaching in a particular interdisciplinary area with participation by the American Studies Association's Crossroads Project, the American Social History Project (City University of New York Graduate Center), the Center for History and New Media (George Mason University), the TLT (Teaching, Learning, and Technology) Group of the American Association for Higher Education, and the Carnegie Foundation for the Advancement of Teaching. The Visible Knowledge Projects leave a rich legacy of case studies and the potential for an ongoing networked learning community.

3.6.5 The Role of Professional Organizations

How are other national organizations helping to advance teaching and learning through the application of new technologies? The American Studies Association (ASA) aims to provide its members with an integrated platform to Communities, Technology & Learning, Curriculum, and Reference & Research (23). Now celebrating its tenth anniversary, Crossroads is fully integrated into ASA's Web site, and Randy Bass, who serves as project director, enjoys the same status as the editor of ASA's flagship journal, *American Quarterly*. Regrettably, neither the Curriculum nor Technology & Learning sections are as actively maintained as one might hope, but there are some useful entry points. For example, Innovistas (Technology & Learning) showcases "high-quality, content-rich online projects" in the categories of exhibits, curriculum, collections, and directories, asking their creators to reflect on four questions:

1. What is the content and purpose of your site?
2. How does your site enhance the *accessibility* of these materials beyond what is available in print?
3. How does new media technology change *the reader's experience* with these materials? How are these materials enhanced by being in electronic form?
4. How do concepts and scholarship of American culture and history studies influence the way your site presents material? (24)

Turning to other scholarly associations, the Society of Early Americanists' Web site promotes a syllabus exchange and has a section on "Teaching Early American Topics" with links to bibliographies, Internet resources, films, graphics, student assignments, student Web projects, study aids, and online articles on pedagogy (25). Not as up-to-date or well maintained as one would hope, it nonetheless points to useful materials, including Scott Ellis's 2003 article, "Early American Print Culture in a Digital Age: Pedagogical Possibilities." Ellis describes how his course design deliberately reflected the progressive stages of print culture and the public sphere in early America that Michael Warner discusses in *Letters of the Republic* through the increasingly open use of technology to encourage public debate.[66]

Joanna Brooks's (2004) "New Media Prospect: A Review of Web Resources in Early American Studies," published in *Early American Literature*, stands out as a lonely example of a broad, discipline-based review of digital resources appearing in a core American literature journal. Brooks astutely points out (as discussed in elsewhere in this report) that teachers of American literature, in sharp contrast to historians, have no Web site comparable to History Matters, "a beautifully designed, impeccably maintained, multidimensional web resource" (26). History Matters carefully selects its content to illustrate the very best work. "Secrets of great history teachers" features inter-

---

[66] See also Ellis 2002.

views with only 14 teachers; likewise, "syllabus central" annotates just 14 creative approaches to teaching. The "digital blackboard" has 77 annotated entries, including many developed by the Library of Congress in conjunction with American Memory and the National Archives and Records Administration's Digital Classroom. "Students as historians" presents examples of innovative projects undertaken by history students, from high school to graduate school, ranging from oral histories to visual essays or exhibits. In "making sense of evidence" teachers of American literature will find expert advice about the effective use of primary sources. This section features a series of guides about how historians use different types of documents (oral history, films, maps, numbers, letters and diaries, advertisements, popular song and photography) also relevant to literary scholars, and "scholars in action" provides audio interviews with teachers who analyze their strategies when confronted by evidence in political cartoons, household inventories, songs, photographs, letters, speeches, newspapers, and literature. American literary scholar, Hans Bergmann (now dean of the College of Liberal Arts at Quinnipiac University) discusses approaches to interpreting Herman Melville's short story "Bartleby, the Scrivener," published in 1853 (27).

Instructors of American literature who turn to the MLA's Web site will be hard pressed to find many useful resources pertaining to teaching (28). A number of the links are out of date or broken. "Teaching with the Web: Two Approaches" connects to an article that appeared in the February 1998 Teaching column of the AHA's *Perspectives* newsletter.

3.6.6 Engaging Departments of English, American Studies, and Students

Some departments of English and American Studies programs are sponsoring long-term collaborative Web projects such as Voices from the Gap at the University of Minnesota (29) or those featured by the American Studies Program at Washington State University (30). The English Department at the University of Virginia features faculty e-text and hypertext projects prominently at its Web site, offering visible evidence of the extent to which their faculty's electronic projects are integral to the institution's teaching and research mission (31). Living up to its motto, "We DO American Studies," Virginia's American Studies program Web site is maintained by students who are also involved in digital conversion of print texts and the development of collateral satellite projects (32). In addition, students collaborate in the creation of the Yellow Pages, a directory of links to American Studies content on the Web. Students have also created other innovative Web content, the most technically advanced of which is America in the 1930s. The Web directory of students' Master of Arts final projects, going back to 1995, is a digital showcase for the American Studies program. In "New Paradigms for Teaching and Learning: Four Case Studies," Alan B. Howard, associate professor of American Studies, argues that AS@UVA, along with three faculty-driven projects (Uncle Tom's Cabin, The Valley of the Shadow: Two Communities in the Civil War, and The Salem Witchcraft Trials Documentary Archive and Transcription Project) are transforming teaching and learning at the University of Virginia (Howard 2004) (33).67

The English Department at University of California-Santa Barbara, offers another model of innovation through the integration of technology into the curriculum and research. Its undergraduate major was recently redesigned with several specializations, including Literature & Culture of Information, intended for students interested in the relationships between literature and digital technology. The Transcriptions project supports advanced research that is then applied to the new major (34). It is one of few examples where the laboratory research environment is embedded within an academic department rather than located in a separate humanities computing institute or e-text center.

Two faculty members from liberal arts colleges report on their experience in introducing text encoding into the undergraduate curriculum. They advise: "Faculty, students, and librarians from six colleges are analyzing archival and literary texts by applying standards developed by the TEI. One developing pedagogical model involves history students producing comparative editions of a document by transcribing and encoding the primary source material from the college archives" (Ebert-Zawasky and Tomasek [n.d.]).

At Emory University, Sheila Cavanagh, professor of English, uses the Emory Women Writers Project as a pedagogical tool to train new literary professionals by giving graduate students the opportunity to edit their own texts (35).68 At the University of Maryland, Martha Nell Smith, editor of the Dickinson Electronic Archives, regularly teaches a graduate seminar related to digital culture (36). There will be, no doubt, a growing body of digital content resulting from dissertation research such as American Women and Dime Novels: Dime Novels for Women, 1870–1920, created by Felicia L. Carr (George Mason University) (37). In a letter to readers, Carr acknowledges that while the "project is still in its infancy," she envisions it "as the premiere on-line source for information about women's dime novels." Even in its present state, Carr's site is a valuable resource and has unique information, including an annotated list of archival and special collections around the country that contain women's dime novels.

As a new generation of Ph.D.s with experience in humanities computing and digital text production moves into full-time teaching appointments, the curriculum is bound to change. To cite two examples: Stephen Ramsay (38) and Matthew Kirschenbaum (39) received their Ph.D.s in English at the University of Virginia, where they were also trained in humanities computing at IATH. Now on the faculty

---

67 For other thought-provoking articles by leading thinkers about whether or not technology is "transforming" teaching, refer to the 2004 issue of *Rethinking History*, in particular to Brown, Cohen, Dennis et al., and Gallagher. See also Claxton and Cooper 2000.

68 See Flanders 2002 for a discussion about the pedagogical aims of Brown University's Women Writers Online.

in the English departments at the University of Georgia and the University of Maryland, respectively, they teach courses such as "Digital Narratives," "Introduction to Humanities Computing," and "Computer and Text." It should come as no surprise that they are both researchers on the national team led by John Unsworth (University of Illinois, Urbana-Champaign) to develop NORA, a suite of analytical tools for large, full-text archives, under development with support from The Andrew W. Mellon Foundation (40).

3.6.7 Resource Links

(1) American Literature: Post-Civil War to the Present (Karen Graffney, Raritan Valley Community College, North Branch, New Jersey). Available at http://www.raritanval.edu/departments/English/fulltime/Gaffney/gaffney.htm. See spring 2004 course, which makes use of Bartleby, Project Gutenberg, and the Heath anthology Web site, among other publicly accessible resources.

(2) Digital Classroom (National Archives and Records Administration). Available at http://www.archives.gov/digital_classroom/index.html.

(3) EEBO in Education. Available from the Text Creation Partnership Web site, this suite of pages gives examples of assignments, projects, syllabi, and EEBO undergraduate student essay award winners. Available at http://www.lib.umich.edu/tcp/eebo/.

(4) CONTENTdm. Available at http://contentdm.com/index.html.

(5) *The Heath Anthology of American Literature,* 4th edition, Paul Lauter (Trinity College), et al., eds. Available at http://college.hmco.com/english/lauter/heath/4e/students/index.html. The companion Web site to the print anthology offers free access to timelines, author profiles, and resources for instructors. "The Internet Research Guide," contributed by Jason Snart (University of Florida) at the Student Resource Center, covers such topics as the purpose of research, evaluating information, constructing arguments, and plagiarism.

The Norton Anthology of American Literature, 6th edition, Nina Baym (University of Illinois, Urbana-Champaign), et al., eds. This resource is adopted for use by more than 1,640 college and universities worldwide. Available at http://wwnorton.com/college/titles/english/naal6/. It offers a publicly accessible ancillary Web site with timelines and maps, self-grading quizzes, and overviews by period; author resource pages for 160 of the writers included in the anthology; and searchable "Explorations" sections that provide generative questions and projects that help students draw connections, close-read text, and link texts to contexts." Links to full text from the anthology are accessible to subscribers only, but there is a wealth of free material, including links to other public Web sites. http://wwnorton.com/college/titles/english/naal6/emedia.htm.

Houghton Mifflin. EduSpace is a classroom-management system powered by Blackboard and designed to bring customizable Houghton Mifflin content and interactive communication tools to any classroom. Available at http://college.hmco.com/eduspace/.

(6) Laura Arnold Liebman (English Department, Reed College). Professor Liebman's home page offers links to her pedagogy, emphasizing problem-based learning and featuring use of the Web and her course syllabi. Available at http://academic.reed.edu/english/faculty/laura.html.

(7) American Literature (Donna M. Campbell, Washington State University). American Literature is discussed in section 3.1 of this report. Available at http://www.wsu.edu/~campbelld/index.html.

(8) Ralph Bauer (Department of English, University of Maryland). Available at http://www.mith2.umd.edu/fellows/bauer/home.html. Follow the course links from Professor Bauer's home page to see how he populates his syllabi with "Online Anthology" and "Resources" (print and digital).

(9) The Jesuit Relations and Allied Documents, 1610 to 1791 (Raymond A. Bucko, Department of Anthropology and Sociology, Creighton University). Available at http://puffin.creighton.edu/jesuit/relations/.

(10) The Jesuit Plantation Project (American Studies Program, Georgetown University). Available at http://www.georgetown.edu/departments/amer_studies/jpp/coverjpp.html.

(11) American Literature since 1865 (Steven Railton, English Department, University of Virginia). Available at http://etext.lib.virginia.edu/railton/enam312/index.html.
> *Absalom, Absalom!* **Electronic, Interactive! Chronology**
> http://etext.lib.virginia.edu/railton/absalom/
> **Mark Twain in His Times**
> http://etext.lib.virginia.edu/railton/index2.html
> **Uncle Tom's Cabin & American Culture: A Multi-Media Archive**
> http://www.iath.virginia.edu/utc/

(12) American West (California Digital Library). Available at http://www.cdlib.org/inside/projects/amwest/.
> **eScholarship Editions** at http://texts.cdlib.org/escholarship/
> **Online Archive of California** at http://www.oac.cdlib.org/

(13) Syllabi and Teaching Projects, Women Writers Project (Brown University). Available at http://www.wwp.brown.edu/texts/syllabi/index.html.

(14) The Classroom Electric: Dickinson, Whitman and American Culture (sponsored in part by the U.S. Department of Education's Fund for the Improvement of Post-Secondary Education). Available at http://jefferson.village.virginia.edu/fdw/.

(15) Syllabus Finder (Daniel J. Cohen, Center for History and New Media, George Mason University). Available at http://chnm.gmu.edu/tools/syllabi/.

(16) Graduate Seminars (English Department, Louisiana State University). Available at http://www.english.lsu.edu/dept/programs/grad/courses.doc.

(17) Visible Knowledge Project (Georgetown University). Available at http://crossroads.georgetown.edu/vkp/.

(18) Enola Gay Controversy (Edward J. Gallagher, Lehigh University). Available at http://www.lehigh.edu/~ineng/enola/.
    The Vietnam Memorial (Edward J. Gallagher, Lehigh University). Available at http://www.lehigh.edu/~ejg1/vietnam/.

Virtual Americana (from Students as Historians, History Matters, George Mason University). Describes the team-taught online course offered at Lehigh University, relying on the Library of Congress's American Memory for primary source material. Available at http://www.lehigh.edu/~ineng/VirtualAmericana/VA-title.html .

(19) Improving the Discussion Board: A Scholarship of Teaching and Learning Project for The Visible Knowledge Project by Edward Gallagher, Professor of English, and Lehigh Lab Fellow, Lehigh University, with assistance from Stephen A. Tompkins, December 2004. Available at http://www.lehigh.edu/~ineng/discussion/1overview/0-title.html.

(20) Reel American History (Edward J. Gallagher, Lehigh University). Available at http://www.lehigh.edu/~ineng/ejg/ejg-first.htm.

(21) VKP Gallery (Georgetown University). Available at http://crossroads.georgetown.edu/vkp/.

(22) VKP Gallery: Active and Critical Reading (Georgetown University). Available at http://crossroads.georgetown.edu/vkp/themes/poster_showcase_reading.htm. From here, link to the projects and posters of Randy Bass, Wyn Kelley, and others.

(23) American Studies Crossroads Project (Georgetown University). Available at http://crossroads.georgetown.edu/.

(24) Innovistas (Georgetown University). Available at http://www.georgetown.edu/crossroads/innovistas/index.html.

(25) Society of Early Americanists (School of Humanities, University of California, Irvine). Available at http://www.hnet.uci.edu/mclark/seapage.htm. **Teaching Early American Topics** at http://www.mnstate.edu/seateaching/.

(26) History Matters: The U.S. Survey Course on the Web (George Mason University). Available at http://historymatters.gmu.edu/.

(27) Analyze a Melville Short Story (Scholars in Action, History Matters). Available at http://historymatters.gmu.edu/mse/sia/melvillestory.htm.

(28) Teaching Resources (Modern Language Association). A stale list of eight links leading to many dead ends. Available at http://www.mla.org/grad_portal_teach/.

(29) English Department (University of Minnesota). Projects and publications. Available at http://english.cla.umn.edu/projects/.

(30) Program in American Studies (Washington State University). Available at http://libarts.wsu.edu/amerst/.

(31) English Department (University of Virginia). Available at http://www.engl.virginia.edu/.

(32) AS@UVA (University of Virginia). Available at http://xroads.virginia.edu/.

> **Hypertexts**
> http://xroads.virginia.edu/~HYPER/hypertex.html
> **Henry Nash Smith's** *Virgin Land: The American West as Symbol and Myth*
> http://xroads.virginia.edu/~HYPER/HNS/hns_home.html
> **Alexis de Tocqueville's** *Democracy in America*
> http://xroads.virginia.edu/~HYPER/DETOC/home.html
> **Allan Trachtenberg's** *The Incorporation of America*
> http://xroads.virginia.edu/~HYPER/INCORP/cover.html
> **Herman Melville's** *Billy Budd*
> http://xroads.virginia.edu/~HYPER/bb/bb_main.html
> **Herman Melville's** *The Confidence Man: His Masquerade*
> http://xroads.virginia.edu/~MA96/atkins/cmmain.html
> **Cultural Maps**
> http://xroads.virginia.edu/~MAP/map_hp.html
> **The Capitol Project**
> http://xroads.virginia.edu/~CAP/cap_home.html
> **Yellow Pages**
> http://xroads.virginia.edu/~YP/yp_home.html
> **America in the 1930s (**a directory of links to American Studies content on the Web)
> http://xroads.virginia.edu/~1930s/front.html

M.A. Final Projects in American Studies at UVa
http://xroads.virginia.edu/~AS@UVA/theses.html

(33) Uncle Tom's Cabin & American Culture: A Multimedia Archive (Stephen Railton, University of Virginia). Available at http://www.iath.virginia.edu/utc/. See "Interpret Mode" for timeline, virtual exhibits, lesson plans (high school and undergraduate).

The Valley of the Shadow: Two Communities in the Civil War (Edward Ayers and Will Thomas, University of Virginia). Available at http://valley.vcdh.virginia.edu/.
   Teaching Resources (topics for high school and undergraduate student papers).
   http://www.vcdh.virginia.edu/teaching/vclassroom/vclass contents.html

The Salem Witchcraft Trials Documentary Archive and Transcription Project (Benjamin Ray, University of Virginia). Available at http://etext.virginia.edu/salem/witchcraft/.
   Salem Witch Trials in Literature and History, An undergraduate course, University of Virginia, Fall 2002
   http://cti.itc.virginia.edu/%7Ebcr/relg415_02/

(34) English Department (University of California-Santa Barbara). Available at http://english.ucsb.edu/.
   Literature and Culture of Information
   http://transcriptions.english.ucsb.edu/curriculum/index.asp
   Transcriptions Project
   http://transcriptions.english.ucsb.edu/

(35) Emory Women Writers Resource Project (Sheila Cavanagh, Emory University). Available at http://chaucer.library.emory.edu/wwrp/.

(36) Archives in the Classroom (Martha Nell Smith, University of Maryland). Available at http://www.emilydickinson.org/classroom/classdex.html.

(37) American Women and Dime Novels: Dime Novels for Women, 1870–1920 (Felicia L. Carr, George Mason University). Available at http://chnm.gmu.edu/dimenovels/about.html.
   Dime Novel Archives at http://chnm.gmu.edu/dimenovels/archives.html.

(38) Stephen Ramsay (University of Georgia). Available at http://cantor.english.uga.edu/cocoon/home/cantor.html.
   Digital Narratives
   http://cantor.english.uga.edu/cocoon/home/engl4890.html
   Introduction to Humanities Computing
   http://cantor.english.uga.edu/cocoon/home/engl4888.html

(39) Matthew G. Kirschenbaum (University of Maryland). Available at http://www.otal.umd.edu/~mgk/blog/.
> **Computer and Text**
> http://www.otal.umd.edu/~mgk/courses/spring2004/467/
> **Digital Studies**
> http://www.otal.umd.edu/~mgk/courses/spring2004/668/

(40) NORA (John Unsworth et al., Graduate School of Library and Information Science, University of Illinois, Urbana-Champaign). Available at http://noraproject.org.

APPENDIX 1:

Interviewees

Douglas Basford
Douglas Basford is a Johns Hopkins University alumnus who lectures for the university's Writing Seminars Department in the School of Arts and Sciences.

Randall Bass
Randy Bass is executive director of Georgetown's Center for New Designs in Learning and Scholarship, a university-wide center supporting faculty work in new learning and research environments. He directs the Visible Knowledge Project (VKP), which explores the impact of technology on learning in the humanities. In conjunction with the VKP, he is director of the American Studies Crossroads Project. Bass is associate professor of English and a member of the American Studies Committee at Georgetown University.

Ralph Bauer
Ralph Bauer is associate professor and director of English Honors, Department of English, at the University of Maryland. He serves as director of the Early Americas Digital Archive supported by the Maryland Institute for Technology in the Humanities.

Peg Bessette
Peg Bessette, product manager in the Academic/Public/ARL market group at Thomson Gale, is responsible for the development of print and electronic resources in the areas of literature, performing arts, and humanities, including such resources as the *Literature Resource Center, Dictionary of Literary Biography, Contemporary Literary Criticism—Select, What Do I Read Next?* and Gale's *MLA International Bibliography* offerings on InfoTrac and the Literature Resource Center.

Nicole Bouché
Nicole Bouché is Pacific Northwest curator, Special Collections, University of Washington Libraries. She was formerly head of the Manuscript Unit of the Beinecke Rare Book and Manuscript Library at Yale University.

Donna M. Campbell
Donna M. Campbell is associate professor of English at Washington State University. She is the author of *Resisting Regionalism: Gender and Naturalism in American Fiction, 1885–1915* (1997). Recent publications

include essays in *Twisted from the Ordinary: Essays on American Literary Naturalism*, edited by Mary E. Papke, *Middlebrow Moderns: Popular Women Writers of the 1920s*, edited by Lisa Botshon and Meredith Goldsmith, and *The Novel and the American Left*. She writes the annual Fiction: 1900–1930 chapter for *American Literary Scholarship* (Duke University Press).

Rosemary Feal

Rosemary Feal is executive director of the Modern Language Association. Feal's active involvement with the MLA began in 1988, when she was appointed to the association's delegate assembly. Prior to her appointment as executive director she was a professor of Spanish and chair of the Department of Modern Languages and Literatures in the College of Arts and Sciences at the University at Buffalo.

Wayne Franklin

Wayne Franklin is Davis Professor of English at Northeastern University. He was recently awarded a Guggenheim Fellowship for his work on James Fenimore Cooper, the American novelist credited with the invention of the frontier novel, the sea novel, and the American historical romance.

Todd Gilman

Todd Gilman is librarian for literature in English at Yale University. He is a member of the Modern Language Association, secretary of the Literatures in English Section of the Association of College & Research Libraries of the American Library Association, and board member of the Northeast American Society for Eighteenth-Century Studies.

Michael Grossberg

Michael Grossberg is professor of history and law at Indiana University and editor of the *American Historical Review*. He has published several articles on scholarly editing and is a founder of the History Cooperative, an electronic publishing project devoted to historical scholarship. Through the cooperative he has overseen the development of projects in digital scholarship and participated in the creation of policies on such issues as the review of electronic books and the archiving of digital journals.

James L. Harner

James Harner is Samuel Rhea Gammon Professor of Liberal Arts and Professor of English at Texas A&M University. In addition to editing the *World Shakespeare Bibliography Online*, he is the author of 12 books, including *Literary Research Guide: A Guide to Reference Sources for the Study of Literatures in English and Related Topics* (5th ed. forthcoming) and *On Compiling an Annotated Bibliography* (2nd ed.). He received the Besterman Medal (1977) and Besterman/McColvin Medal (2001) from the Library Association (London).

Mark Kamrath

Mark Kamrath is associate professor of English at the University of Central Florida and is actively involved in its Ph.D. program in texts and technology. He has worked on the Willa Cather Scholarly Edition for several years and served as a Modern Language Association Committee on Special Editions' inspector. He is general editor of the *Charles Brockden Brown Electronic Archive and Scholarly Edition* and is working with a collective of scholars to publish Brown's later writing in both print and digital formats. He also serves on the NINES Steering Committee.

Eileen Lawrence

Eileen Lawrence is vice president of sales and marketing at Alexander Street Press. She has worked with academic libraries since 1980. Before launching Alexander Street Press, she was vice president of sales for the former Chadwyck-Healey Company, where she introduced more than a dozen new products to libraries and built in-house and field sales teams. She developed innovative pricing models, making possible patron access to previously out-of-reach data, and created innovative ways for consortia of all sizes to acquire electronic materials.

Alan Liu

Alan Liu is a professor in the English Department at the University of California, Santa Barbara (UCSB). His central interests are British Romantic literature and art, information culture, new media, literary theory, and cultural studies. He is the author of *Wordsworth: The Sense of History* and *The Laws of Cool: Knowledge Work and the Culture of Information*. His major Web projects include the Voice of the Shuttle, Palinurus: The Academy and the Corporation, and the Romantic Chronology, (coedited with Laura Mandell). He is director of the English Department's curricular development project titled Transcriptions: Literary History and the Culture of Information. He codirects (with Rita Raley) the Literature and Culture of Information specialization in the UCSB English Department and co-organized the department's Public Humanities Initiative. He serves on the NINES editorial board for Romantic scholarship.

Mary Loeffelholz

Mary Loeffelholz is professor of English at Northeastern University and editor of *Studies in American Fiction*. Selected publications include *Dickinson and the Boundaries of Feminist Theory; Experimental Lives: Women and Literature, 1900–1945; From School To Salon: Reading Nineteenth-Century American Women's Poetry* (2004); "Dickinson's 'Decoration,'" forthcoming in *English Literary History*; "Stedman's Black Atlantic," forthcoming in *Victorian Poetry*; "The Religion of Art in the City at War," *American Literary History*; and "Who Killed Lucretia Davidson? or Poetry in the Domestic-Tutelary Complex," in the *Yale Journal of Criticism*.

Jack Lynch

Jack Lynch is associate professor in the English Department of the Newark campus of Rutgers University, specializing in English literature of the eighteenth century. He has edited a number of publications, including most recently *Anniversary Essays on Johnson's Dictionary* (2005), a collection that he co-edited with Anne McDermott. Among his Web sites are Literary Resources on the Web and Eighteenth-Century Resources.

Shawn Martin

Shawn Martin is the Text Creation Partnership outreach librarian at the University of Michigan. He has worked for several years in digital libraries, including the Digital Library Project at the Colonial Williamsburg Foundation and the Ohio Memory Project at the Ohio Historical Society. He has served as adjunct faculty at the School of Library and Information Science at Indiana University. He serves on the board of the American Association for History and Computing and is working on his master of science in information at the University of Michigan's School of Information.

Jerome McGann

Jerome McGann is the John Stewart Bryan University Professor at the University of Virginia (UVa). He is a cofounder of UVa's Institute for Advanced Technology in the Humanities and the founder of NINES. His online The Rossetti Archive has been a highly influential digital humanities project, and his book *Radiant Textuality: Literature after the World Wide Web* (2001) won the Modern Language Association's James Russell Lowell Award. He is a member of the American Academy of Arts and Sciences and of the American Council of Learned Societies' Commission on Cyberinfrastructure for the Humanities and Social Sciences. Most recently, he founded the tools development group Applied Research in Patacriticism, which is building several important tools for high-level interpretative investigation of humanities and social sciences materials, including Ivanhoe, Juxta, and Collex.

Meredith McGill

Meredith McGill is associate professor and director of the graduate program in the English Department at Rutgers University, New Brunswick. Her primary fields of research are nineteenth-century American literature, history of the book, law and literature, American poetry and poetics, and literary and cultural theory.

William McPheron

William McPheron is William Saroyan Curator for British and American Literature and head of the Humanities Resource Group at Stanford University Libraries. He has played a leading role in the Lots of Copies Keeps Stuff Safe (LOCKSS) Humanities Project, which seeks to identify and preserve "born-digital" journals that have long-term value to scholars.

Eric Lease Morgan

Eric Lease Morgan is head of the Digital Access and Information Architecture Department at the University Libraries of Notre Dame. He also maintains the Alex Catalogue of Electronic Texts, a small, full-text collection of American and English literature as well as of Western philosophy. Some of his other work in the maintenance of digital collections includes the Mr. Serials Process, a method for systematically collecting electronic serials, and MyLibrary, a user-driven, customizable interface to digital library collections and services.

Jeffrey Moyer

Jeff Moyer, Publisher–Research Collections in the Academic/Public/ARL market group at Thomson Gale, is responsible for the film and digital collection publishing programs, including Eighteenth Century Collections Online, The Making of the Modern Economy, and The Making of Modern Law. Moyer oversees publishing under the Primary Source Microfilm and Scholarly Resources brands.

James Nagel

James Nagel is the J. O. Eidson Distinguished Professor of American Literature at the University of Georgia. Early in his career he founded the scholarly journal *Studies in American Fiction* and the series Critical Essays on American Literature, which published 156 volumes of scholarship. Among his 20 books are *Stephen Crane and Literary Impressionism*, *Hemingway in Love and War*, and *The Contemporary American Short-Story Cycle*. His current projects include *The Houghton-Mifflin Anthology of the American Short Story*, *The Blackwell Companion to the American Short Story* (with Alfred Bendixen), and two more volumes on the story cycle in the United States. He is also the executive coordinator of the American Literature Association.

John Mark Ockerbloom

John Ockerbloom is a digital library architect and planner for the University of Pennsylvania Library. His areas of interest include digital preservation, online learning systems and their relationships to digital repositories, distributed knowledge bases, and enhancing open access to information. Since the 1990s, he has worked on systems to aid in the documentation and use of digital formats (including his current work on TOM and Fred), which is funded by The Andrew W. Mellon Foundation. He founded and edits The Online Books Page.

Kenneth M. Price

Kenneth Price is Hillegass Professor of Nineteenth-Century American Literature in the English Department at the University of Nebraska, Lincoln. He is coeditor with Ed Folsom (University of Iowa) of The Walt Whitman Hypertext Archive and with Martha Nell Smith of The Classroom Electric: Dickinson, Whitman, and American Culture. Price teaches courses in American literature and culture. He is finishing a book on Whitman and cultural iconography and is engaged in a long-term effort to reedit Whitman's works on the Web. He serves on the NINES Steering Committee.

Stephen Railton

Stephen Railton is professor of English at the University of Virginia. He has created three Web sites for UVa: Mark Twain in His Times: An Electronic Archive; Uncle Tom's Cabin and American Culture: A Multi-Media Archive; and *Absalom, Absalom!* Electronic, Interactive! Chronology.

Roy Rosenzweig

Roy Rosenzweig is Mark and Barbara Fried Professor of History and New Media at George Mason University, where he also heads the Center on History and New Media. He is the coauthor, with Elizabeth Blackmar, of *The Park and the People: A History of Central Park*, which won the 1993 Historic Preservation Book Award and the 1993 Urban History Association Prize for Best Book on North American Urban History. He also coauthored (with David Thelen) *The Presence of the Past: Popular Uses of History in American Life*, which won prizes from the Center for Historic Preservation and the American Association for State and Local History. He was coauthor of the CD-ROM *Who Built America?*, which won the James Harvey Robinson Prize of American Historical Association for its "outstanding contribution to the teaching and learning of history." He is currently vice president for research of the American Historical Association and a member of the ACLS Commission on Cyberinfrastructure for the Humanities and Social Sciences.

Mark Sandler

Mark Sandler is collection development officer at the University of Michigan University Library with general oversight responsibilities for the collection budget, resource selection and licensing, and collections management. In this capacity, he has an interest in how libraries, publishers, and users are managing the transition from print to electronic resources. He has been involved with developing the Text Creation Partnership at the University of Michigan, a library collaboration that is creating thousands of accurately keyboarded and encoded editions of early texts. He writes and presents about mass-digitization strategies, public domain rights, and the use of e-resources in the humanities.

Mary Sauer-Games

Mary Sauer-Games is ProQuest's vice president of publishing for Chadwyck-Healey products. She has more than 15 years' experience in electronic publishing, of which the past 10 years have been spent in library publishing. She first worked for Gale Research and was responsible for the development of their newspaper publishing program, including the digitization of *The Times* of London. Since arriving at ProQuest, she has had responsibility for the reconfiguration and relaunch of Literature Online and for the further development of Early English Books Online and the American Periodical Series.

Robert Scott

Robert Scott is head, Electronic Text Service, Columbia University Libraries, and chair, Electronic Text Centers Discussion Group of the Association of College & Research Libraries.

David Seaman

David Seaman is executive director of the Digital Library Federation (DLF). He joined the DLF in 2002 from the Electronic Text Center at the University of Virginia Library, where he was the founding director (1992–2002). In this role, he oversaw the creation and development of an online archive of XML and SGML texts, of which many are available in multiple e-book formats. He has lectured and published extensively in the fields of humanities computing and digital libraries and since 1993 has taught e-text and Internet courses at the annual Book Arts Press Rare Book School at the University of Virginia.

Martha Sites

Martha Sites is associate university librarian for information technology at the University of Virginia. Her focus is on leadership of activities that support libraries and technology-related research, instruction, and administration in higher education. With her colleagues, she is engaged in developing the "Library of Tomorrow," which blends digital and traditional library activities and programs to enable digital scholarship to thrive. Areas of direct responsibility include acquisitions, cataloging, information technology systems, digital library research and development, digital research and instructional services, and digital library production services.

Martha Nell Smith

Martha Smith is professor of English and director of the Maryland Institute for Technology in the Humanities at the University of Maryland. Her numerous publications include three award-winning books—*Open Me Carefully: Emily Dickinson's Intimate Letters to Susan Dickinson*, coauthored with Ellen Louise Hart (1998); *Comic Power in Emily Dickinson*, coauthored with Cristanne Miller and Suzanne Juhasz (1993); and *Rowing in Eden: Rereading Emily Dickinson* (1992). With Mary Loeffelholz, she is editing the *Blackwell Companion to Emily Dickinson* (forthcoming in 2005). Smith is also coordinator and general editor of the Dickinson Electronic Archives projects at the Institute for Advanced Technology in the Humanities at the University of Virginia. With Lara Vetter, Smith is a general editor of the forthcoming *Emily Dickinson's Correspondences*. She serves on the NINES Steering Committee.

John Unsworth

John Unsworth is dean of the Graduate School of Library and Information Science (GSLIS) at the University of Illinois, Urbana-Champaign, with appointments as professor in GSLIS, in the Department of English, and on the library faculty. From 1993 until 2003, he served as the first director of the Institute for Advanced Technology in the

Humanities (IATH) and was a faculty member in the English Department at the University of Virginia. For his work at IATH, he received the 2005 Richard W. Lyman Award from the National Humanities Center (Research Triangle Park, N.C.). He has supervised research projects across the disciplines in the humanities and published widely on the topic of electronic scholarship. In 1990, at North Carolina State University, he cofounded *Postmodern Culture*, the first peer-reviewed electronic journal in the humanities (now published by Johns Hopkins University Press, as part of Project Muse). He is chair of the ACLS Commission for Cyberinfrastructure for the Humanities and Social Sciences and project director of NORA.

Amanda Watson

Amanda Watson is a Council on Library and Information Resources postdoctoral fellow who has worked on two projects with University of Virginia faculty: a small digitized collection of materials from special collections related to the poet Hart Crane (in collaboration with Stephen Cushman) and a Web site to supplement an interdisciplinary undergraduate course on the Enlightenment (with David Morris). She is also serving the public at the reference desk of the Alderman Library, teaching user-education courses, and helping create metadata for the E-text Center's Early American Fiction digital collection. Before her fellowship began at UVa, she worked for the Early English Books Online Text Creation Partnership project at the University of Michigan.

Perry Willett

Perry Willett is head of the Digital Library Production Service at the University of Michigan. Previously, he was assistant director of the Digital Library Program and librarian for English and American Literature at Indiana University. He is the general editor of the Wright American Fiction Project and founding editor of the Victorian Women Writers Project. He currently serves on the Text Encoding Initiative Council and the Steering Committee of NINES.

Helene C. Williams

Helene Williams is English bibliographer for the humanities at Harvard University's Widener Library and the former chair of the Literatures in English Section of the Association of College & Research Libraries.

Patricia Willis

Patricia Willis is curator of the Yale Collection of American Literature, Beinecke Rare Book and Manuscript Library, Yale University. Her scholarship centers on twentieth-century modernism, particularly on Marianne Moore, Ezra Pound, and William Carlos Williams. She is the editor of the *Yale University Library Gazette*.

APPENDIX 2:

Guiding Questions for Vetters of Scholarly Editions

Excerpt from Guiding Questions for Vetters of Scholarly Editions (August 3, 2005). Prepared by the Committee on Scholarly Editions, Modern Language Association of America. Available at http://www.mla.org/cse_guidelines#d0e354.

For each question listed below, the vetter should enter Yes, No, or Not applicable as appropriate. Vetter should also indicate whether additional comment on this point is made in the attached report.

V. Electronic Editions (see glossary for expansion of abbreviations)

22.1 Does the edition include help documentation that explains the features of the user interface and how to use them?

22.2 Does the edition carry a clear statement of the appropriate re-use of its constituent elements, especially those protected by copyright or used by permission?

23.0 Is the text of the edition encoded in an ISO standard grammar such as XML or SGML?

23.1 Is the XML or SGML applied using relevant community guidelines (e.g., the *Text Encoding Initiative Guidelines*)?

23.2 If the answer to the previous question is "No," then does the essay on technical methods provide a rationale for departing from community practice?

23.3 Is the edition designed to make its underlying markup (rather than markup that results from a rendering process) available to the reader for examination?

24.0 Is character encoding in the edition done according to an ISO standard (e.g., Unicode)?

24.1 Are rendering or transformation instructions (e.g., stylesheets) encoded in an ISO standard grammar such as XSL?

24.2 Does the edition use ISO standard formats (e.g., JPEG, PNG) for the distribution copies of its digital images?

24.3 If there are time-dependent media elements in the edition (for example, audio or video) are these encoded using ISO standard formats (e.g., MPEG/MP3)?

25.0 Are the distribution copies of multimedia elements (image, sound, video) sufficiently high resolution to allow close study?

25.1 Are the distribution copies of multimedia elements stored at reasonable file size, given the intended method of distribution?

25.2 Are the sources for those distribution copies archived?

25.3 Are those sources captured at sufficiently high resolution to allow for the future derivation of higher-resolution distribution copies?

26.0 Does the edition have, and does it validate against, a DTD or schema?

26.1 Is the DTD or schema used in marking up the edition adequately documented (e.g., with a tag library)?

26.2 If the edition includes one or more databases, is referential integrity enforced within the database(s)?

26.3 Are the database schema(s) documented?

26.4 Are the style sheets (or other rendering instructions) documented as to their intended effect?

27.0 Is there a definitive and documented method for determining what constitutes the electronic edition?

27.1 Is there a definitive and documented method for determining whether all the constituent elements of the edition actually exist?

27.2 Is technical, descriptive, and administrative metadata provided for all of the components of the edition, using a library-approved schema (such as METS)?

27.3 If any software has been uniquely developed for this edition, is source code for that software available and documented?

27.4 Has a copy of the edition, its images, software, stylesheets, and documentation been deposited with a library or other long-term digital object repository?

APPENDIX 3: Indexes of E-Books

	Digital Book Index	The Online Books Page	Celebration of Women Writers	Alex Catalogue of Electronic Texts	Oxford Text Archive (OTA)
Web site URL	http://digitalbookindex.com/	http://digital.library.upenn.edu/books	http://digital.library.upenn.edu/women	http://www.infomotions.com/alex	http://ota.ahds.ac.uk/
Sponsor	Site developed by Advocate Systems Development Group. No attribution given for the site's content development.	Founded and edited by John Mark Ockerbloom, digital library planner and researcher at University of Pennsylvania Library, which hosts the site.	Edited by Mary Mark Ockerbloom and developed in collaboration with the Online Books Page.	Independently produced by University of Notre Dame digital librarian Eric Lease Morgan.	Oxford University Computing Service, Joint Information Systems Committee, Arts and Humanities Data Service, under direction of Lou Burnard, Oxford University.
Purpose	Metasite indexing e-books and e-texts.	Index to free books on the Web.	Promote awareness of the breadth and variety of women's writings.	Catalog of e-texts in public domain.	Collects, catalogs, and preserves high-quality, noncommercial e-texts for teaching and research. Source files made available for redistribution with permissions.
Coverage	Multidisciplinary adult, professional, business, technical, reference, and children's books.	Multidisciplinary. Geared to academic users and general readers. Criteria for inclusion are identified but coverage is idiosyncratic, based in part on user interest. Special features on women writers, banned books, and prize winners.	Aims to provide comprehensive list of links to biographical and bibliographical information about women writers and access to complete published books written by women.	Focuses on American and English literature; philosophy.	Full text in the humanities, with priority to literary and linguistic disciplines, covering any literary genre, period, or language.
Size	Links to 105,000 title records, of which more than 66,000 are freely available. Claims 12,000 basic texts in English and American literature.	22,000 books, of which American literature comprises 2,347 entries (Library of Congress Classification: PS).	Not readily available. Estimated by Ockerbloom at 20 percent of Online Books Page's titles or more than 4,000 titles, of which 230 are locally produced. Search of writers from the United States. retrieved more than 4,800 records.	600 texts.	2,500 texts in 26 languages, of which more than 950 are in English. No separate category to distinguish American authors.
Sources	1,800 commercial and noncommercial publishers, universities, and private sites. Lists free and fee-based sources. Predominantly United States, but also Canada, United Kingdom, Ireland, Australia, Japan, and others.	Noncommercial e-book publishers, universities, projects, and individuals. Invites contributors. Maintains a list of titles in progress and suggested titles.	Same as Online Books Page; however, does digitize some texts itself, which are listed as Local Editions, focusing on older, often rare, out-of-copyright works.	Public domain e-book providers. Each record links to the "original" source, making it possible to identify from where the text is derived, and to a "local copy." Even when original location link is broken, local copy link functions.	Accepts texts on deposit according to certain standards, including e-texts, text bases and corpora, databases, digital image data, and hypermedia. Materials are out of copyright or appropriate permissions have been granted to the OTA for their use.

Appendix 3, continued

	Digital Book Index	The Online Books Page	Celebration of Women Writers	Alex Catalogue of Electronic Texts	Oxford Text Archive
Access	Requires free registration to search. One-third of material is not in public domain; links to publisher for purchase or subscription.	Freely accessible materials in public domain.	Freely accessible. Some materials may not be in public domain.	Freely accessible. Materials in public domain.	All contributors must grant OTA a nonexclusive license to redistribute their texts. All texts are free, but some require a written order form.
Browse Functions	By subject, author, or publisher. Browse NetLibrary by subject and American studies (forthcoming). Browse Reference Sources by category and title.	Browse by author, title, or LC subject classification. Browse serials by title. Browse new listings by date and title. Latest book listings, by date, added.	Browse by author. Browse Local Editions by author or by category. What's New listing by date. Specialty Collections links to other Web sites related to women writers.	Browse by author, title, or date.	Browse by author, title, or language. Print catalog available in PDF format in alphabetic order by author.
Search Functions	By author, title (keywords), or author and title.	By author or title.	By author, date ranges when author lived, country, and ethnicity. Not all books are completely indexed according to these fields.	Simple search only by author or title. Concordance/word-search functions can be run against items in the catalog.	Basic search by author or title keyword in addition to advanced search delimiters by subject keyword or language. Supports full-text searches with delimiters, including SGML tags.
Book Formats and Down-loading	Multiple formats covered and explained on main Help page. Links to reader devices to download or purchase.	ASCII text and HTML preferred.	ASCII text and HTML preferred.	Plain text files preferred over HTML. Can download individual texts or a complete file of all American texts (57 MB uncompressed).	Download from Web site catalog. Charges for transfer to diskette, data cartridge, or CD-ROM.
Alerts Service	Will send new e-book title information from publishers.	Maintains a list for those who contribute digital texts.	Runs a blog.		
Comments	Well organized. Sites from which texts are derived clearly indicated.	Promotes collaborative contribution of texts, but there are extensive waiting lists for addition to the index.	Promotes collaborative contribution of texts. An uneven and eclectic mix of titles. Derivation of titles not always identified at level of upper link.	Collection Policy page identifies qualities of texts accepted and file format preferences. A pilot version of Alex includes a full-text indexed subset of the collection that supports downloading in various e-book reader formats.	Clearly stated collection policy and standards.

APPENDIX 4:

Checklist for the Evaluation of Free e-Books

Excerpt from Berglund, Ylva, Alan Morrison, Rowan Wilson, and Martin Wynne. *An Investigation into Free eBooks: Final Report*, March 2004. (Revised 2004-03-12). Available at http://www.ahds.ac.uk/litlangling/ebooks/report/FreeEbooks.html#back.1_div.6.

In view of the importance given to quality assurance by potential users, we have considered it useful to develop some ad hoc procedures for evaluation of free e-books. Here is the draft checklist developed for our in-house quality evaluation:

Is it what it says it is?
1. Is the text really available and free to the user?
2. Check for existence of metadata;
3. If the metadata claims to conform to an external standard (e.g., Dublin Core) check its grammaticality, completeness, and relevance;
4. Is the relevant information about the particular edition of the text present and accurate; and
5. Are intellectual property issues covered in the metadata or text? Is the treatment accurate? Does the resource provider have the right to distribute the resource, and are the creators of the resource credited in the documentation or metadata or text (as appropriate)?
6. Check the accuracy and completeness of the metadata for individual texts, where the resource is a collection of texts or samples;
7. Where there is no metadata covering these issues, check in particular whether the following particulars are as expected: text, language, file type, and text-encoding format.
8. Where there is more than one file, check that all relevant resource files are present in the correct file structure (i.e., as documented), and that file naming conventions are suitable;
9. Assess the file format: Is it as documented, is it valid according to the normal standards for that format, and is this a suitable format for interchange, storage, use, and preservation?

Fitness for purpose
1. Assess the appropriateness of the format for the intended purpose (e.g., quality of design, representativeness, sampling);
2. Duplication: is the text available elsewhere in a usable way, or even in a more useful form?

3. Is this text likely to be of use in HE [Higher Education] and/or FE [Further Education]? If so, where and how?

Text integrity

1. Check integrity of textual material (Are bits missing? Have some elements been silently omitted?);
2. Check for erroneously repeated textual material;
3. Are footnotes, endnotes, other editorial interventions encoded, and if so are they done correctly;
4. Are front matter such as foreword, preface, introduction etc. correctly encoded;
5. Are appendices such as afterword, endnotes, bibliography present and correctly encoded?

Text format and encoding

1. Assess the character sets which are used: is the character set as per the documentation, if this exists? Is it suitable? Are there any invalid characters or entities?
2. Assess the choice of textual markup scheme: is it suitable for interchange, use and migration?
3. Validate the textual markup and evaluate the semantic accuracy and appropriateness (e.g., are chapter or paragraph tags correctly used?);
4. Validate the design, markup, and annotation against external criteria; check that it actually works with software for the processing of the format (e.g., check that XML is valid and parses, check [that] Acrobat Reader can read PDF files);

Factors external to the text

1. Search for and follow up on documented bug reports, comments, and reviews that may be available at the repository or elsewhere;
2. Contact, and maintain ongoing dialogue with, the resource provider (where this is possible) to ensure the accuracy and completeness of metadata, and to manage enhancement of the resource where necessary.

Reprinted with permission of authors. Copyright 2004. Arts and Humanities Data Service/Joint Information Systems Committee.

APPENDIX 5: Alternative Publishing Communities

	EServer	Electronic Literature Organization	NINES	eScholarship Program	Rotunda Electronic Imprint
Web Site URL	http://www.eserver.org	http://www.eliterature.org	http://www.nines.org	http://www.cdlib.org/programs/escholarship.html	http://www.ei.virginia.edu/
Year Established	1990	1999	2004	1999; 2002 (repository); 2003 (editions)	2004
Main Sponsors	English Department, Iowa State University; formerly at Carnegie Mellon University.	English Department, Center for Digital Humanities, and other programs at the University of California, Los Angeles	North American Society for the Study of Romanticism, North American Victorian Studies Association, American Studies Association, American Literature Association	California Digital Library with University of California (UC) departments, UC Press, and other academic publishers	University of Virginia (UVa) Press
External Funding		Ford Foundation and Rockefeller Foundation	The Andrew W. Mellon Foundation		The Andrew W. Mellon Foundation
Purpose	Online community where writers, artists, editors, and scholars gather to publish and discuss their works.	To promote and facilitate the writing, publishing, and reading of literature in electronic media.	To protect, sustain, and enhance digital scholarship and criticism in 19th-century English-language studies.	To facilitate innovation and support experimentation in the production and dissemination of scholarship.	To combine the traditional roles of university press publishing with technological innovation to disseminate high-quality, peer-reviewed work.
Editorial Board	Overseen by membership consisting of editors and contributors (estimated at 226).	Membership organization. Anyone may contribute to the ELO Directory if their work meets inclusion criteria. Authors have control over their material.	18-member academic steering committee and three editorial boards: Americanist, Romantic, and Victorian.	Varies by collection and service from UC departmental control (eScholarship Repository) to peer reviewed (UC Press titles in eScholarship editions).	UVa Press.
Content	Previously published, reformatted editions and new work in the arts and humanities, including scanned texts, journals and Web sites.	Born-digital literature with significant use of electronic media in poetry, fiction, drama, and creative nonfiction.	Aggregated body of primary and secondary 19th-century digital scholarship, British and American.	Born-digital scholarship and reformatted editions in all disciplines, ranging from open-access preprints to peer-reviewed content.	Born-digital scholarship and reformatted editions in two series—Founding Era and 19th-century American literature and culture.
Access	Publicly accessible	Publicly accessible	Publicly accessible	Subset freely available	For purchase or licensed

Appendix 5, continued

	EServer	Electronic Literature Organization	NINES	eScholarship Program	Rotunda Electronic Imprint
Quality Control	Acceptable-use policy for collections (e.g., project Web sites and publications).	No qualitative content criteria, but works must meet inclusion criteria for genres and electronic elements.	Peer reviewed.	Mix of in-progress and peer reviewed.	Peer reviewed.
Features	Work space for contributors and editors. Advice for project developers. Discussion forum. Access to open-source software and tools.	Discussion forum. Directory of electronic literature. Preservation, archiving, and dissemination program to sustain endangered literature. Annual award. Sponsor events. Matchmaker initiative to pair writers, artists, and programmers for collaboration and creation of electronic literature.	Common interface to aggregated resources. Archiving of projects. Standards-compliant, open-source suite of tools and markup schemes. Codifying peer-review process. Summer fellowships to develop projects.	Repository for research and scholarly output. Web-based publications of digitally reformatted content. Electronic editions of academic monographs.	Fully searchable online editions.
Size	More than 30,000 works in 45 collections.	Directory includes more than 2,000 works by more than 1,150 authors, representing nearly 200 publishers. Large number of works are self-published.	Not yet actively soliciting content.	eScholarship Repository: nearly 7,000 papers eScholarship Editions: 1,400 titles	American Founding Era • *Dolley Madison Digital Edition* • *Papers of George Washington* (forthcoming) 19th-Century Literature and Culture • *Emily Dickinson Correspondences* (forthcoming) • Melville's *Typee* (forthcoming) • Five reformatted UVa Press titles (forthcoming)

APPENDIX 6:

Checklist of Criteria Used in the *Literary Research Guide*

James L. Harner uses this checklist to evaluate resources for inclusion in the fifth edition of *Literary Research Guide: An Annotated Listing of Reference Sources in English Literary Studies* (forthcoming in 2007). Some questions are borrowed or adapted from the "Minimal Guidelines for Authors of Web Pages," prepared by the Modern Language Association's Committee on Information Technology, available at http://www.mla.org/web_guidelines.

Does the resource

- Identify author(s) or editor(s) and provide contact information.
- Identify, if appropriate, designer(s) and contact information.
- Identify the institution/group/organization funding/sponsoring/publishing the database and contact information.
- Provide a statement of copyright (and contact information for copyright permissions).
- Provide a privacy statement that indicates what information is collected on users and how that information is used.
- Note any special software requirements (and provisions for users with special needs).
- Provide a precise description of scope (e.g., what kinds of documents are included/excluded; what years are covered; what languages, if any, are excluded).
- Offer a description of sources of data (e.g., are records based on firsthand examination of documents or are they taken secondhand from other sources [a list of which should be included]).
- Indicate who (author/professional abstracter/volunteer) writes abstracts for and/or indexes documents.
- Describe editorial practices that might affect search strategies/capabilities.
- Spell out the frequency of updates.
- Explain record structure.
- Explain the relationship to any print version (e.g., what is omitted/what is added).
- Provide a way for users to report errors/omissions.
- Explain how the database complements/supersedes/mirrors other resources.
- Provide a Help file that explains search techniques and alerts users to quirks in searching.

- Provide a site map.
- Offer a description of the taxonomy of the database if it replicates a print source and allows browsing based on the taxonomy.
- Provide a way of sorting records by accession number/date and/ or identifying records added within each update.

Reprinted with permission of James L. Harner.

APPENDIX 7:

Glossary

ABELL: Annual Bibliography of English Language and Literature
http://www.proquest.com/products/pd-product-ABELL.shtml

ACLS: American Council of Learned Societies
http://www.acls.org

ACRL: Association of College & Research Libraries
http://www.acrl.org

ADE: Association for Documentary Editing
http://etext.virginia.edu/ade/

AHA: American Historical Association
http://www.historians.org

ALA: American Literature Association
http://www.calstatela.edu/academic/english/ala2/

AQ: American Quarterly (journal of the ASA)
http://www.americanquarterly.org

ASA: American Studies Association
http://www.georgetown.edu/crossroads/asainfo.html

ASCII: American Standard Code for Information Interchange
"Dirty" or "rough" ASCII refers to OCR-generated ASCII text format that has not been proofread. Also referred to as "dirty OCR" or "rough OCR."

CDWA: Categories for the Descriptions of Works of Art
Product of the Art Information Task Force funded by the J. Paul Getty Trust with two-year matching grants from the National Endowment for the Humanities to the College Art Association.
http://www.getty.edu/research/conducting_research/standards/cdwa/

CETH: Center for Electronic Texts in the Humanities, Rutgers University
http://www.ceth.rutgers.edu/

CIC: Committee on Institutional Cooperation
http://www.cic.uiuc.edu/index.shtml

CSDGM: Content Standard for Digital Geospatial Metadata
Under development by the Federal Geographic Data Committee of
the U.S. Geological Survey.
http://www.fgdc.gov/metadata/contstan.html

CSE: Committee on Scholarly Editions (of the MLA)
http://www.iath.virginia.edu/~jmu2m/cse/

CWW: Celebration of Women Writers
http://digital.library.upenn.edu/women/

DBI: Digital Book Index
http://www.digitalbookindex.org/

DEA: Dickinson Electronic Archives
http://www.emilydickinson.org/

DRM: Digital Rights Management
Any of several technical methods used to control or restrict the use
of digital media content on electronic devices with such technologies
installed.

DTD: Document Type Definition
The set of rules that specifies how the SGML or XML grammar will
be applied in a particular document instance.

Dublin Core Metadata Initiative: An open forum engaged in the
development of interoperable online metadata standards that support a broad range of purposes and business models.
http://dublincore.org

EAD: Encoded Archival Description
The EAD Document Type Definition (DTD) is a standard for encod-
ing archival finding aids using extensible markup language (XML).
The standard is maintained in the Network Development and
MARC Standards Office of LC in partnership with the Society of
American Archivists.
http://www.loc.gov/ead/

EADA: The Early Americas Digital Archive
http://www.mith2.umd.edu:8080/eada/index.jsp

ECCO: Eighteenth Century Collections Online
http://www.gale.com/EighteenthCentury/find.htm

EEBO: Early English Books Online
http://eebo.chadwyck.com/home

ELO: Electronic Literature Organization
http://www.eliterature.org/

ESTC: English Short Title Catalogue
http://www.rlg.org/en/page.php?Page_ID=179

GIF: Graphics Interchange Format
A graphics file format used to transmit raster images on the Internet.
http://www.w3.org/Graphics

HTML: HyperText Markup Language
The lingua franca for publishing on the World Wide Web.
http://www.w3.org/MarkUp

IATH: Institute for Advanced Technology in the Humanities,
University of Virginia
http://www.iath.virginia.edu

ICT: Information and Communication Technologies

IEEE: Institute of Electrical and Electronics Engineers, Inc.
http://www.ieee.org/portal/site

IMLS: Institute of Museum and Library Services
http://www.imls.gov

ISO: International Organization for Standardization
http://www.iso.org/iso/en/ISOOnline.frontpage

JAH: *Journal of American History* (journal of the AHA)
http://www.indiana.edu/~jah/

JISC: Joint Information Systems Committee
http://www.jisc.ac.uk/

JSTOR: Journal Storage, the Scholarly Journal Archive, The Andrew
W. Mellon Foundation
http://www.jstor.org

LC: Library of Congress
http://www.loc.gov

LION: Literature Online
http://www.proquest.com/products/pd-product-Lion.shtml

LoCC: Library of Congress Classification Outline
http://www.loc.gov/catdir/cpso/lcco/lcco.html

LOM: Learning Object Metadata, Learning Technology Standards
Committee, IEEE
http://ltsc.ieee.org/wg12/

LRG: Literary Research Guide
http://www-english.tamu.edu/pubs/lrg/

MARC: Standards for the representation and communication of bibliographic and related information in machine-readable form.
http://www.loc.gov/marc/

MBP: Million Book Project
http://www.archive.org/details/millionbooks

MEP: Model Editions Partnership
http://mep.cla.sc.edu/

METS: Metadata Encoding and Transmission Standard
A standard for encoding descriptive, administrative, and structural metadata regarding objects within a digital library, expressed using the XML schema language of the World Wide Web Consortium. The standard is maintained in the Network Development and MARC Standards Office of the Library of Congress, and is being developed as an initiative of the Digital Library Federation.
http://www.loc.gov/standards/mets/

MITH: Maryland Institute for Technology in the Humanities, University of Maryland
http://www.mith.umd.edu/

MLA: Modern Language Association of America
http://www.mla.org

MODS: Metadata Object Description Scheme
A schema for a bibliographic element set that may be used for a various purposes, and particularly for library applications. MODS is intended to be able to carry selected data from existing MARC 21 records as well as to enable the creation of original resource description records.
http://www.loc.gov/standards/mods/

MPEG: Moving Picture Experts Group
http://www.mpeg.org

NDNP: National Digital Newspaper Program
http://www.neh.fed.us/projects/ndnp.html

NEH: National Endowment for the Humanities
http://www.neh.gov

NINES: Nineteenth-Century Electronic Scholarship
http://www.nines.org

NISO: National Information Standards Organization
http://www.niso.org

NITLE: National Institute for Technology and Liberal Education
http://www.nitle.org

NORA: A project to produce software for discovering, visualizing, and exploring significant patterns across large collections of full-text humanities resources in digital libraries.
http://www.noraproject.org

NSF: National Science Foundation
http://www.nsf.gov

NUCMC: National Union Catalogue of Manuscript Collections
http://www.loc.gov/coll/nucmc/

NYPL: The New York Public Library
http://www.nypl.org

OAH: Organization of American Historians
http://www.oah.org

OAI-PMH: Open Archives Initiative Protocol for Metadata Harvesting
Defines a mechanism for harvesting XML-formatted metadata from repositories.
http://www.openarchives.org/

OAIS: Open Archival Information System
An archive, consisting of an organization of people and systems, that has accepted the responsibility to preserve information and make it available for a "designated community."
http://ssdoo.gsfc.nasa.gov/nost/wwwclassic/documents/pdf/CCSDS-650.0-B-1.pdf

OAIster: University of Michigan Digital Library Production Service
http://oaister.umdl.umich.edu/o/oaister

OBP: Online Books Page
http://digital.library.upenn.edu/books/

OCLC: Online Computer Library Center
http://www.oclc.org

OCR: Optical Character Recognition
The process by which images of typewritten text, usually captured by a scanner, are translated into machine-editable text, or by which pictures of characters are translated into a standard encoding scheme representing them in ASCII or Unicode.
http://en.wikipedia.org/wiki/Optical_character_recognition

OTA: Oxford Text Archive
http://ota.ahds.ac.uk/

PAD: The Preservation, Archiving, and Dissemination of Electronic Literature (of the ELO)
http://www.eliterature.org/programs/pad/

PCI: Periodical Contents Index
http://pcift.chadwyck.com

PDF: Portable Document File
A proprietary file format developed by Adobe Systems for representing documents in a manner that is independent of the original application software, hardware, and operating system used to create those documents.
http://en.wikipedia.org/wiki/Pdf

PG: Project Gutenberg
http://www.gutenberg.org

PNG: Portable Network Graphics
An extensible file format for the lossless, portable, well-compressed storage of raster images.
http://www.libpng.org/

SFX: The proprietary name for the link server devised by Ex Libris, used generically to refer to context sensitive linking services.
http://www.exlibrisgroup.com/sfx.htm

SGML: Standard Generalized Markup Language
A grammar for text encoding defined in International Organization for Standardization, ISO 8879.
http://xml.coverpages.org/sgml.html

TCA: *The Charleston Advisor: Critical Review for Web Products for Information Professionals*
http://www.charlestonco.com/

TCP: Text Creation Partnership, University of Michigan
http://www.lib.umich.edu/tcp/

TEI: Text-Encoding Initiative
An international and interdisciplinary standard that helps libraries, museums, publishers, and individual scholars represent all kinds of literary and linguistic texts for online research and teaching, using an encoding scheme that is maximally expressive and minimally obsolescent.
http://www.tei-c.org/

TIFF: Tagged Image File Format
The de facto standard graphics format for high-color-depth (32-bit) graphics; widely used in image manipulation applications.
http://en.wikipedia.org/wiki/TIFF

TLT: Teaching and Learning Technology

URL: Uniform Resource Locator. An address for a resource on the Internet.
http://www.w3.org/Addressing/

VKP: Visible Knowledge Project, Georgetown University
http://crossroads.georgetown.edu/vkp

VLE: Virtual Learning Environment

VoS: Voice of the Shuttle
http://vos.ucsb.edu/

VRA Core: Visual Resource Association Core
http://www.vraweb.org/vracore3.htm (version 3.0)

XML: Extensible Markup Language
A simple, flexible text format derived from SGML (ISO 8879). Designed to meet the challenges of large-scale electronic publishing, XML is playing an increasingly important role in the exchange of a wide variety of data on the Web and elsewhere.
http://www.w3.org/XML/
"A Gentle Introduction to XML" is available from http://www.tei-c.org/P4X/SG.html.

Z39.50: A client server protocol for searching and retrieving information from remote databases. It is covered by ANSI standard Z39.50, and ISO standard 23950.
http://en.wikipedia.org/wiki/Z39.50

See also

Glossary from *Introduction to Metadata*, edited by Murtha Baca. Available at http://www.getty.edu/research/conducting_research/standards/intrometadata/4_glossary/index.html.

"Glossary of Terms Used in the Guiding Questions for Vetters of Scholarly Editions." August 3, 2005. Committee on Scholarly Editions, Modern Language Association. Available at http://www.mla.org/cse_guidelines#d0e1937.

W3C: A–Z (Glossary of Home Pages)
http://www.w3.org

References

American Library Association. Association of College & Research Libraries. 1998–2005. *Index to Internet Resources from C&RL News*. Links to full text of published articles are freely accessible; recent updates are restricted to members only. Available at http://www.ala.org/ala/acrl/acrlpubs/crlnews/internetresourcestopic.htm.

American Library Association. Association of College & Research Libraries. 1988. *Books for College Libraries: A Core Collection of 50,000 Titles*, 3rd ed. Chicago: ALA.

Ayers, Edward L. 2005a. Revolution in the Archives. Unpublished notes from a talk delivered at the Library of Congress, Washington, D.C., March 14, 2005. Webcast archive available from C-SPAN at http://www.c-span.org/congress/digitalfuture.asp.

Ayers, Edward L. 2005b. Scholarship in the Digital Age. Paper presented at the University of Minnesota, Minneapolis, Minn., April 19, 2005. Webcast archive available until September 30, 2005, at http://www.lib.umn.edu/ppp.

Bass, Randy. 2001. New Canons and New Media: American Literature in the Electronic Age. Hypertext version, expanded from the *Heath Anthology of American Literature*, 3rd ed., Paul Lauter, general editor. Available at http://college.hmco.com/english/lauter/heath/4e/instructors/articles/editorintro.html and http://www.georgetown.edu/faculty/bassr/heath/editorintro.html.

Bass, R., T. Derrickson, B. Eynon, and M. Sample, eds. 1998. Intentional Media: the Crossroads Conversations on Learning and Technology in the American Culture and History Classroom. *Works and Days* 16(1/2). As cited by Edward Gallagher (2004a).

Bauer, Ralph. 2003. Notes on the Comparative Study of the Colonial Americas: Further Reflections on the Tucson Summit. *Early American Literature* 38(2): 281–304.

Beagrie, Neal. 2005. Digital Preservation: Best Practice and Its Dissemination. *Ariadne* 43. Available at http://www.ariadne.ac.uk/issue43/beagrie/.

Beer, Emma. 2005. Waking up in the British Library. *Ariadne* 43. Available at http://www.ariadne.ac.uk/issue43/wakingupinbl-rpt.

Berglund, Ylva, Alan Morrison, Rowan Wilson, and Martin Wynne. 2004. *An Investigation into Free eBooks: Final Report.* Commissioned by the JISC E-books Working Group. Arts and Humanities Data Service, AHDS Literature, Languages and Linguistics. Available at http://www.ahds.ac.uk/litlangling/ebooks/.

Brooks, Joanna. 2004. New Media's Prospect: A Review of Web Resources in Early American Studies. *Early American Literature* 39(3): 577–590.

Brown, Joshua. 2004a. Commentary: Rambling Thoughts While on a Virtual Stroll . . . *Rethinking History* 8(2): 333–335.

Brown, Joshua. 2004b. Forum: History and the Web. *Rethinking History* 8(2): 253–275.

Bryant, John. 2002. *The Fluid Text: A Theory of Revision and Editing for Book and Screen.* Ann Arbor, Mich.: University of Michigan Press.

Burnard, Lou, Katherine O'Brien O'Keeffe, and John Unsworth, eds. 2004. *Electronic Textual Editing.* Available at http://www.tei-c.org/Activities/ETE/Preview/index.xml. Scheduled for publication in paper form by the Modern Language Association in late 2005.

Carpenter, Leona. 2005. Supporting Digital Preservation and Asset Management in Institutions. *Ariadne* 43. Available at http://www.ariadne.ac.uk/issue43/carpenter/.

Case, Mary, and David Green. 2004. Rights and Permissions in an Electronic Edition. In Burnard et al., eds. *Electronic Textual Editing.* Available at http://www.tei-c.org/Activities/ETE/Preview/case.xml.

The Charleston Advisor: Critical Reviews of Web Products for Information Professionals. Subscription-based review journal with some freely available content. Available at http://www.charlestonco.com/.

Chodorow, Stanley. 1997. "The Once and Future Monograph." Paper presented at The Specialized Scholarly Monograph in Crisis or How Can I Get Tenure If You Won't Publish My Book? Washington, D.C., September 11, 1997. Available at http://www.arl.org/scomm/epub/papers/chodorow.html.

Claxton, Mae Miller, and C. Camille Cooper. 2000. Teaching Tools: American Literature and the World Wide Web. *English Journal* 90(2): 97–103.

Cohen, Daniel J. 2005. By the Book: Assessing the Place of Textbooks in U.S. Survey Courses. *Journal of American History* 91 (March): 1405–1415. Available at www.indiana.edu/~jah/textbooks/2005/cohen.shtml.

Cohen, Daniel J. 2004a. Digital History: the Raw and the Cooked. *Rethinking History* 8(2): 337–340.

Cohen, Daniel J. 2004b. History and the Second Decade of the Web. *Rethinking History* 8(2): 293–301.

Cronin, Blaise, and Kathyrn La Barre. 2004. Mickey Mouse and Milton: Book Publishing in the Humanities. *Learned Publishing* 17(2): 85–98.

Darnton, Robert. 2000. An Early Information Society: News and Media in Eighteenth-Century Paris. *American Historical Review* 105 (February): 1–35.

Darnton, Robert. 1999. The New Age of the Book. *New York Review of Books* 46(5): 5–8.

Davidson, Cathy N. 2004. The Futures of Scholarly Publishing. *Journal of Scholarly Publishing* 35(3): 129–142.

Davidson, Cathy N. 2003. Understanding the Economic Burden of Scholarly Publishing. *Chronicle of Higher Education* 50(6): B7–10.

Day, Betty H., and William A. Wortman, eds. 2000. *Literature in English: A Guide for Librarians in the Digital Age*. ACRL Publications in Librarianship no. 54. Chicago: Association of College & Research Libraries, a division of the American Library Association.

Deegan, Marilyn, and Simon Tanner. 2004. Conversion of Primary Sources. In Susan Schreibman, Ray Siemans, and John Unsworth, eds. *A Companion to Digital Humanities*. Blackwell Companions to Literature and Culture, number 26. Oxford: Blackwell Publishing, 488–504.

Dennis, Brian, Carl Smith, and Jonathan Smith. 2004. Using Technology, Making History: A Collaborative Experiment in Interdisciplinary Teaching and Scholarship. *Rethinking History*. 8(2): 303–317.

Digital Library Federation. 2004a. DLF Scholars' Panel. Washington, D.C., June 2–3, 2004. Available at http://www.diglib.org/use/scholars0406/.

Digital Library Federation. 2004b. *Registry of Digital Masters Record Creation Guidelines*. Version 1.0. July 2004. Prepared by DLF Registry of Digital Masters Working Group. Available at http://www.diglib.org/collections/reg/digregguide.htm.

Ebert-Zawasky, Kathleen, and Kathryn Tomasek. [n.d.] *Examining Scholarly and Pedagogical Implications of the Text Encoding Initiative (TEI) for Small Liberal Arts Colleges.* Available at http://www.nitle. org/downloads/conference/TEI.doc.

Ellis, Scott. 2003. Early American Print Culture in a Digital Age: Pedagogical Possibilities. *Pedagogy: Critical Approaches to Teaching Literature, Language, Composition, and Culture* 3(2): 288–291.

Ellis, Scott. 2002. Digitizing the Past: Using Electronic Texts in Scholarship and the Classroom. *Legacy* 19(1): 115–120.

Estabrook, Leigh, and Beija Warner. 2003. The Book as the Gold Standard for Tenure and Promotion in Humanistic Disciplines. [Urbana-Champaign, Ill.: Committee on Institutional Cooperation] Available at http://lrc.lis.uiuc.edu/web/ScholarlyCommunicationsSummitReport_Dec03.pdf.

Flanders, Julia. 2002. Learning, Reading, and the Problem of Scale: Using Women Writers Online. *Pedagogy: Critical Approaches to Teaching Literature, Language, Composition, and Culture* 2(1): 49–59.

Flanders, Julia. 1998. Trusting the Electronic Edition. *Computers and the Humanities* 31: 301–310.

Flanders, Julia, and John Unsworth. 2002. The ACH Page: The Evolution of Humanities Computing Centers. *Computers and the Humanities* 36: 279–280.

Gallagher, Edward J. 2004a. History and the New Technology: the Missing Link. *Rethinking History* 8(2): 319–332.

Gallagher, Edward J. 2004b. Pompous Prolegomenon to a Serious Program. *Rethinking History* 8(2): 341–342.

Gallagher, Edward J., with Stephen A. Tompkins. 2004. Improving the Discussion Board, a Scholarship of Teaching and Learning Project for the *Visible Knowledge Project.* Available at http://www.leigh. edu/~ineng/discussion/1overview/0-title.html.

Gilbaldi, Joseph. 2003. *MLA Handbook for Writers of Research Papers,* 6th ed. New York: The Modern Language Association.

Gilliland-Swetland, Ann J. 2000. Introduction to Metadata: Setting the Stage. In Murtha Baca, ed. *Introduction to Metadata: Pathways to Digital Information.* Los Angeles, Calif.: Getty Research Institute. Available at http://www.getty.edu/research/conducting_research/ standards/intrometadata/.

Goldenberg-Hart, Diane. 2004. Libraries and Changing Research Practices: A Report of the ARL/CNI Forum on E-Research and Cyberinfrastructure. *ARL Bimonthly Report* 237 (December): 1–5. Available at http://www.arl.org/newsltr/237/cyberinfra.html.

Greenblatt, Stephen. 2002. A Letter to MLA Members. Available at http://chronicle.com/jobs/2002/07/2002070202c.htm.

Greenstein, Daniel. 2004. *Aquifer: A Progress Report*. Available at http://www.diglib.org/aquifer/aqreport041111.htm.

Hagedorn, Katerina. 2005. Looking for Pearls. *Research Information* (March/April). Available at http://www.researchinformation.info/rimarapr05oaister.html.

Hall, Steven. 1998. Literature Online—Building a Home for English and American Literature on the World Wide Web. *Computers and the Humanities* 32: 285–301.

Hanlon, Christopher. 2005. History on the Cheap: Using the Online Archive to Make Historicists out of Undergrads. *Pedagogy: Critical Approaches to Teaching Literature, Language, Composition, and Culture* 5(1): 97–101. (The text of the original paper, Using the Online Archive to Make Historicists Out of Undergrads, delivered at the Illinois Philological Association, Millikin University, Decatur, Ill., March 2003, is available at http://www.eiu.edu/~agora/Sept03/Hanlall.htm.)

Harner, James L. 2003. Some Suggestions for the Future of the MLA *International Bibliography*. In David William Foster and James R. Kelly, eds. *Bibliography in Literature, Folklore, Language and Linguistics: Essays on the Status of the Field*. Jefferson, N.C.: McFarland & Co., 153–160.

Harner, James L. 2002. *Literary Research Guide: An Annotated Listing of Reference Sources in English Literary Studies*, 4th ed. New York: Modern Language Association. Harner maintains an ongoing list of updated annotations available at http://www-english.tamu.edu/pubs/lrg/.

Hatch, Thomas, Randy Bass, Toru Iiyoshi, and Desiree Pointer Mace. 2004. Building Knowledge for Teaching and Learning: The Promise of Scholarship in a Networked Environment. *Change Magazine* (September/October): 42–49.

Hayles, N. Katherine. 1999. *How We Became Posthuman: Virtual Bodies in Cybernetics, Literature, and Informatics*. Chicago: University of Chicago Press.

Hockey, Susan. 2004. The History of Humanities Computing. In Susan Schreibman, Ray Siemans, and John Unsworth, eds., *A Companion to Digital Humanities*. Blackwell Companions to Literature and Culture, number 26. Oxford: Blackwell Publishing.

Hockey, Susan. 2000. *Electronic Texts in the Humanities*. Oxford: Oxford University Press.

Howard, Alan B. 2004. American Studies and the New Technologies: New Paradigms for Teaching and Learning. *Rethinking History* 8(2): 277–291.

Kamrath, Mark. 2002. *Eyes Wide Shut* and the Cultural Poetics of Eighteenth-Century American Periodical Literature. *Early American Literature* 37(3): 497–536.

Karlsson, Lina, and Linda Malm. 2004. Revolution or Remediation? A Study of Electronic Scholarly Editions on the Web. *Human IT: Journal for Information Technology Studies as a Human Science* 7(1): 1–46. Available at http://www.hb.se/bhs/ith/1-7/lklm.pdf.

Killingsworth, M. Jimmie. 2004. Whitman and Dickinson. In David Norloh, ed., *American Literary Scholarship 2002*. Chapel Hill, N.C.: Duke University Press, 59–83.

Killingsworth, M. Jimmie. 2003. Whitman and Dickinson. In David Norloh, ed., *American Literary Scholarship 2001*. Chapel Hill, N.C.: Duke University Press, 67–95.

Kirschenbaum, Matthew. 2004. Getting Out of the Tool Box: Text and Data Mining for the Humanities. Presentation delivered at the Modern Language Association Annual Conference, Philadelphia, Pa., December 27–30, 2004. Available at http://www.iath.virginia.edu/nora/wiki/uploads/Main/Matt-MLAslides-Dec04.ppt.

Koch, Traugott. 2000. Quality-controlled Subject Gateways on the Internet. *Online Information Review* 24(1). Available at http://www.lub.lu.se/tk/demos/SGin.html.

Kornblith, Gary J., and Carol Lasser, contributing eds. 2003. Editors' Introduction: More than Bells and Whistles? Using Digital Technology to Teach American History. *Journal of American History* 89(4): 1465–1466. Available to subscribers from the History Cooperative http://www.historycooperative.org. Annual *JAH* Textbooks and Teaching section freely available at companion Web site http://www.indiana.edu/~jah/textbooks/.

Lin, Nancy. 2003. ACLS History E-Book Project: Report on Technology Development and Production Workflow for XML Encoded E-Books. ACLS History E-Book Project White Paper 1, (October 3), v. 1.0. Available at http://www.historyebook.org/heb-whitepaper-1.html.

Liu, Alan. 2003. The Humanities: A Technical Profession. MLA Panel on Information Technology and the Profession. Paper presented at the Modern Language Association Convention, San Diego, Ca., December 28, 2003. Available at http://www.english.ucsb.edu/faculty/ayliu/research/talks/2003MLA/Liu_Talk.pdf.

Liu, Alan, David Durand, Nick Montfort, Merrilee Proffitt, Liam R.E.Quin, Jean-Hugues Réty, and Noah Wardrip-Fruin. 2004. *Born-Again Bits: A Framework for Migrating Electronic Literature* beta 1.13 (September 30). Forthcoming from the Electronic Literature Organization's PAD Project Web site at http://www.eliterature.org/.

Luther, Judy, Maureen Kelly, and Donald Beagle. 2005. Visualize This. *Library Journal* (March 1): 34–37. Available at http://www.groxis.com/archives/lib_journal_030105.htm.

Mach, Michelle. 2004. *Twentieth-Century Authors: Biographic and Bibliographic Information Is Just a Click Away*. September 17 update. Available to ACRL members at http://www.ala.org/ala/acrl/acrlpubs/crlnews/internetresources.htm.

Manning, Patrick. 2004. Gutenberg-e: Electronic Entry to the Historical Professoriate. *American Historical Review* 109(5): 1505–1526. Available from the Gutenberg-e Web site at http://www.gutenberg-e.org/aboutframe.html.

McCarty, Willard. 2005 (forthcoming). *Humanities Computing*. New York: Palgrave Macmillan. (Online access provided to the unpublished manuscript by the author.)

McCarty, Willard, and Matthew Kirschenbaum. 2003. Institutional Models for Humanities Computing. *Literary and Linguistic Computing*. 18(4): 465–489. Updated annotated directory published annually since 2003 and available at http://www.allc.org/imhc/.

McGann, Jerome. 2002. Textonics: Literary and Cultural Studies in a Quantum World. Paper presented at the Richard W. Lyman Award Lecture, National Humanities Center, Research Triangle Park, N.C., October 3, 2002. Available at http://www.nhc.rtp.nc.us/newsrel2002/mcgannlecture.pdf.

McGann, Jerome. 2001. *Radiant Textuality: Literature after the World Wide Web*. New York: Palgrave Macmillan.

Modern Language Association. Committee on Scholarly Editions. 2005. Guidelines for Editors of Scholarly Editions. August 3, 2005. Available at http://www.mla.org/cse_guidelines.

____. Committee on Scholarly Editions. 2005. Guiding Questions for Vetters of Scholarly Editions. August 3, 2005. Available at http://www.mla.org/cse_guidelines#d0e354.

____. MLA Executive Council. 2003. Statement on Publication in Electronic Journals. Available at http://www.mla.org/statement_on_publica.

____. Ad Hoc Committee on the Future of Scholarly Publishing. 2002. The Future of Scholarly Publishing. *Profession*: 172–86. Available at http://www.mla.org/resources/documents/issues_scholarly_pub/repview_future_pub.

____. Committee on Information Technology. 1999 (reviewed in 2002). Minimal Guidelines for Authors of Web Pages. Available at http://www.mla.org/web_guidelines.htm.

Monfort, Nick, and Noah Wardrip-Fruin. 2004. Acid-Free Bits: Recommendations for Long-Lasting Electronic Literature, v.1.0 (June 14). Available at http://www.eliterature.org/pad/afb.html.

Morrison, Alan, Michael Popham, and Karen Wikander. [n.d.] *Creating and Documenting Electronic Texts: A Guide to Good Practice*. London: Arts & Humanities Data Service. Available at http://ota.ahds.ac.uk/documents/creating/.

Mueller, Martin. 2004. The Book of Life and the Book of English, or the Query Potential of the Digital Surrogate. Presented before the ACLS Commission on Cyberinfrastructure for the Humanities & Social Sciences at a public hearing, Northwestern University, Evanston, Ill., May 22, 2004. Available at http://www.acls.org/cyberinfrastructure/cyber_meeting_notes_may.htm#mueller_summary.

National Historical Publications and Records Commission. 2000. *Historical Documentary Editions 2000. A Descriptive List of Documentary Publications Supported or Endorsed by the National Historical Publications and Records Commission*. Washington, D.C.: National Archives and Records Administration. Available at http://www.archives.gov/grants/documentary_editing/documentary_editions_catalog.pdf.

National Information Standards Organization (NISO). 2004. *Understanding Metadata*. Bethesda, Md.: NISO. Available at http://www.niso.org/standards/resources/UnderstandingMetadata.pdf.

National Information Standards Organization. NISO Framework Advisory Group. 2004. *A Framework of Guidance for Building Good Digital Collections*, 3rd ed. Bethesda, Md.: NISO. Available at http://www.niso.org/framework/framework2.html.

O'Donnell, James. 2004. Testimony presented before the ACLS Commission on Cyberinfrastructure for the Humanities and Social Sciences at a public hearing, Baltimore, Md., October 26, 2004. Available at http://www.acls.org/cyberinfrastructure/cyber_meeting_notes_october.htm#odonnell_summary.

Open eBook Forum. 2002. Open eBook™ Publication Structure 1.2: Recommended Specification. Available at http://www.openebook. org/oebps/oebps1.2/download/oeb12-xhtml.htm. FAQs about the OeBPS available at http://www.openebook.org/oebps/oebps_faq. htm.

Palmer, Carole L. 2004. Thematic Research Collections. In Susan Schreibman, Ray Siemans, and John Unsworth, eds., *A Companion to Digital Humanities*. Blackwell Companions to Literature and Culture, number 26. Oxford: Blackwell Publishing, 348–365.

Pizer, Donald, Richard W. Dowell, and Frederic E. Rusch. 1991. *Theodore Dreiser: A Primary Bibliography and Reference Guide*. Boston: G. K. Hall.

Price, Kenneth M. 2001. Dollars and Sense in Collaborative Digital Scholarship: The Example of the Walt Whitman Hypertext Archive. *Documentary Editing* 23(2): 29–33.

Price-Wilkin, John. 1997. Just-in-Time Conversion, Just-in-Case Collections: Effectively Leveraging Rich Document Formats for the WWW. *D-Lib Magazine* May 1997. Available at http://www.dlib.org/ dlib/may97/michigan/05pricewilkin.html.

Ramirez, Victoria. 2004. Rewriting: Postmodern Narrative and Cultural Critique in the Age of Cloning/Radiant Textuality: Literature after the World Wide Web (book review). *American Literature* 76(3): 626–628.

Ramsay, Stephen. 2004. Tool-Time Architectures. Paper presented at the 2004 Association for Literary & Linguistic Computing/Association for Computers and the Humanities Conference, Gothenburg, Sweden, June 13–17, 2004. Available at http://cantor.english.uga. edu/docs/tool-time/tool-time.html#tex2html1.

Renear, Allen H. 2004. Text Encoding. In Susan Schreibman, Ray Siemans, and John Unsworth, eds. *A Companion to Digital Humanities*. Blackwell Companions to Literature and Culture, number 26. Oxford: Blackwell Publishing, 218–239.

Roberson, Julie, Debora Richey, and Mona Kratzert. 2002. Literary Theory: A Guide to Critical Theory Resources on the Internet. *C&RL News* 63(3): 176–180. Available to ACRL members at http://www.ala. org/ala/acrl/acrlpubs/crlnews/internetresources.htm.

Rockwell, Geoffrey. 2003. The ACH Page: Graduate Education in Humanities Computing. *Computers and the Humanities* 37: 242–244.

Roemer, Kenneth. 1999. The Tales Tables (of Contents) Tell. Reproduced by permission of the editor of *The Heath Anthology of American*

Literature Newsletter 19 (Fall). Available at http://www.uta.edu/english/roemer/ctt/intro.html.

Rommel, Thomas. 2004. Literary Studies. In Susan Schreibman, Ray Siemans, and John Unsworth, eds. *A Companion to Digital Humanities.* Blackwell Companions to Literature and Culture, number 26. Oxford: Blackwell Publishing, 88–96.

Rosenzweig, Roy. 2005. Should Historical Scholarship be Free? *Perspectives* (April). Available at http://www.historians.org/perspectives/issues/2005/0504/0504vic1.cfm.

Rosenzweig, Roy. 2000. The Riches of Hypertext for Scholarly Journals. *Chronicle of Higher Education* 46(28): B4.

Sandler, Mark. 2004. New Uses for the World's Oldest Books: Democratizing Access to Historic Corpora. *ARL Bimonthly Report* 232 (February): 4–6. Available at http://www.arl.org/newsltr/232/textcreation.html.

Sandler, Mark. 2003. Advisor Op-Ed: Public Domain: To Be or Not To Be. *The Charleston Advisor* 5 (1). Available to subscribers at http://www.charlestonco.com/features.cfm?id=135&type=ed.

Schreibman, Susan, Ray Siemans, and John Unsworth, eds. 2004. *A Companion to Digital Humanities.* Blackwell Companions to Literature and Culture, number 26. Oxford: Blackwell Publishing.

Shaw, Elizabeth J., and Sarr Blumson. 1997. Making of America: Online Searching and Page Presentation at the University of Michigan. *D-Lib Magazine* July/August 1997. Available at http://www.dlib.org/dlib/july97/america/07shaw.html.

Shirkey, Cynthia D. 2003. E-poetry: Digital Frontiers for an Evolving Art Form. *C&RL News* (April): 249–251.

Sklar, Kathryn Kish. 2002. Teaching Students to Become Producers of New Historical Knowledge on the Web. *Journal of American History* 88(4): 1471–1475.

Smith, Abby. 2003. *New-Model Scholarship: How Will It Survive?* Washington D.C.: Council on Library and Information Resources. Available at http://www.clir.org/pubs/reports/pub114/contents.html.

Smith, Martha Nell. 2002. Computing: What's American Literary Study Got to Do with IT? *American Literature* 74(4): 833–857.

Smith, Roger W. 2003. Review-Essay: Dreiser on the Web. *Dreiser Studies* 34(1): 66–91.

Sparr, Lisa Russ. 2003. Lines Online: Poetry Journals on the Web. *Chronicle of Higher Education* 50(11): B9.

Stebelman, Scott. 2000. English and American Literature Internet Resources: A Selective List. Published simultaneously in *Journal of Library Administration* 30(1/2): 209–229 and in Helen Laurence and William Miller, eds., *Academic Research on the Internet: Options for Scholars & Libraries.* 2000. New York: Haworth Information Press, 209–229.

Tennant, Roy. 2005. Google Out of Print. *Library Journal* (February 15). Available at http://www.libraryjournal.com/article/CA502014.

Thomas, William G., and Edward L. Ayers. 2003. An Overview: The Differences Slavery Made: A Close Analysis of Two American Communities. *The American Historical Review* 108(5): 1299–1307.

Townsend, Robert B. 2004. Is History Falling Behind the Times? *Perspectives* (February). Available at http://www.historians.org/perspectives/issues/2004/0402/0402new3.cfm.

Townsend, Robert B. 2001. Lessons Learned: Five Years in Cyberspace. *Perspectives* (May). Available at http://www.historians.org/perspectives/issues/2001/0105/0105aha1.cfm.

Unsworth, John. 2005. The Last Rites of the Humanities. Presented at a seminar at University College London, Senate House, London, March 22, 2005. Available at http://www3.isrl.uiuc.edu/~unsworth/unction.html.

Unsworth, John. 2003. Tool-Time, or "Haven't We Been Here Already?" Ten Years in Humanities Computing. Paper presented at Transforming Disciplines: The Humanities and Computer Science, Washington D.C., January 18, 2003. Available at http://www3.isrl.uiuc.edu/~unsworth/carnegie-ninch.03.html.

Unsworth, John. 2000a. Scholarly Primitives: What Methods Do Humanities Researchers Have in Common, and How Might Our Tools Reflect This? Paper presented at a symposium on Humanities Computing: Formal Methods, Experimental Practice, King's College, London, May 13, 2000. Available at http://jefferson.village.virginia.edu/~jmu2m/Kings.5-00/primitives.html.

Unsworth, John. 2000b. Thematic Research Collections. Paper presented at the Modern Language Association Annual Conference, Washington D.C., December 28, 2000. Available at http://www3.isrl.uiuc.edu/~unsworth/MLA.00/.

Walter, Katherine L., and Kenneth M. Price. 2004. An Online Guide to Walt Whitman's Dispersed Manuscripts. *Library Hi Tech* 22(3): 277–282.

Waters, Donald J. 2005. "Managing Digital Assets: An Overview of Strategic Issues." Keynote presentation at Managing Digital Assets: A Primer for Library and Information Technology Administrators, Charleston, S.C., February 4, 2005. Available at http://www.clir.org/activities/registration/feb05_spkrnotes/waters.htm.

Werre, Pam, and Ru Story-Huffman. 2000. Children's Literature: Useful Sites for Teachers, Librarians, and Students. *C&RL News* 61(7). Available to ACRL members at http://www.ala.org/ala/acrl/acrl-pubs/crlnews/internetresources.htm.

Willett, Perry. 2004. Electronic Texts: Audiences and Purposes. In Susan Schreibman, Ray Siemans, and John Unsworth, eds. *A Companion to Digital Humanities*. Blackwell Companions to Literature and Culture, number 26. Oxford: Blackwell Publishing, 240–253.

For Further Reading

Ayers, Edward L. 2004. Doing Scholarship on the Web: 10 Years of Triumphs and a Disappointment. *Chronicle of Higher Education* 50(21): B24.

Ayers, Edward L., and Charles M. Grisham. 2003. Why IT Has Not Paid Off As We Hoped (Yet). *EDUCAUSE Review* 38(6): 40–51.

Institute of Museum and Library Services. 2004. *Digital Resources for Cultural Heritage: A Strategic Assessment Workshop on Current Status and Future Work*. Available at http://www.imls.gov/pubs/pdf/LibraryBrochure.pdf.